TIME
100

TIME 100

Editor	Kelly Knauer
Art Director	Anthony Wing Kosner
Picture Editor	Patricia Cadley
Copy Editor	Bruce Christopher Carr
Designers	Scott G. Weiss, Heath Brockwell
Production Director	John Calvano
Photo Technology	Urbano Delvalle
TIME Special Projects Editor	Barrett Seaman

SPECIAL ISSUE STAFF

This book is based on two special issues of TIME. The editorial staff for those issues includes:

Managing Editor	Walter Isaacson
Editors: Builders & Titans	Bill Saporito, Steve Koepp
Editors: Great Minds of the Century	Philip Elmer-DeWitt, Christopher Porterfield
Picture Editor	Jay Colton, Jessica Taylor Taraski (Assistant)
Art Director	Marti Golon
Research Director: Builders & Titans	Bernard Baumohl
Research Director: Great Minds of the Century	Andrea Dorfman

Thanks to: Ames Adamson, Andy Blau, Anne Considine, Elena Falaro,
Brian Fellows, Kevin Kelly, Denise Lynch, Ellin Martens, Cornelis Verwaal

TIME INC. HOME ENTERTAINMENT

President	David Gitow
Director, Continuities and Single Sales	David Arfine
Director, Continuities and Retention	Michael Barrett
Director, New Products	Alicia Longobardo
Group Product Manager	Jennifer McLyman
Product Managers	Christopher Berzolla, Roberta Harris, Stacy Hirschberg, Carlos Jiminez, Kenneth Maehlum, Daniel Melore
Manager, Retail and New Markets	Thomas Mifsud
Associate Product Managers	Daria Raehse, Dennis Sheehan, Meredith Shelley, Betty Su, Niki Viswanathan, Lauren Zaslansky, Cheryl Zukowski
Assistant Product Managers	Victoria Alfonso, Jennifer Dowell
Editorial Operations Director	John Calvano
Book Production Manager	Jessica McGrath
Assistant Book Production Manager	Jonathan Polsky
Book Production Coordinator	Kristen Travers
Fulfillment Director	Michelle Gudema
Assistant Fulfillment Manager	Richard Perez
Financial Director	Tricia Griffin
Associate Financial Manager	Amy Maselli
Assistant Financial Manager	Steven Sandonato
Marketing Assistant	Ann Gillespie

Copyright 1999 by Time Inc. Home Entertainment
Published by TIME Books
Time Inc., 1271 Ave. of the Americas, New York, NY 10020
ISSN: 1521-5008
ISBN: 1-883013-62-3

We welcome your comments and suggestions about TIME Books. Please write to us at:
TIME Books
Attention: Book Editors
P.O. Box 11016
Des Moines, IA 50336-1016

To order additional copies, please call 1-800-327-6388
(Monday through Friday 7:00 a.m.–8:00 p.m. or Saturday 7:00 a.m.–6:00 p.m. Central Time)

Printed in the United States of America

BUILDERS & TITANS

TIME 100

GREAT MINDS OF THE CENTURY

TIME 100

Big Wheels Turning by Norman Pearlstine 2

Henry Ford by Lee Iacocca 6

Cars That Shaped a Century 10

L.B. Mayer by Budd Schulberg 12

David Sarnoff by Marcy Carsey and Tom Werner 16

Video Visionaries 19

A.P. Giannini by Daniel Kadlec 20

Charles Merrill by Joseph Nocera 22

Moguls of the Market 25

Willis Carrier by Molly Ivins 26

Good Things: Innovative Products 28

Stephen Bechtel by George J. Church 30

Monuments of the Age 34

Walt Disney by Richard Schickel 36

Juan Trippe by Richard Branson 40

Lucky Luciano by Edna Buchanan 43

William Levitt by Richard Lacayo 46

Walter Reuther by Irving Bluestone 49

A Bestiary of Bosses: The Good, the Bad & the Ugly 52

Leo Burnett by Stuart Ewen 54

Brought to You By: Great Advertising Minds 57

Thomas Watson Jr. by John Greenwald 58

Screen Saviors: Computer Pioneers 61

Ray Kroc by Jacques Pepin 62

Estée Lauder by Grace Mirabella 65

Cracking the Ceiling: Women in Business 68

Pete Rozelle by Michael Lewis 70

Milestones of TV Sports 73

Akio Morita by Kenichi Ohmae 74

High Tech, Big Bucks 77

Sam Walton by John Huey 78

The Customer Is King 81

Bill Gates by David Gelernter 82

The Most Influential People Of the 20th Century

GREAT MINDS OF THE CENTURY

Faust's Pact by Philip Elmer-DeWitt **86**

The Wright Brothers by Bill Gates **90**

Albert Einstein by James Gleick **94**

    Particle Pioneers **98**

Ludwig Wittgenstein by Daniel Dennett **99**

Sigmund Freud by Peter Gay **102**

    Magellans of the Mind **105**

Leo Baekeland by Ivan Amato **106**

Alexander Fleming by Dr. David Ho **109**

Philo T. Farnsworth by Neil Postman **112**

Jean Piaget by Seymour Papert **115**

    Putting Science to Work **118**

Kurt Gödel by Douglas Hofstadter **120**

Robert Goddard by Jeffrey Kluger **123**

Edwin Hubble by Michael D. Lemonick **126**

    The Century of the Countdown **130**

Enrico Fermi by Richard Rhodes **132**

    Behind the Bomb **135**

John Maynard Keynes by Robert B. Reich **136**

Alan Turing by Paul Gray **139**

    Homeric Hackers **142**

William Shockley by Gordon Moore **143**

James Watson & Francis Crick by Robert Wright **146**

Jonas Salk by Wilfrid Sheed **150**

Rachel Carson by Peter Matthiessen **153**

    Cranks, Villains & Unsung Heroes **156**

The Leakeys by Donald C. Johanson **158**

    The Delvers: Great Anthropologists **161**

Tim Berners-Lee by Joshua Quittner **162**

    Weavers of the Web **165**

Index 166

Picture Credits 170

Foreword

The TIME 100

The two young men who founded TIME, Henry Luce and Briton Hadden, strongly believed in the power of the individual to influence history: week after week for many decades, the cover of the magazine always featured a portrait of a man or woman in the news. In the first issue of 1928, five years after TIME's debut, the editors named aviation pioneer Charles Lindbergh the "Man of the Year 1927." This designation of the individual who had done the most in the past year to affect the news for good or for ill became the magazine's signature journalistic act, the annual embodiment of its belief in the power of individual deeds to change the destiny of men and nations.

As the 20th century was drawing to a close, TIME managing editor Walter Isaacson conceived a project that reflected the magazine's deepest roots: to select and profile the 100 most influential people of the century in a series of special issues of the weekly magazine. The list would be divided into five groups of 20 individuals: Leaders and Revolutionaries, Artists and Entertainers, Builders and Titans, Scientists and Thinkers, Heroes and Inspirations. Noted authorities would be invited to write the profiles of the individuals named to the list. The entire project would culminate at the end of 1999 in the naming of a Person of the Century.

To select the 100 individuals, TIME solicited nominations from editors and journalists around the world, consulted outside experts and historians and registered opinions from millions of readers who sent in suggestions by mail and e-mail. The final selection was made in a series of occasionally contentious (but always stimulating) meetings that included journalists from CBS News, which produced a series of television specials on the project.

This second of three hardbound volumes comprising the complete sereies of TIME 100 profiles includes the third and fourth installments of the series: 20 Builders and Titans and 20 "Great Minds of the Century." (The original title for this group, Scientists and Thinkers, came to seem too narrow during the selection process).

In transforming the special issues of the weekly magazine into book form, each story has been completely redesigned, and a number of new pictures and related articles have been added. In addition, TIME assistant managing editor Philip Elmer-DeWitt, who oversaw the Great Minds of the Century issue, has written a new introductory essay specifically for this volume.

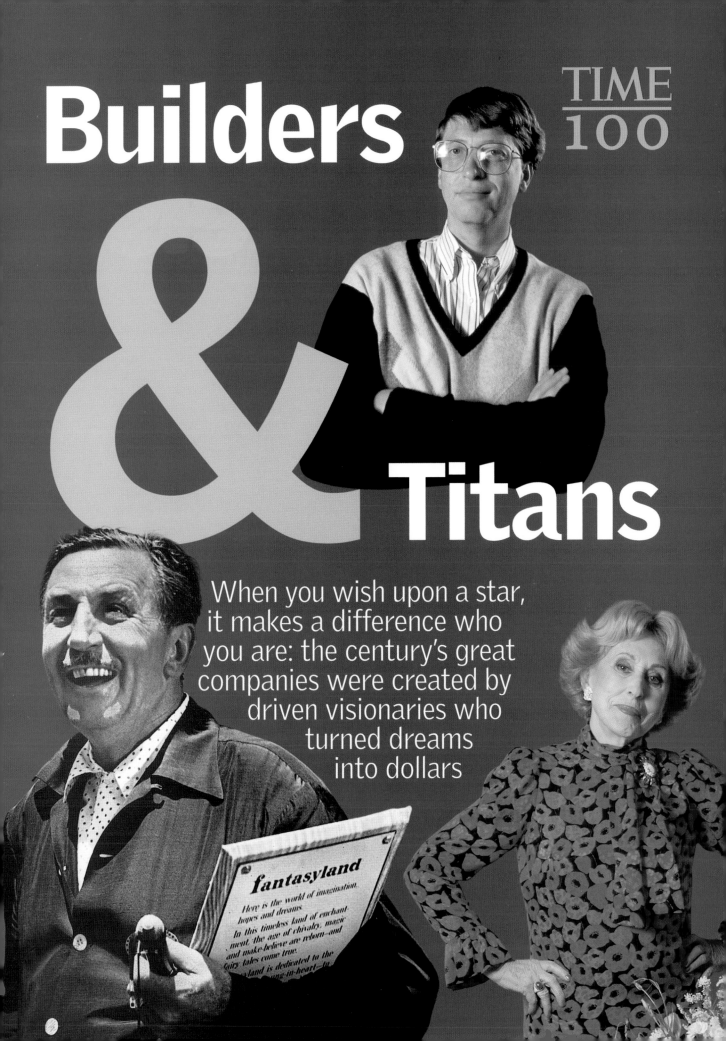

Builders
&
Titans

TIME
100

When you wish upon a star,
it makes a difference who
you are: the century's great
companies were created by
driven visionaries who
turned dreams
into dollars

fantasyland

Here is the world of imagination.
hopes and dreams.
In this timeless land of enchant-
ment, the age of chivalry, magic
and make-believe are reborn—and
fairy tales come true.
...yland is dedicated to the
...ng-in-heart—to...

Big Wheels
Turning

By **NORMAN PEARLSTINE**

*"Make money, be proud
of it; make more money,
be prouder of it."* —HENRY R. LUCE, 1937

With those words, TIME magazine's co-founder joined Calvin Coolidge ("The chief business of the American people is business"), former General Motors president Charles E. Wilson ("What is good for the country is good for General Motors, and what's good for General Motors is good for the country") and, alas, *Wall Street's* Gordon Gekko ("Greed ... is good. Greed is right. Greed works") in defining and defending the 20th century as the century of business.

"Capitalism not only won, it turned into a marvelous machine of prosperity, led by people who could take an idea and turn it into an industry

The first half of this book, TIME's second in a series of three that chronicles the 100 most influential people of the century, is devoted to the 20 remarkable builders and titans who most embody capitalism and its triumphs. It also creates the occasion for this writer, who has covered business for more than three of this century's decades, to make a few observations and bestow a few honors of his own.

From Henry Ford at one end of the century to Bill Gates at the other, these 20 people influenced lives far beyond the business world. Indeed, TIME defines the business realm broadly, including anyone who works for a living: our list extends to pro football's Pete Rozelle, organized labor's

Walter Reuther and even organized crime's Lucky Luciano, whose syndicate was better managed than was Al Capone's.

It is no accident that our list is almost entirely American. It does include Sony's Akio Morita, and it arguably could include a handful of other leaders from abroad, notably Japan's Soichiro Honda and Eiji Toyoda (Toyota), Italy's Giovanni Agnelli (Fiat) and Australia's Rupert Murdoch (now a U.S. citizen). But if the 20th century was, as Luce also said, the American Century, it was largely because our system, espousing freedom of markets and freedom of the individual, rewarding talent instead of class and pedigree, bred a group of leaders whose single-minded fixation on

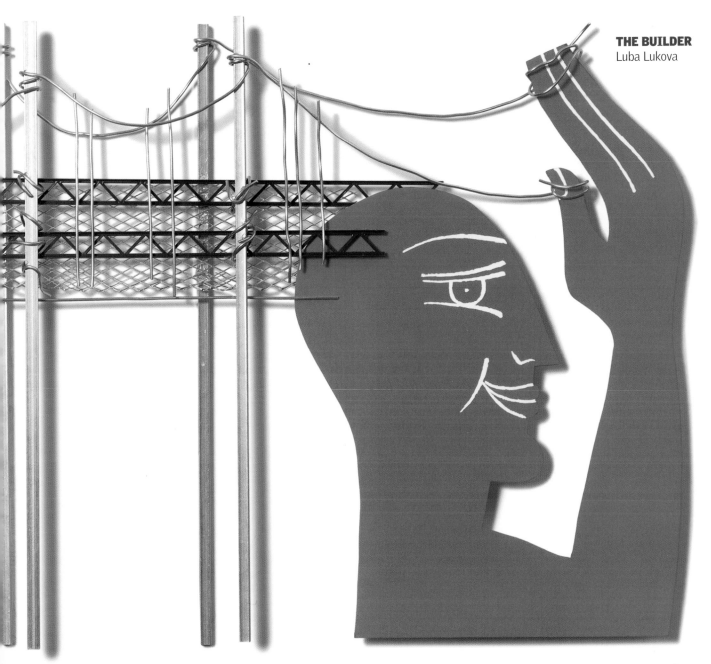

THE BUILDER
Luba Lukova

getting rich—and creating great products to do so—led to unheard-of levels of productivity and prosperity. It was America's industrial might that enabled it to win wars and rebuild continents. Other countries may have had the capital, the natural resources or the skilled workers needed to industrialize, but their economic and political systems usually favored consensus management and faceless bureaucrats while denigrating the kind of individual initiative required to take an idea and turn it into an industry. The 21st century will no doubt include a larger number of great business leaders from outside the U.S. as more nations embrace capitalism and come to understand the importance of rewarding individual initiative.

I T IS ALSO NO ACCIDENT THAT THE LIST INCLUDES only one woman, Estée Lauder, and only one industry, cosmetics, in which other women—including Elizabeth Arden, Helena Rubinstein and Mary Kay Ash—also flourished as entrepreneurs. And although the book includes a reference to an influential black entrepreneur, no people of color make our Top 20. Through most of this century, American business has been dominated by men, white men, despite more than 25 years of modern feminism and some ambitious corporate efforts to achieve racial equality. The next century will certainly be different, although I don't see meaningful change coming soon enough. Yes, TIME's sister publication FORTUNE assembled a credible list of the 50 most powerful women in U.S. business in 1998. But only two women head companies included in FORTUNE's annual list of America's 500 largest firms. Meanwhile, many of America's most talented female executives, tired of trying to fit into the boys' clubs, are leaving large corporations to start their own businesses. The status of African Americans and other racial minorities in big business is, if anything, even more dismal. The diversity of America's population and the entry of women into the workplace give the U.S. an important competitive advantage over other countries. But that advantage will be squandered if our largest corporations don't figure out how to benefit from these resources more fully.

Financiers, including A.P. Giannini (Bank of America) and Charles Merrill (Merrill Lynch), make our list, but some might argue that finance is underrepresented, since it was the availability of capital, as much as or more than individual genius or initiative, that so often created the conditions for business success. By that measure, Drexel Burnham's Michael Milken, who raised billions for the likes of Ted Turner, Rupert Murdoch and MCI Corp., should be included in the list, notwithstanding his conviction for violating securities laws and his time spent in jail. Other financial innovators who changed the way we spend and save might also have made the list, including Dee Hock, a little-known businessman who made the Visa credit card a success, and Peter Lynch, who as head of Fidelity's Magellan Fund was America's most successful money manager.

J.P. Morgan, a titan of the 19th century who helped set

the stage for the 20th, acted in his day as a cross between today's Federal Reserve Board and the Goldman Sachs mergers-and-acquisitions department, providing the money and acumen needed to launch the prototypes of modern industrial corporations. Under Morgan's leadership, this century began much as the 19th century ended, with heavy industry—steel, rails, electricity and oil—ascendant. Automobiles were in short supply until 1913, when Henry Ford introduced the assembly line and mass production, making ours a consumer as well as an industrial society. As the century progressed, the service economy began to compete with industry as fortunes were made in

THE TITAN
Luba Lukova

carbonated drinks (Coca-Cola), processed foods (Heinz), insurance (Travelers, AIG) and retail (Sears, Wal-Mart). The information age began in the 1920s, when Walt Disney, Louis B. Mayer and the rest of Hollywood began to build businesses of scale. But it wasn't until the 1950s, with the emergence of television as a mass medium, and the two most recent decades, with the computer's coming of age, that information has replaced manufacturing as the primary source of growth. In fact, it is really too soon to pass judgment on most of the information age's brightest lights—among them Apple's Steve Jobs, America Online's Steve Case and Netscape's Marc Andreessen—who may wind up contributing even more to the 21st century than to the 20th.

Nor do we honor economists here, preferring to include them in a subsequent list devoted to scientists and thinkers. But surely our nation and the world would be less strong today, and many of our most famous business leaders would seem less prescient, absent the guidance of the Federal Reserve Board's Alan Greenspan. John Maynard Keynes, who convinced us of the value of fixed exchange rates and the need to use deficit financing to spend our way out of recessions, had tremendous influence over economic policy through the Depression and in the years after World War II. My own vote for economist of the century goes to Milton Friedman, whose books, including *Capitalism and Freedom* and *Free to Choose* (written with his wife Rose), articulate the importance of free markets and the dangers of undue government intervention. Friedman's work is back in vogue in the late 1990s, as many nations cope with the most serious economic crisis since the Depression.

Our list, recognizing only 20 people, is by definition subjective, especially since we sought to recognize leadership in several different industries. If, as I believe, the automobile is the product of the century, we could easily have filled the list with the names of famous automakers, including Alfred P. Sloan, Charles Kettering and William Durant (all from General Motors), Walter Chrysler, Ransom Olds, Ferdinand Porsche (Porsche and Volkswagen), the Dodge brothers and Clement Studebaker. Henry J. Kaiser not only built cars but also played a key role in shipbuilding, housing,

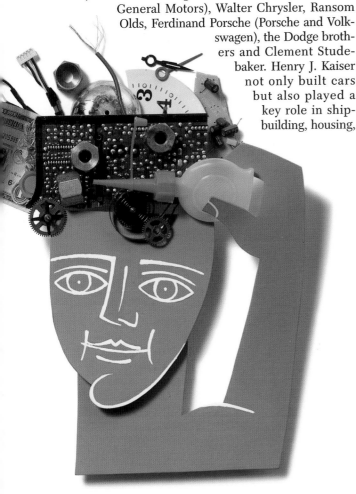

construction and hospitals. In the end, however, we settled on Henry Ford because his individual genius was so responsible for automating the assembly line and lowering the price to make cars affordable, thus building the industry.

Our bias toward innovators and company founders and against managers kept several famous names off the list—not only Sloan, whose organizational and management skills helped consolidate several disparate automakers into General Motors, but also a number of chief executives best known for their ability to manage large enterprises and increase shareholder value. It should be remembered that Ford Motor Co. was foundering when Henry Ford died,

and it was left to his grandson Henry Ford II to revive the company after World War II with the help of a group of button-down managers, the "Whiz Kids," including Robert McNamara, Arjay Miller and Charles Thornton. Similarly, Walt Disney wouldn't be so well thought of today had Michael Eisner not saved the company and its founder's name in the years that he has run the company.

M Y OWN CHOICE FOR COMPANY OF THE CENTURY is General Electric, which began the century as an industrial company with sales of less than $16 million and, catching almost every wave, evolved into a diversified manufacturing and finance colossus with strong positions in media and information. This year's sales are expected to exceed $100 billion, and with market capitalization of $302 billion, the company is in a close race with Microsoft for the title of Most Valuable. GE chairman Jack Welch isn't the innovator that GE's founder Thomas A. Edison was, but this son of a railroad conductor and lifelong GE employee would certainly get my vote for CEO of the century.

While our issue venerates business leaders and the economic system that allows them to flourish, we should be mindful of the limitations of both. Most successful entrepreneurs and executives benefit from their single-minded focus on creating wealth, and when talking about their businesses, they do so with passion. But when discussing society's broader issues, they are too often simplistic and uninformed, and they rarely understand that government's stakeholders have different interests from their own company's shareholders'. Moreover, they tend to be authoritarian, and they aren't often very tolerant of contrary opinions.

Lee Iacocca, the charismatic auto executive who did great work at Ford and Chrysler, was one CEO who recognized his limitations. Following the publication of his autobiography, *Iacocca,* which sold 7 million copies, he flirted briefly with making a run for the presidency. In the end, Iacocca decided against it, realizing he would never have the patience required to deal with Congress. Compromising to achieve consensus wasn't his long suit, he told me. It would be good if others seeking the presidency, such as Ross Perot and son-of-a-businessman Steve Forbes, better understood this handicap.

Finally, we must recognize that markets are always messy—they frequently overshoot or undershoot desired targets—and that it is ordinary working people, not investors, bankers and business leaders, who suffer most when they do. When that happens, it is worth remembering that there is a role for government in protecting society's weakest members from the markets' excesses while encouraging the animal spirits that free markets unleash. Getting that balance right will be a challenge for business and government in the century ahead. ∎

Norman Pearlstine is the editor-in-chief of Time Inc. and former managing editor of the Wall Street Journal.

MOTOR — COMPANY.

Henry
Ford

He produced an affordable car, paid high wages and helped create a middle class. Not bad for an autocrat

By LEE IACOCCA

THE ONLY TIME I EVER MET HENRY FORD, he looked at me and probably wondered, "Who is this little s.o.b. fresh out of college?" He wasn't real big on college graduates, and I was one of 50 in the Ford training course in September 1946, working in a huge drafting room at the enormous River Rouge plant near Detroit.

One day there was a big commotion at one end of the floor and in walked Henry Ford with Charles Lindbergh. They walked down my aisle asking men what they were doing. I was working on a mechanical drawing of a clutch spring (which drove me out of engineering forever), and I was worried that they'd ask me a question because I didn't know what the hell I was doing—I'd been there only 30 days. I was just awestruck by the fact that there was Colonel Lindbergh with my new boss, coming to shake my hand.

The boss was a genius. He was an eccentric. He was no prince in his social attitudes and his politics. But Henry Ford's mark in history is almost unbelievable. In 1905, when there were 50 start-up companies a year trying to get into the auto business, his backers at the new Ford Motor Co. were insisting that the best way to maximize profits was to build a car for the rich.

But Ford was from modest, agrarian Michigan roots. And he thought that the guys who made the cars ought to be able to afford one themselves, so that they too could go for a spin on a lazy Sunday afternoon. In typical fashion, instead of listening to his backers, Henry Ford eventually bought them out.

In 1907, the year before he rolled out his Model T, Ford showed off a precursor on Broadway in New York City

And that proved to be only the first smart move in a crusade that would make him the father of 20th century American industry. When the black Model T rolled out in 1908, it was hailed as America's Everyman car—elegant in its simplicity and a dream machine not just for engineers but for marketing men as well.

Ford instituted industrial mass production, but what really mattered to him was mass consumption. He figured that if he paid his factory workers a real living wage and produced more cars in less time for less money, everyone would buy them.

Almost a half-century before Ray Kroc sold a single hamburger, Ford invented the dealer-franchise system to sell and service cars. In the same way that all politics is local, he knew that business had to be local. Ford's "road men" became a familiar part of the American landscape. By 1912 there were 7,000 Ford dealers across the country.

In much the same fashion, Ford worked on making sure that an automotive infrastructure developed along with the cars. Just like horses, cars had to be fed—so he pushed for gas stations everywhere. And as his tin lizzies bounced over the rutted tracks of the horse age, he campaigned for better roads, which eventually led to an interstate-highway system that is still the envy of the world.

His vision would help create a middle class in the U.S., one marked by urbanization, rising wages and some free time in which to spend them. When Ford left the family farm at age 16 and walked eight miles to his first job in a Detroit machine shop, only 2 out of 8 Americans lived in the cities. By World War II that proportion would double, and the affordable Model T was one reason. People flocked to Detroit for jobs, and if they worked in one of Henry's factories, they could afford one of his cars—it was a virtuous circle, and he was the ringmaster.

Nobody was more of an inspiration to Ford than Thomas Alva Edison. At the turn of the century the great inventor

had blessed Ford's pursuit of an efficient, gas-powered car during a chance meeting at Detroit's Edison Illuminating Co., where Ford was chief engineer. After the Model T's enormous success, the two visionaries from rural Michigan became friends and business partners. Ford asked Edison to develop an electric storage battery for the car and funded the effort with $1.5 million. Ironically, despite all his other great successes, Edison never perfected the storage battery. Yet Ford immortalized his mentor's inventive genius by building the Edison Institute in Dearborn.

FORD'S GREAT STRENGTH WAS THE MANUFACTURING process—not invention. Long before he started a car company, he was an inveterate tinkerer, known for picking up loose scraps of metal and wire and turning them into machines. He'd been putting cars together since 1891. Although by no means the first popular automobile, the Model T showed the world just how innovative Ford was at combining technology and markets.

The company's assembly line alone threw America's Industrial Revolution into overdrive. Instead of having workers put together the entire car, Ford's cronies, who were great tool- and diemakers from Scotland, organized teams that added parts to each Model T as it moved down a line. By the time Ford's sprawling Highland Park plant was humming along in 1914, the world's first automatic conveyor belt could churn out a car every 93 minutes.

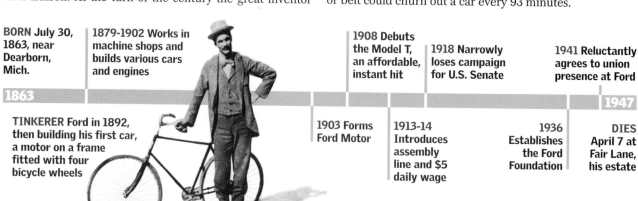

By 1913 Ford's assembly line had reduced a car's construction time from 12 hours to 93 minutes

BORN July 30, 1863, near Dearborn, Mich.

1879-1902 Works in machine shops and builds various cars and engines

1908 Debuts the Model T, an affordable, instant hit

1918 Narrowly loses campaign for U.S. Senate

1941 Reluctantly agrees to union presence at Ford

1863

1947

TINKERER Ford in 1892, then building his first car, a motor on a frame fitted with four bicycle wheels

1903 Forms Ford Motor

1913-14 Introduces assembly line and $5 daily wage

1936 Establishes the Ford Foundation

DIES April 7 at Fair Lane, his estate

TIME 100

> # "I will build a car for the great multitude ... so low in price that no man will be unable to own one."
>
> **HENRY FORD, in 1907, on his soon-to-debut Model T**

The same year, Henry Ford shocked the world with what probably stands as his greatest contribution ever: the $5-a-day minimum-wage scheme. The average wage in the auto industry then was $2.34 for a 9-hr. shift. Ford not only doubled that; he also shaved an hour off the workday. In those years it was unthinkable that a guy could be paid that much for doing something that didn't involve an awful lot of training or education. The *Wall Street Journal* called the plan "an economic crime," and critics everywhere heaped "Fordism" with equal scorn. But as the wage increased later to a daily $10, it proved a critical component of Ford's quest to make the automobile accessible to all. The critics were too stupid to comprehend that because Ford had lowered his costs per car, the higher wages didn't matter—except for making it feasible for more people to buy cars.

When Ford stumbled, it was because he wanted to do everything his way. By the late 1920s the company was so vertically integrated that it was completely self-sufficient. Ford controlled rubber plantations in Brazil, a fleet of ships, a railroad, 16 coal mines and thousands of acres of timberland and iron-ore mines in Michigan and Minnesota. All this was combined at the River Rouge plant, a sprawling city of a place where more than 100,000 men worked.

The problem was that for too long they had worked on only one model. People told Ford to diversify, but he had developed tunnel vision. To hell with the customer: he could have any color as long as it was black. Ford didn't bring out a new design until the Model A in '27, and by then General Motors was gaining on him.

In a sense Henry Ford became a prisoner of his own success. He turned on some of his best and brightest when they launched design changes or plans he had not approved. On one level you have to admire his paternalism. He was so worried that his workers would go crazy with their five bucks a day that he set up a "Sociological Department" to make sure that they didn't blow the money on booze and vice. He banned smoking because he thought, correctly as it turned out, that tobacco was unhealthy. "I want the whole organization dominated by a just, generous and humane policy," he said.

Naturally, Ford, and only Ford, determined that policy. He was violently opposed to labor organizers, whom he saw as "the worst thing that ever struck the earth," and entirely unnecessary—who, after all, knew more about taking care of his people than he? Only when he was faced with a general strike in 1941 did he finally agree to let the United Auto Workers organize a plant.

By then Alfred P. Sloan had combined various car com-

panies into a powerful General Motors, with a variety of models and prices to suit all tastes. He had also made labor peace. That left Ford in the dust, its management in turmoil. And if World War II hadn't turned the company's manufacturing prowess to the business of making B-24 bombers and jeeps, it is entirely possible that the 1932 V-8 engine might have been Ford's last innovation.

THERE WAS NO INTELLIGENT MANAGEMENT AT FORD in the prewar years. When I arrived at the end of the war, the company was a monolithic dictatorship. Its balance sheet was still being kept on the back of an envelope, and the guys in purchasing had to weigh the invoices to count them. College kids, managers, anyone with book learning was viewed with suspicion. Ford had done so many screwy things—from terrorizing his own lieutenants to canonizing Adolf Hitler—that the company's image was as low as it could go.

It was Henry Ford II who rescued the legacy. He played down his grandfather's antics, and he made amends with the Jewish business community that Henry Ford had alienated so much with the racist attacks that are now a matter of historical record. Henry II encouraged the "whiz kids" like Robert McNamara and Arjay Miller to modernize management, which put the company back on track.

Ford was the first company to get a car out after the war, and it was the only auto manufacturer that had a real base overseas. In fact, one of the reasons that Ford is so competitive today is that from the very beginning, Henry Ford went anywhere there was a road—and usually a river. He took the company to 33 countries at

In 1942 Ford once again takes the wheel of his first "quadricycle" at his Greenfield Village museum

his peak. These days the automobile business is becoming more global every day, and in that, as he was about so many things, Ford was prescient.

Henry Ford died in his bed at his Fair Lane mansion seven months after I met him, during a blackout caused by a storm in the spring of 1947. He was 83. The fact is, there probably couldn't be a Henry Ford in today's world. Business is too collegial. One hundred years ago, business was done by virtual dictators—men laden with riches and so much power they could take over a country if they wanted to. That's not acceptable anymore. But if it hadn't been for Henry Ford's drive to create a mass market for cars, America wouldn't have a middle class today. ∎

Lee Iacocca was president of Ford and later chairman of Chrysler. In 1996 he founded EV Global Motors.

Cars That Shaped a Century

The automobile is one of the inventions that defined the 20th century from start to finish. Hundreds of companies have produced millions of cars over the past 99 years, but a handful of models stand out for their technical, cultural or commercial significance

—By JOSEPH R. SZCZESNY

1. Ford Model T

Henry Ford used a single design and inexpensive, mass-produced parts to make his pioneering vehicle affordable to millions. His tin lizzies created a new dynamic that reshaped the American city, landscape and life-style.

2. Volkswagen Beetle

The "people's car" became a 20th century icon despite its provenance as a project of Hitler's. The Bug slowly caught on in the '50s among practical-minded buyers, and then in the '60s became a groovy symbol of peace and love.

3. Willys Jeep

The general-purpose vehicle that carried G.I.s during World War II created the off-road market, then enjoyed a renaissance as the progenitor of sport-utility vehicles.

4. 1966 Toyota Corona

This model was the forerunner of the Corolla, which has become one of the best-selling cars ever. Its durability and economy made it the first Toyota popular with Americans.

5. 1912 Cadillac
The first car equipped with an electric starter opened up the road for women. Cadillac president Henry Leland pressed engineer Charles Kettering to devise the starter after a friend was killed trying to crank a car by hand.

6. 1960 Corvair
The novel "compact" car with its rear-mounted engine is much prized by collectors, but its glaring deficiencies helped launch the automotive-safety movement that led to today's seat belts, air bags and antilock brakes.

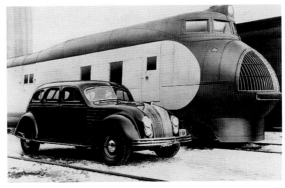

7. 1934 Citroën 7CV
This was the first successful front-wheel-drive car; its revolutionary drive system was first adopted by an American company in the 1966 Oldsmobile Toronado and is now standard on most automobiles.

8. 1934 Chrysler Airflow
The first car designed using a wind tunnel, it sported the first fully streamlined body. Chrysler put the engine over the front axle and moved the passenger cabin forward to create a more comfortable ride, a design still in use.

9. 1949 Cadillac
The first post–World War II car to boast tail fins and V-8 power, the '49 model set a mood of exuberance that reached its peak with the shark-finned Caddy of 1959.

10. 1914 Dodge Touring Car
This was the first automobile manufactured with a steel frame, which meant the car was heavier, sturdier and could hold the road better under all kinds of conditions.

Louis B. Mayer

His MGM was a film factory, with stars working the assembly line to fabricate his dreams: apple pie, chaste romance and Andy Hardy

By BUDD SCHULBERG

Singin' in the reins: L.B. on the set of MGM's smash hit in the 1920s, *Ben-Hur*

DAN QUAYLE WOULD HAVE LOVED LOUIS B. MAYER, a man for whom the words family values had real meaning. Motherhood, the Stars and Stripes and God were equal parts of a lifelong strategy that would establish Metro Goldwyn Mayer as the industry's dominant film factory, from the silent era through the talkies revolution. While Hollywood's other early moguls were simply trying to make the best movies they could, young Mayer was an ideologue intent on using the power of the new medium to exert what he considered the proper moral influence on the American public.

Mayer went West in 1918, just after the first wave of Hollywood pioneers. He had been on the move since his threadbare family left its Cossack-plagued Ukrainian village in the late 1880s and a few years later settled in Saint John, New Brunswick. There his father Jacob Mayer struggled as a junkman. Little Louie, half starved, battled anti-Semitic bullies and helped his father—whom he despised as much as he adored his mother. Escaping Saint John in his late teens, he moved on to Boston, where he discovered the Nickelodeon, the embryo of the moving-picture business.

Quick to seize his opportunities in the young business of film distribution, Mayer earned a breakthrough $500,000 by putting up $50,000 for a lopsided 90% of the New England ticket sales on the first movie blockbuster, *The Birth of a Nation.* Now ready to produce his own pictures, he inveigled a popular actress, Anita Stewart, into breaking her contract with Vitagraph, and in 1918-19 starred her in a series of teary films at the modest studio leased from the Selig Zoo in downtown Los Angeles, where my father B.P. Schulberg joined him in the now vanished Mayer-Schulberg Studio in 1920.

Mayer took a major step up when entertainment tycoon Marcus Loew hired him to lead a new company merging Metro and Goldwyn. Mayer soon added his big M to the mix. He raised the contract system to an art, ruling over a stable of stars who were legally bound to the company for years. With frail, dedicated Irving Thalberg at his side, L.B. worked hard to project himself as a father figure to his extended family of stars, directors and producers.

He was the master manipulator, and it was generally acknowledged that of all the great actors on the lot—the Barrymores, Spencer Tracy, Lon Chaney, Garbo—L.B. was No. 1. When Robert Taylor tried to hit him up for a raise, L.B. advised the young man to work hard, respect his elders, and in due time he'd get everything he deserved.

BORN July 4,
1885, in
Minsk, Russia

1917-18 Starts Louis B.
Mayer Pictures; first
release: *Virtuous Wives*

1925 Signs
Greta Garbo

1939 MGM
releases, *The
Wizard of Oz*,
one of Mayer's
biggest hits

1948
Relinquishes
control of MGM.
Retires in 1951

1885

1957

1907 Buys and
rebuilds a movie
theater near Boston

1924 With Marcus
Loew, forms Metro
Goldwyn Mayer.
Goldwyn backs out

1932 Rift with
production chief
Irving Thalberg
divides studio

DIES
Oct. 29 in
Los Angeles

Mayer, front row, center, of course, boasted MGM had "more stars than there are in heaven." (If you can't name them, see page 169)

L.B. hugged him, cried a little and walked him to the door. Asked, "Did you get your raise?" the now tearful Taylor is said to have answered, "No, but I found a father."

There were ways to get to him. When ingenue Ann Rutherford asked for a supplement to her modest salary in the highly profitable Andy Hardy series, L.B. began his familiar ploy. Then Rutherford took out her little bank book, showed him her meager savings and said she had promised her mother a house. Mother was the magic word. L.B. embraced her, but chastely; down his cheeks came the obligatory tears; and Rutherford left with her raise.

Mayer was building a roster of household names that almost lived up to MGM's slogan, "More stars than there are in heaven": Judy Garland, Clark Gable, Joan Crawford, Elizabeth Taylor, Katharine Hepburn, Lana Turner, the Marx Brothers, Ava Gardner and, of course, Greta Garbo, L.B.'s personal discovery.

He kept them in line with hand holding and falling to his knees in tears, but if that failed, he'd reverse field, as he did with Gable. When Gable was getting $1,000 a week and

wanted $5,000, L.B. blackmailed him by threatening to reveal Gable's affair with Crawford to his wife. Both knew Gable was worth $12,000, but he settled for $2,000. The indentured servitude had its benefits, though, for the kind of power that L.B. wielded on the studio lot extended to local politics. When a drunken Gable hit and killed a pedestrian near Hollywood Boulevard, L.B. sent Gable into hiding and then conspired with the local D.A. to have a minor executive take the rap in return for staying on the payroll for life at a higher salary. A pliant press hushed the story.

While L.B.'s moral code was complicated, his zeal was not. When his biggest star at the time, Jack Gilbert, used the word whore in reference to his co-star Mae Murray, and then—gasp—about his own mother, the president of MGM rushed from around his desk and knocked down his million-dollar meal ticket.

Having learned not to say "ain't" or use double negatives or drop his Gs, a more polished L.B. found a new role model in Herbert Hoover. He worked so effectively for Hoover that he dared hope he might be the new President's

Wizard of Oz. Thalberg was increasingly resistant to playing Andy to Mayer's Judge Hardy. By 1936, Mayer was the highest-salaried executive in America, breaking the million-dollar barrier. Thalberg felt entitled to an equal share. For his part, L.B. had begun to resent the prevailing opinion that Thalberg was the genius behind MGM, and Mayer the engineer who kept the plant humming.

By the mid-'30s, MGM was divided between Mayer loyalists and "Thalberg people," and by the time the strong-willed, weak-hearted Thalberg collapsed and went to Europe for treatment, he and his former mentor were no longer speaking to each other. When Thalberg returned, Mayer offered a production deal in place of his old job. An angry Thalberg threatened to leave MGM. It was at this impasse that he died at age 37. L.B. cried, sent a spectacular spray of gardenias to the funeral and, soon after, remarked to my mother, "God saw fit to take Irving away."

God wasn't L.B.'s co-pilot; he was his senior partner, reaching out to remove those who dared get in L.B.'s way. For almost 15 years, L.B. would continue to reign, and with its host of prizewinning and profitable movies, MGM's decline as Film Factory No. 1 was almost imperceptible. But in the postwar years, the Mayer formula of sentimental family fare and glossy romantic productions was wearing thin.

THE GOLDEN YEARS OF THE MOGULS WERE COMING to an end too. The government forced the industry to divest its lucrative theater chains, and top stars and directors were demanding the profit participation that Mayer & Co. had always denied them. Mayer was forced to accept writer-producer Dore Schary in Thalberg's old job, and at first it seemed once again that Mayer had found the son he had always wanted. But the liberal Schary found L.B. an overbearing and stultifying influence. A bitter showdown prompted Marcus Loew's successor Nick Schenck to make a choice. To Mayer's shock, Schenck picked Schary.

After 27 years of arbitrary power, L.B. was out. Even his vaunted patriotism had now become shrill. He identified with right-wing fanatic Senator Joe McCarthy and opposed General Eisenhower as too moderate at the '52 G.O.P. convention. When Mayer died in 1957, the apostle of family values left a contentious, meanspirited will disinheriting family members, including his daughter Edith, because of her husband's liberal politics. No happy ending there. No movie-star hero to set everything right at the rosy fade-out.

Had L.B. been making his own movie, it would have been different. He knew how to turn American life into pipe dreams. But give the devil his due: this self-inflated, ruthless and cloyingly sentimental monarch presided over the most successful of all the Hollywood fantasy factories, leaving a legacy of classic, inimitable films that defined America's aspirations, if not its realities. ∎

choice as ambassador to England. An ambassadorship to Turkey was dangled, but Mayer chose to oversee his studio's triumphant transition from silence to sound: "Garbo Talks!" Mr. and Mrs. Mayer did claim the privilege of being Hoover's first guests at the White House. From then on L.B. felt free to phone the President, and frequently did, to make suggestions for running the government.

Meanwhile he was cashing in on his conviction that morality sold. With films like the Andy Hardy series, featuring teenage star Mickey Rooney, sage father Judge Hardy (Lewis Stone) and charming mother (Fay Holden), Mayer was defining American society according to his fantasies. He took his responsibility for the country's values so seriously that when Rooney, a precocious womanizer and partygoer, got out of hand, L.B. was overheard screaming at him, "You're Andy Hardy! You're the United States! You're Stars and Stripes! You're a symbol! Behave yourself!"

But as praise and profits soared, a conflict was building between Mayer and his brilliant production chief Thalberg. An intense perfectionist who never lost his schoolboy looks, Thalberg oversaw MGM's hits: *The Big Parade, Ben-Hur, Anna Christie, Grand Hotel, Mutiny on the Bounty* and *The*

Novelist and screenwriter Budd Schulberg is the author of the classic tale of Hollywood, What Makes Sammy Run?

David
Sarnoff

RCA's General turned radio into a mass medium carried by a network, then did the same for television, changing lives (and living rooms) forever

By MARCY CARSEY and TOM WERNER

WHEN DICK SOLOMON, THE ALIEN HIGH commander in *3rd Rock from the Sun*, declares, "God bless television," he is merely reflecting the feeling of most earthlings: that television is the most influential medium of the 20th century. While some people critique its content, no one debates television's power. It is the window through which we see reality, as well as the window that permits us to escape from it. In the late 1990s the average American family watched the ubiquitous box more than 50 hours a week.

So it is nearly impossible to imagine that it was as recently as 1939 when David Sarnoff told a crowd of curious viewers, "Now we add sight to sound." Sarnoff went on to say, "It is with a feeling of humbleness that I come to this moment of announcing the birth in this country of a new art so important in its implications that it is bound to affect all society. It is an art which shines like a torch of hope in the troubled world. It is a creative force which we must learn to utilize for the benefit of all mankind. This miracle of engineering skill which one day will bring the world to the home also brings a new American industry to serve man's material welfare ... [Television] will become an important factor in American economic life."

And how. On that fateful day in 1939, with America recovering from its greatest depression and war rumbling in the distance, Sarnoff gave the world a look into a new life. Not only was he instrumental in creating both radio

and television as we know them, he was also nearly clairvoyant in seeing how each medium would develop. He regarded black-and-white TV as only a transitional phase to color and even predicted the invention of the VCR. His stubborn pursuit of technology turned his employer, Radio Corp. of America, into a powerhouse in less than a decade.

Sarnoff was born in Uzlian, Russia, in 1891 (the year the electron was christened; he often bragged they were born the same year) and traveled steerage to New York nine years later with his family. Knowing no English, he helped support his family by selling newspapers. At 15 he bought a telegraph key, learned Morse code and, after being hired as an office boy for the Marconi Wireless Telegraph Co. of America, became a junior operator in 1908.

Then, like so many people in the communications business, he was at the right place at the right time. On April 14, 1912, Sarnoff was working at the Marconi station atop Wanamaker's department store when he picked up a message relayed from ships at sea: "S.S. *Titanic* ran into iceberg, sinking fast." For the next 72 hours, the story goes, he remained at his post, giving the world the first authentic news of the disaster. Did someone say CNN?

Sarnoff's technical ability propelled him quickly through the ranks at Marconi, and in 1915 he submitted an idea for a "radio music box" at a time when radio was mainly used in shipping and by amateur wireless enthusiasts. He believed his device would make radio a "household utility" like the piano or phonograph. "The idea is to bring music into the

BORN
Feb. 27, 1891,
in Uzlian,
Russia

1915 Proposes a
"radio music box"
to receive
broadcasts

1926 Creates NBC,
the first radio
network

1939
Introduces TV
broadcasting
to the U.S.

1970 Retires
from RCA

1891

1971

1900
Immigrates
to U.S.

1921 Appointed
RCA general
manager; debuts
the first sports
broadcast

1930 Named
RCA president

1947 Named
CEO of RCA

DIES
in New York

DASHING Sarnoff at
the telegraph, 1912

> ## "Television service requires the creation of a system, not merely the ... development of apparatus.
>
> **DAVID SARNOFF, at RCA's annual meeting, May 1935**

Sarnoff gives television its sign-on at the 1939 New York World's Fair

His strong-willed management style gave him the label of not always being "talent-friendly," although he was close to great musicians like Arturo Toscanini. Sarnoff managed to survive a major raid orchestrated by CBS boss William S. Paley, who lured several major NBC stars. But if Sarnoff lost a battle, you could always bet on his winning the war. Under his leadership NBC had the first videotape telecast and the first made-for-television movie.

Sarnoff retired as RCA chairman in 1970 and died a year later. RCA became a conglomerate, diversifying broadly—and unsuccessfully—before being taken over in 1986 by GE, the outfit that had started RCA and was forced to divest it in 1932.

From our earliest days as network executives and, before that, as students of the medium and charter members of the first generation of TV viewers, we have lived and worked in his giant shadow. Having established our own production company, we are humbled by the success of a man who started with nothing and by force of will ignited a revolution that has had an unparalleled effect on our society.

When we first teamed up at ABC in the mid-'70s, broadcast television was still a heady and vibrant place. We were thrilled when we heard someone mention a show we had helped get on—*Soap*, maybe, or *Barney Miller* or *Taxi*. We learned from our two favorite bosses, Fred Silverman and Michael Eisner, that a good programmer respects the audience, takes risks, has showman-like instincts and lives to bring the best and brightest talent to the people.

house by wireless," he wrote in a memo. It was regarded as commercial folly. But he would soon have another opportunity to find backing for his idea. After the Great War, in 1919, RCA was formed by General Electric to absorb Marconi's U.S. assets (which included him).

Sarnoff had it all figured out: for RCA to sell radios, it had to have programming—music, news, sports. On July 2, 1921, he arranged the broadcast of the Jack Dempsey–Georges Carpentier prizefight (great ratings in the male demos), which was a watershed event. Within three years the radio music box, now called the Radiola (price: a hefty $75), was a success, with sales of $83.5 million.

The visionary's career took off. His next epiphany: the fastest path to profits would be to create national broadcasts by stringing together hundreds of stations. In other words, a network. In 1926, as general manager of RCA, he formed the National Broadcasting Co. as a subsidiary.

Next Sarnoff saw the potential of the iconoscope, a proto-television patented by Vladimir Zworykin in 1923. Within five years Sarnoff had set up a special NBC station called B2XBS to experiment with what came to be known as television. In 1941 NBC started commercial telecasting from station WNBT in New York City, but once again progress was delayed by war. Sarnoff served as communications consultant for General Dwight D. Eisenhower, who later named him a brigadier general. The title stuck. And in the halls of 30 Rockefeller Plaza, Sarnoff became known as "the General."

After the war, television was unleashed. As a shrewd businessman who mixed as easily with scientists as with corporate leaders, Sarnoff fought for patents and the right to advance the technology of the medium. Called ruthless by his rivals, he once said, "Competition brings out the best in products and the worst in men." And when others would complain that his focus was more on technology than on programming, he said, "Basically, we're the delivery boys."

THE BROADCAST INDUSTRY HAS CHANGED SINCE then, and is undergoing the same kind of technological revolution that occurred when Sarnoff introduced television. Still there are programmers and producers with great passion for the medium, and we count ourselves among them. But now these broadcasters have had to embrace other media as well—cable and the Internet—to avoid being crushed by the furious pace of technology.

For that very reason, our latest venture is a new kind of hybrid production company called Oxygen, in which we will fuse a new cable channel with an Internet base to program for women. The heady feeling is back with another technology revolution. But the basic truth Sarnoff articulated—television is a beneficial, creative force—still holds despite the tumult of vertical integration, ratings wars, new-media breakthroughs and Internet companies with zooming stock prices. Certainly, the General would have caught the new wave, if not led it, and embraced television's transformation by the digital age. His channel was always dialed to the future. ∎

Marcy Carsey and Tom Werner produced the hit TV series The Cosby Show, Roseanne *and* 3rd Rock from the Sun.

Video Visionaries

First came radio, then television, then lots and lots of television. These farsighted entrepreneurs helped build TV's global village

Ted Turner

He turned a tiny UHF station in Atlanta into America's first superstation. Then he decided, against all odds, that an all-news TV channel could succeed. Result: TBS and CNN helped define the transforming world of cable TV—and the unpredictable Turner (now vice chairman of Time Warner) enlivened it with his buccaneering bravado.

William Paley

The founder of CBS brought to the infant medium both a showman's instincts and a public-service mission. He staged TV's first big talent raid, hiring Jack Benny and other top stars from NBC. And he invented modern broadcast news, giving Ed Murrow and his protégés the corporate backing that still inspires TV journalists.

Gerald Levin

For decades America's TV programming was controlled by the broadcasting trio of CBS, NBC and ABC. Levin, the head of a small cable channel, HBO, broke the network stranglehold in 1975 when he put HBO on a satellite, making it a national presence. But in the 1990s, Levin, as head of Time Warner, saw his dreams of a video "information superhighway" collapse before the computer Internet juggernaut.

Rupert Murdoch

With Turner and Levin, the Australia-born mogul broke the oligopoly that defined the TV landscape for much of the century. When everyone said three networks were enough, he created a fourth, Fox. When TV was still a parochial business, he made it global, with satellite ventures around the world. And that's not to mention his newspaper empire.

Giving a boost to actor Jackie Coogan, small depositor

A.P.
Giannini

Anyone with a bank account owes a debt to a produce seller who refused to say no

By DANIEL KADLEC

LIKE A LOT OF FOLKS IN THE San Francisco area, Amadeo Peter Giannini was thrown from his bed in the wee hours of April 18, 1906, when the Great Quake shook parts of the city to rubble. He hurriedly dressed and hitched a team of horses to a borrowed produce wagon and headed into town—to the Bank of Italy, which he had founded two years earlier. Sifting through the ruins, he discreetly loaded $2 million in gold, coins and securities onto the wagon bed, then covered the bank's resources with a layer of vegetables and headed home.

In the days after the disaster, the man known as A.P. broke ranks with his fellow bankers, many of whom wanted area banks to remain shut to sort out the damage. Giannini quickly set up shop on the docks near San Francisco's North Beach. With a wooden plank straddling two barrels for a desk, he began to extend credit "on a face and a signature" to small businesses and individuals in need of money to rebuild their lives. His actions spurred the city's redevelopment.

That would have been legacy enough for most people. But Giannini's mark extends far beyond San Francisco, where his dogged determination and unusual focus on "the little people" helped build what was at his death the largest bank in the country, Bank of America, with assets of $5 billion. (In 1998 it was No. 2, with assets of $572 billion, behind Citigroup's $751 billion.)

Giannini's innovations—including home mortgages, auto loans and other installment credit—are taken for granted by most bank customers today. Heck, most of us take *banks* for granted. But they didn't exist, at least not for working stiffs, before Giannini.

A.P. was also the architect of what has become nationwide banking in the 1990s—although parochial interests prevented him from realizing it in his lifetime. His great vision was that a bank doing business in all parts of a state or the nation would be less vulnerable to any one region's difficulties. It would therefore be strong enough to

TIME 100

> I have worked without thinking of myself. This [is] the largest factor in whatever success I have attained.

A.P. GIANNINI, on his approach to business

lend to troubled communities when they were most in need. That same model is applied today in both national and international banking. Fittingly, the first bank in the U.S. to have branches coast to coast is that same Bank of America, which accomplished the feat in 1998 through its $48 billion merger with NationsBank of Charlotte, N.C.

A.P. Giannini was born in San Jose, Calif., in 1870, the son of immigrants from Genoa, Italy. His father, a farmer, died in a fight over a dollar when A.P. was seven. His mother later married Lorenzo Scatena, a teamster who went into the produce business. Young A.P. left school at 14 to assist him, and by 19 he was a partner in a thriving enterprise, built largely on his reputation for integrity. At 31 he declared that he would sell his half-interest to his employees and retire, which he did. But then fate intervened, and his real career began.

At 32, A.P. was asked to join the board of the Columbus Savings & Loan Society, a modest bank in North Beach, the Italian section of town. Giannini soon found himself at odds with the other directors, who had little interest in extending loans to hardworking immigrants. In those days banks existed mainly to serve businessmen and the wealthy. Giannini tried to convince the board that it would be immensely profitable to lend to the working class, which he knew to be credit worthy.

He was soundly rebuffed. So in 1904 he raised $150,000 from his stepfather and 10 friends and opened the Bank of Italy—in a converted saloon directly across the street from the Columbus S&L. He kept the bartender on as an assistant teller. There he began to exploit his guiding principle: that there was money to made lending to the little guy. He promoted deposits and loans by ringing doorbells and buttonholing people on the street, painstakingly explaining what a bank does. Traditional bankers were aghast. It was considered unethical to solicit banking business.

Giannini also made a career out of lending to out-of-favor industries. He helped the California wine industry get started, then bankrolled Hollywood at a time when the movie industry was anything but proven. In 1923 he created a motion-picture loan division and helped Mary Pickford, Charlie Chaplin, Douglas Fairbanks and D.W. Griffith start United Artists. When Walt Disney ran $2 million over budget on *Snow White,* Giannini stepped in with a loan.

In 1919 he had organized Bancitaly Corp. as a launching pad for statewide expansion; it was succeeded in 1928 by TransAmerica Corp., a holding company with wide interests in financial services, including some overseas banks. That same year he bought Bank of America, one of New York City's most venerable lending institutions.

Giannini retired again in 1930 and moved to Europe, believing his successor would carry on in his spirit. But when TransAmerica management switched focus during the Depression, the betrayed Giannini returned to retake control. He had always urged employees and depositors to become shareholders of the bank; now he won a 1932 proxy fight by knocking on doors again, asking working-class shareholders for their votes. He then consolidated TransAmerica's California bank holdings under the Bank of America name, which survived when regulators forced Trans-America to break up in the '50s, after A.P.'s death.

When Giannini died at age 79, his estate was worth less than $500,000, at his choosing. He could have been a billionaire, but he disdained great wealth, believing it would make him lose touch with the people he wanted to serve. For years he accepted virtually no pay, and when he was granted a surprise $1.5 million bonus one year, he promptly gave it all to the University of California. "Money itch is a bad thing," A.P. once said. "I never had that trouble." ∎

The earthquake that destroyed San Francisco breathed life into Giannini's financial empire

Daniel Kadlec writes a column about personal finance and Wall Street for TIME'*s weekly section* Personal Time.

BORN May 6, 1870, in San Jose, Calif.

1904 Founds the Bank of Italy to serve the working classes

1928 Buys the Bank of America and consolidates his vast bank properties

1945 Bank of America is the largest bank in the country

1870

1949

FATHER With his family, around 1920

1906 Rescues the bank's money after San Francisco's Great Quake

1932 Ends his retirement to regain control of TransAmerica

DIES in San Mateo, Calif., on June 3

Charles
Merrill

With a fervent belief in the small investor as the foundation of the stock market, "Good Time Charlie" made America the shareholder nation

By JOSEPH NOCERA

IN 1940, THE YEAR CHARLES EDWARD MERRILL founded the investment firm we now know as Merrill Lynch & Co., he was 54 years old and had already lived an extraordinarily productive and visible life. A poor boy from the backwaters of Florida, Merrill was forced to leave college by lack of funds. But he schemed his way to Wall Street and made himself wealthy by the time he was 31.

He was the first investment banker to realize that chain stores would one day dominate retailing, and he got rich by underwriting (and often controlling) such future powerhouses as S.S. Kresge (now K Mart) and Safeway Stores. He set up one of America's first wire houses—brokerage firms with branch offices in different cities connected to the main office by Teletype.

He was also the first big-name Wall Streeter to predict the Great Crash of 1929. Indeed, in the months leading up to the Crash, Merrill pleaded (to no avail) with President Calvin Coolidge to speak out against speculation. By February 1929, Merrill was so sure the end was near that he liquidated his firm's stock portfolio, an act that made him famous in October, when the Crash finally came.

Merrill made the gossip pages as regularly as the financial pages. By 1940, he had been married three times, had had countless affairs ("recharging my batteries" was his euphemism for philandering) and had sired three children, the youngest of whom, James Merrill, became one of America's finest poets. A short, self-absorbed, prideful, flamboy-

ant fellow—"Good Time Charlie Merrill," his friends called him—he had the unconscious expectation that Great Men always have: that he should be at the center of any orbit he entered. And so he was. As his son once wrote, "Whatever he decided to serve, the victim was meant to choke it down and be grateful."

Merrill can't be dismissed as a moneybags who made a lucky guess on the Crash. He truly deserves to be remembered for what he did during that second career of his, the one that began when he was deep into middle age. In founding Merrill Lynch—his partner and sidekick, Edmund C. ("Eddie") Lynch, was a soda-fountain-equipment salesman—Merrill created an important and enduring institution. But more than that, he started the country down an important and enduring path.

Merrill, you see, was the first person to advocate openly that the stock market should not just be a plaything for Wall Street insiders but should also be an avenue for the broad mass of Americans. Decades before founding Merrill Lynch, he coined the phrase "Bringing Wall Street to Main Street." For the last 17 years of his life, that's what he tried to achieve with his new firm, which became a laboratory for his grand experiment. Today when we conjure up the names of the great American financiers, we tend to think of people like J.P. Morgan and Warren Buffett and even Michael Milken. But none of them had the effect on American life that Merrill had. In fact, they're not even close.

Can there be any doubt that the democratization of the

BORN Oct. 19, 1885, in Green Grove Springs, Fla.

1914 Earns his first fortune financing future powerhouses S.S. Kresge (K Mart) and Safeway

1929 Worried by speculation, tells clients to sell portfolios months before the Crash

1885

1956

HIGH LIFE He sought out common folk for customers but enjoyed a society-page lifestyle. He had three wives over the years, and as many mansions

1940 Founds firm now known as Merrill Lynch & Co., vowing to bring "Wall Street to Main Street"

DIES At his death, his firm boasts 115 offices

"We do advise in no uncertain terms that you take advantage of the present high prices."

CHARLES MERRILL, in a letter to customers before the '29 Crash

markets is the single most profound financial trend of the past half-century? The statistics certainly bear this out: by some measures, half of America's households now invest, compared with only 16% in 1945, and mutual funds alone hold more of America's financial assets than banks do. Indeed, a strong argument can be made that the small investor, more than the professional trader, is the true foundation upon which the modern bull market has been built.

Look at how fixated we've become with the daily ups and downs of the Dow—how our hearts race when the market is up and how we sag when the market does. Or look at how we've turned mutual-fund managers like Peter Lynch into celebrities. Most of all, look at the extraordinary extent to which we now rely on stocks to fund our retirement, send our kids to college and allow us to lead the kind of comfortable lives we view as middle class. Our belief in the market today approaches religious faith.

Which, it turns out, is a pretty fair description of how Merrill always viewed the market. Its ability to create wealth broadly was to him an indisputable proposition. And while this is now a more or less universal truth, it was not always so. During the first part of this century, after all, the Street was largely a rigged game. Insiders manipulated the market from behind the curtains, behavior that, while unseemly, was legal then. Small investors were scorned—or fleeced. Yet Merrill was untouched by the cynicism that pervaded Wall Street. Like so many American visionaries, he was marked by a naive and exaggerated optimism that was unshakable, despite the darker reality around him.

Did the events of the Roaring Twenties and the Great Depression change Merrill's views? Quite the contrary. The Crash proved that people should have listened to him rather than those charlatans who encouraged investors to borrow so heavily and speculate so wildly. And if Americans had soured on the market by the end of the 1930s—and how could they not as the Dow Jones average lost 60% of its value and people came to see how rotten the game had been—Merrill eventually concluded that someone would have to rekindle the country's faith in the market. He turned to the only man he thought capable of the task: himself.

IN RETROSPECT, MERRILL LYNCH WAS REALLY CHARLIE Merrill's bully pulpit, the platform from which he could preach the virtues of the stock market and show the country that the small investor could get a fair shake on Wall Street. "Demystification had been the key to [my father's] great success," James Merrill later wrote in his memoir. "No more mumbo-jumbo from Harvard men in paneled rooms; let the stock market's workings henceforth be intelligible even to the small investor." To that end, the firm published an endless stream of reports, magazines, pamphlets—11 million pieces in 1955 alone—with titles like *How to Invest.* Under Merrill the firm gave seminars across the country, with child care provided so that both husband and wife could attend. It set up tents in county fairs. It ran a brokerage on wheels. Once, it even gave away stock in a contest sponsored by Wheaties.

By Merrill's death, in 1956, the firm had some 400,000 clients and had become the country's largest brokerage, a distinction it still held in 1999. But Merrill died a disappointed man. Wall Street had not rushed to follow his example, as he had hoped, and the majority of the country, still scarred by the memory of the Depression, was not ready to plunge back into stocks. He was simply too far ahead of his time.

There are many other people—mutual-fund pioneer Ned Johnson at Fidelity Investments and discount broker Charles Schwab, to name two—who over the course of the next 40 years helped push Wall Street and Main Street closer together. Yet for all their innovations, they remain at bottom Merrill's heirs. Their modern investing mantra is the same basic message he preached so many years ago—that people should invest for the long haul; that they should have a clear understanding of the companies they are buying; that despite the hair-raising ups and downs, stocks have historically outperformed every other form of investment. Today the stock market no longer belongs to insiders. It belongs to all of us, who partake in its gains just as we share in its losses. Good Time Charlie Merrill's lonely voice has become America's common wisdom. ∎

Merrill, second from left, brought Wall Street to local shopping centers

Joseph Nocera is an editor-at-large at FORTUNE *and the author of* A Piece of the Action.

Moguls of the Market

Visionary bankers and brokers married capital to industry to make the U.S. the world's most powerful economy

Andrew Mellon

Through Pittsburgh, Pa.'s Mellon Bank, he became a driving force behind Alcoa, Gulf Oil, Union Steel, McClintic-Marshall and other giants. The key financier of America's industrial boom, Mellon is credited with bringing on the prosperity of the 1920s while serving as Secretary of the Treasury.

Michael Milken

The first to see the potential of using high-yield bonds to raise capital for risky ventures, Milken bankrolled upstart companies and fostered the '80s takeover mania by financing corporate raiders. Imprisoned after pleading guilty to fraud in 1988, he is now a consultant, health activist and philanthropist.

Charles Schwab

Following in the footsteps of Charles Merrill, Schwab pioneered the "discount brokerage." He brought price wars to the sale of securities, put his brokers on salary rather than commission, executed orders quickly—and led millions of new middle-class investors to the market.

Arthur Rock

An early backer of such technology firms as Apple, Teledyne and Fairchild Semiconductor, Rock was also a founder of Intel. Famous for investing his own money in tech start-ups, San Francisco–based Rock has led a new generation of venture capitalists that is driving the greatest creation of wealth in history.

Willis Carrier

So it *was* the humidity! How a kindly engineer from the Snowbelt helped make the Sunbelt boom

By MOLLY IVINS

W OULD YOU LIKE TO WRITE ABOUT WILLIS H. Carrier?" the TIME editor inquired. "And who the hell might he be?" "Man who invented air conditioning." "A lifelong hero of mine!"

And what a splendid fellow he was too, in addition to being such a benefactor to mankind (unless you want to hold all the Yankees who have moved to the South against him). A perfectly Horatio Alger kind of guy was Willis Carrier, struggling against odds, persisting, overcoming. Slapped down by the Great Depression, he fought back to build an enormous concern that to this good day is the world's leading maker of air conditioning, heating and ventilation systems.

And think of the difference he's made. As anyone who has ever suffered through a brutal summer can tell you, if it weren't for Carrier's having made human beings more comfortable, the rates of drunkenness, divorce, brutality and murder would be Lord knows how much higher. Productivity rates would plunge 40% over the world; the deep-sea fishing industry would be deep-sixed; Michelangelo's frescoes in the Sistine Chapel would deteriorate; rare books and manuscripts would fall apart; deep mining for gold, silver and other metals would be impossible; the world's largest telescope wouldn't work; many of our children wouldn't be able to learn; and in Silicon Valley, the computer industry would crash.

The major imponderable in the life of Willis Carrier is whether he was actually a genius, which depends, of course, on the definition. Engineers will tell you that theirs is a craft more of persistence than inspiration. Yet Carrier was without question the leading engineer of his day on the conditioning of air (more than 80 patents). Carrier was also an exceptionally nice man, according to all reports, modest and sometimes droll, and a farsighted manager—he devoutly believed in teamwork and mentoring decades before the management consultants discovered it. One of his other management precepts, born of his own experience, is that time spent staring into space while thinking is not time wasted.

Carrier was the offspring of an old New England family—in fact, his many-times-great-grandmother, who was known for her "keen sense of justice and a sharp tongue," was hanged as a witch by the Puritans in Salem. The son of a farmer and a "birthright Quaker" mother, Carrier was the only child in a houseful of adults, including his grandparents and great-aunt. He seems to have been a born tinkerer. Unfortunately, he was seriously handicapped by lack of wherewithal. He worked

| BORN Nov. 26, 1876, in Angola, N.Y. | 1901 Goes to work in the drafting department of Buffalo Forge Co. | 1915 Forms the Carrier Engineering Corp. | HOT TICKET A movie theater sign in 1940 | DIES at age 73 in New York City |

1876 ——————————————————————————————— 1950

| 1906 U.S. patent issued for "Apparatus for Treating Air" | 1922 First centrifugal refrigerating machine unveiled in Newark, N.J. | 1939 Invents a system for air-conditioning skyscrapers |

TIME 100

if the company hadn't decided in 1914 to kill off its engineering department. Carrier, Lyle and five other young engineers left a year later to start their own operations.

Air conditioning did not begin life as a cooling system for homes and offices. Nor did it begin life as a system. Carrier's first customer, in 1902, was a business with a production problem: a frustrated printer in Brooklyn whose color reproductions kept messing up because changes in humidity and temperature made his paper expand and contract, causing a lot of ugly color runs.

Carrier could solve this problem by controlling humidity. But in '06, a cotton mill in South Carolina gave him a new challenge—heat. "When I saw 5,000 spindles spinning so fast and getting so hot that they'd cause a bad burn when touched several minutes after shutdown, I realized our humidifier was too small for the job."

FOR THE FIRST TWO DECADES OF AIR CONDITIONING, the device was used to cool machines, not people. Eventually, deluxe hotels and theaters called in Carrier. Three Texas theaters, I am pleased to report, were the first to be air-conditioned (the claims of Grauman's Metropolitan in Los Angeles are to be ignored). The hot air generated by Congress was cooled by Carrier in 1928-29—and needs it again today. But it was not until after World War II that air conditioning lost its luxury status and became something any fool would install.

Willis Carrier, who read and sought out knowledge until his death at 73, married three times (twice a widower) and adopted two children. In classic American-businessman fashion, he was a Presbyterian, a Republican and a golfer.

Alas, there is a downside to this tale. Scientists now believe the chlorofluorocarbons (CFCs) used in refrigeration systems are largely responsible for blowing a hole in the ozone, and that will cause potentially zillions of cases of skin cancer, cataracts and what-have-you. That's quite a big Oops! for our exemplary Horatio Alger figure.

The First Rule of Holes is, When You Are *in* One, Stop Digging; and that is what Carrier's namesake has done. In 1994 the company, now part of giant United Technologies, produced the first chlorine-free, non-ozone-depleting residential air-conditioning system. It has since produced two generations of chlorine-free cooling units, well before the Montreal Accords or the still unratified Kyoto Accords have come into play. Much in the fashion of its founder, the company is trying to fix all this without a grand scheme, but simply by doing the next right thing.

Now, the premise that technology got us into this mess and technology will surely get us out seems to be a dubious proposition. But if you had your druthers, wouldn't you really want to see the biologists backed up by engineers? Rachel Carson backed by Willis Carrier: the Chief really did know how to get things done. ∎

his way through high school, taught for three years and finally won a four-year scholarship to Cornell University.

I picked up some of these nuggets from a wonderfully dated biography by Margaret Ingels (*Father of Air Conditioning;* 1952). The introduction to this respectful book is by a Chicago banker, Cloud Wampler, who helped bail out Carrier's firm in the Depression and later became its CEO. He writes, "[In] my unforgettable first meeting with 'The Chief' ... Right off the bat Dr. Carrier made it clear he had a dim view of bankers ... I remember so well the ring in his voice when he said: 'We will not do less research and development work'; 'We will not discharge the people we have trained'; and 'We will all work for nothing if we have to.'"

The Father of Air Conditioning's first job was with a heating outfit, the Buffalo Forge Co. In appropriate young-genius fashion, his research had soon saved the company $40,000 a year, and they put him in charge of a new department of experimental engineering. At Buffalo Forge he met Irvine Lyle, a gifted salesman and ultimately his partner in Carrier Corp. We'd all know the name Buffalo Forge today

Syndicated columnist Molly Ivins' latest book is You Got to Dance with Them What Brung You. *She lives in Texas.*

Good Things

In a century that harnessed technology to convenience, an explosion of innovation made everyday life better

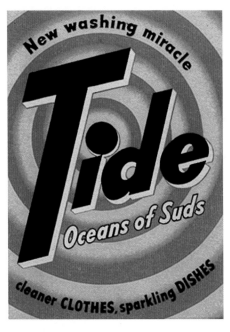

Refrigerator
With the introduction of small electric motors and nontoxic Freon in the 1930s, refrigerators migrated from industry to home, replacing iceboxes and gas-powered refrigerators. In 1927 General Electric established a refrigeration department, and in 1931 Sears sold its first affordable and popular electric refrigerator, for $137.50.

Detergents
By adding surfactants—two-molecule, synthetic surface-active agents—to soap granules, Proctor & Gamble created a washday miracle. Dreft was first, in 1933, but the big gun, Tide, arrived in 1949. Bull's-eye!

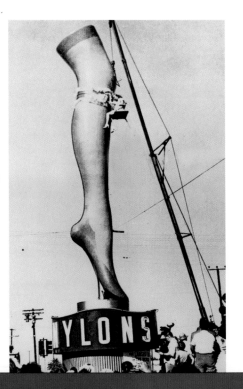

Nylon Stockings
Nylon was created in 1938; DuPont found the killer app in 1940 when the first nylon stockings went on sale. Women gladly paid $1.15 a pair for the durable stuff, twice the price of silk hose.

The Zipper
Swedish immigrant Gideon Sundback invented this nifty device in 1913. B.F. Goodrich coined the term for a fastener on galoshes; it was not used for clothes until the 1930s. By 1941 zippers beat the pants off buttons in the Battle of the Fly.

Neon

In 1910 a French scientist named Georges Claude applied an electrical charge to a tube filled with neon gas (as opposed to a filament in a vacuum) and created a new kind of illumination. Car dealers did the rest.

Paper Clip

The design is perfect. There's been little improvement since Norwegian Johan Vaaler got his American patent in 1901. Only about 20% are actually used to clip papers.

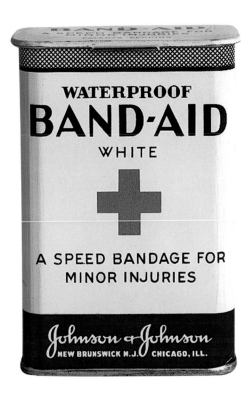

WATERPROOF
BAND-AID
WHITE
A SPEED BANDAGE FOR MINOR INJURIES
Johnson & Johnson
NEW BRUNSWICK N.J. CHICAGO, ILL.

Band-Aid

Johnson & Johnson sold $3,000 worth of handmade Band-Aids in 1921, the year it introduced them. A company cotton buyer, Earle Dickson, had created them at home for his accident-prone wife. He then convinced his boss that the strips had merit.

Automatic Washing Machine

Among those credited with making electric washing machines around 1910 was Alva J. Fisher. The machines used wringers to remove water from clothes. Truly automatic machines appeared in the 1930s. An early ad for a GE washer read, "If every father did the family washing next Monday, there would be an electric washing machine in every home by Saturday night."

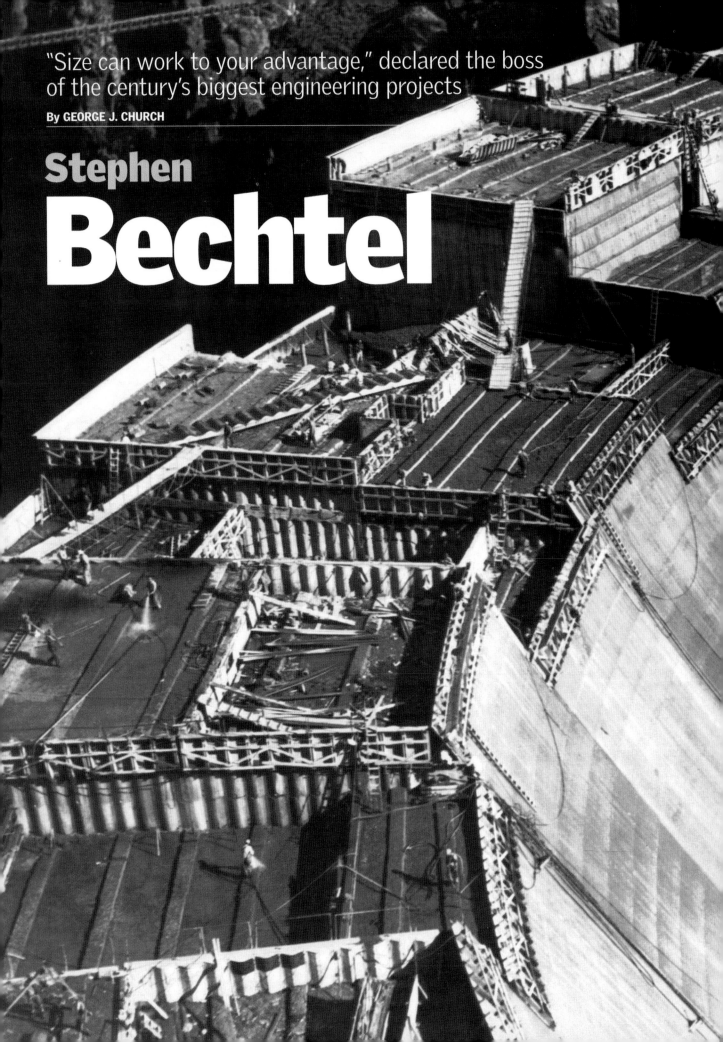

"Size can work to your advantage," declared the boss of the century's biggest engineering projects

By GEORGE J. CHURCH

Stephen
Bechtel

Hoover Dam swallowed 4.4 million cu. yds. of concrete and provided work for 5,000 laborers at a time, who built it in just five years. Price: $54.7 million

IN THE EARLY DAYS OF WORLD WAR II, GERMAN U-boats were sending Allied merchant ships to the bottom twice as fast as shipyards could build them. The U.S. Maritime Commission, desperately seeking an outfit to build 60 cargo ships for its allies, sent word to the Bechtel construction company that it would be welcome to bid on half the job. Stephen Bechtel, head of the family firm, had no experience in shipbuilding. But he insisted on getting the order for all 60. "Size can work to your advantage if you think big," he said. "You just recognize it and move the decimal point over."

Thinking big was Steve Bechtel's forte. He learned to appreciate scale as the primary manager in the building of Hoover Dam in the early '30s, then the largest public works project in U.S. history. The wartime shipyards Bechtel organized would build 560 vessels—up to 20 ships a month—between 1941 and 1945, an astounding output even in an era of production miracles.

Bechtel was, and remained throughout his nearly 70-year career, a visionary whose imagination was fired by grandiose projects—the more seemingly impossible the better. His motto, endlessly repeated, was "We'll build anything for anybody, no matter what the location, type or size." He and his company built pipelines and power plants in the forbidding reaches of the Canadian Rockies, across the Arabian desert and through South American jungles, as well as in daunting places like downtown Boston, where the Central Artery project unfolds today. His portfolio even includes an entire city (Jubail, Saudi Arabia). Bechtel built in 140 countries and on six continents. It has been said, hyperbolically perhaps, that Bechtel engineers changed the physical contours of the planet more than any other humans.

Bechtel grew up on rugged construction sites where his father Warren, who started the company, punched rail lines and highways through the California wilderness. To the end of the son's long life—he died in 1989, six months short of his 89th birthday—Steve Bechtel enjoyed prowling around job sites, but he neither looked nor sounded like a construction boss. In his prime, in the 1950s, he was well tailored

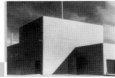

> # "Hoover Dam put us in a prime position as being big-time, real thinkers. We bet our shirts on it."
>
> ## STEPHEN BECHTEL

and soft-spoken, with the ingratiating manner of a salesman.

He was always peering over the horizon. In the 1920s he foresaw an energy boom and took the company into pipeline construction. Later he helped pioneer the now common "turnkey" construction contract, under which Bechtel would design a project, build it and turn it over to the owner by a set date, for a fixed fee. In 1959 he helped produce a study for a tunnel under the English Channel, a project finally realized in the 1990s.

Bechtel got on the map in a place that was almost off it: Black Canyon, Nev. With the Depression raging in 1931, Bechtel's father helped organize a consortium called Six Companies to tackle the massive engineering job that became known as Hoover Dam. The consortium bid $49 million and made a profit. Over the course of five years workers excavated 3.7 million cu. yds. of rock and poured 4.4 million cu. yds. of concrete; the main arch of the dam towers 70 stories high. Steve was first in charge of transportation, engineering and administration. When his father died suddenly in 1933, he became chief executive of the whole project, which transformed the economy of much of the West, as well as Bechtel's company.

After Hoover, Bechtel was convinced he and his outfit had no limits, and he set out to prove it. While the dam was still going up, he began building the 8.2-mile San Francisco–Oakland Bay Bridge. During World War II, Bechtel, in addition to shipyards, built bases and ran plants that modified bombers and rebuilt jeeps. At the same time Steve built a top-secret 1,600-mile pipeline through the Canadian wilderness to Alaska, under primitive conditions. The pace left him so fatigued that in 1946 he briefly retired. But he would not be on the shelf long.

The Trans-Arabian pipeline: a path to power for Bechtel

Returning to active management, Bechtel spent six months every year roaming the world, hobnobbing with kings, presidents and foreign business magnates, fishing for projects. Around 1947 he landed a whopper: construction of what was then the world's longest oil pipeline (1,068 miles), across Saudi Arabia. That was an early step in the building of a powerful economy as well as a fruitful relationship with Saudi kings. According to legend, on one trip to the kingdom Bechtel noticed the flames of natural gas being burned off at wellheads as he flew over. Surely, he thought, the wasted energy could be put to some use. In 1973 he presented a plan to King Faisal, an old acquaintance: use the gas to power factories in a new city that Bechtel would build on the site of a tiny fishing village

at Jubail. The city, still under construction, houses a steel mill and factories that make chemicals, plastics and fertilizer. The town is now home to 70,000 and growing.

THE COMPANY BECHTEL BUILT IS NOT UNIVERSALLY loved. One partner in the wartime shipyards was John McCone, a steel executive who later became CIA director. He was among the first of a long line of men who filled high offices alternately in Bechtel and the Federal Government (most notable: George Shultz and Caspar Weinberger). That led to charges of undue influence—by whom on whom was never quite clear. The company's penchant for secrecy didn't help its reputation either. In 1976 the Justice Department charged that Bechtel had gone too far to please Arab clients by blacklisting potential subcontractors who dealt with Israel. Bechtel signed a consent decree promising not to join any Arab boycott of Israel.

None of that has prevented the company, now headed by Riley Bechtel, a grandson of Steve's, from flourishing mightily. When Steve took over in 1933, Bechtel had revenues of less than $20 million; a quarter-century later, when he officially retired, sales were $463 million. The company, still family controlled, had 1997 revenues of $11.3 billion; its projects range from a transit system in Athens to a semiconductor plant in China. These and others are fruits of Steve Bechtel's forward thinking—decades before the term global economy became a cliché. ∎

George J. Church, now a contributor to TIME, *has written more than 125 cover stories for the magazine.*

Monuments Of the Age

Just as Egyptians, Greeks and Romans built grand projects that defined the culture and technology of their times, builders of this century made big statements in concrete and steel —By **DANIEL S. LEVY**

Panama Canal 1914

The $380 million project, like the Suez Canal that preceded it, was an epic assault on nature that employed as many as 43,400 workers at a time—many of whom succumbed to yellow fever while clearing the mosquito-infested swamps. More than 211 million cu. yds. of earth and rock were moved to create a water link between the Atlantic and Pacific oceans, cutting the voyage from New York to California by 7,800 miles. Leased by the U.S., the canal returns to Panamanian sovereignty in 2000.

Empire State Building 1931

Opened in the Depression as a mighty symbol of rebirth, the 102-floor building got off to a wobbly start financially. Built by General Motors executive John Raskob, it reigned for 42 years as the world's tallest building. Its Art Deco crown, intended as a mooring mast for blimps, was a handy perch in *King Kong*. Skyscrapers have since soared higher, but none have surpassed its limestone majesty.

Interstate Highway System 1956 to the present

Created by Dwight Eisenhower, the 43,000-mile, $330 billion (and still counting) network is the greatest pork barrel in U.S. history. It made America an automobile society, created millions of jobs and laced the country with freeways that increased mobility, spurred trade and opened the countryside to development. It also doomed passenger trains—and diminished regional flavor.

Chunnel 1994

Napoleon dreamed of one, but not until 192 years later would a tunnel under the channel linking England and the Continent be finished. Beginning on their respective shores, teams of French and English sandhogs used 1,000-ton boring machines to burrow through the 24 miles of chalk, clearing 20 million tons. The two sides met on Dec. 1, 1990.

Three Gorges Dam 2009

Mao once dreamed of taming the Yangtze, China's longest river, whose floodwaters have claimed the lives of millions. Officials expect this $24 billion dam to corral the river, giving their nation a great leap forward as it generates electricity for China's burgeoning cities and makes the mighty river more navigable. But as with other major projects, there is controversy. Some see it as a disaster because it will endanger animal species, submerge ancient temples and forcibly uproot 1.2 million people.

Walt
Disney

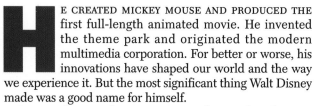

The first multimedia empire was built on animation, but its happy toons masked the founder's darker soul

By RICHARD SCHICKEL

H E CREATED MICKEY MOUSE AND PRODUCED THE first full-length animated movie. He invented the theme park and originated the modern multimedia corporation. For better or worse, his innovations have shaped our world and the way we experience it. But the most significant thing Walt Disney made was a good name for himself.

It was, of course, long ago converted into a brand name, constantly fussed over, ferociously defended, first by Disney, latterly by his corporate heirs and assigns. Acting as a beacon for parents seeking clean, decent entertainment for their children, the Disney logo—a stylized version of the founder's signature—more generally promises us that anything appearing beneath it will not veer too far from the safe, sound and relentlessly cheerful American mainstream, which it defines as much as serves.

That logo also now identifies an institution whose $22 billion in annual sales makes it the world's largest media company. It purveys many products that would have been unimaginable to its founder, a few of which (the odd TV show, the occasional R movie) might have been anathemas to him. Not that one sees him pondering long over such trifles, as his company fulfills the great commercial destiny this complex and darkly driven man always dreamed for it.

The notion of Walt Disney as a less than cheerful soul will ring disturbingly in the minds of older Americans taught by years of relentless publicity to think of Disney as "a quiet, pleasant man you might not look twice at on the

street," to quote an old corporate promotional piece—a man whose modest mission was simply "to bring happiness to the millions." Going along with the gag, Disney implied that the task was easy for him because he always whistled while he worked: "I don't have depressed moods. I'm happy, just very, very happy."

Sure. You bet. It sounded plausible, for if anyone seemed entitled to enjoy late-in-life contentment it was Walt Disney. Did not his success validate the most basic of American dreams? Had he not built the better mouse and had the world not beaten a path to his door, just as that cherished myth promised? Did he not deploy his fame and fortune in exemplary fashion, playing the kindly, story-spinning, magic-making uncle to the world? No entrepreneurial triumph of its day has ever been less resented or feared by the public. Henry Ford should have been so lucky. Bill Gates should get so lucky.

The truth about Disney, who was described by an observant writer as "a tall, somber man who appeared to be under the lash of some private demon," is slightly less benign and a lot more interesting. Uncle Walt actually didn't have an avuncular bone in his body. Though he could manage a sort of gruff amiability with strangers, his was, in fact, a withdrawn, suspicious and, above all, controlling nature. And with good—or anyway explicable—reason.

For he was born to a poverty even more dire emotionally than it was economically. His father Elias was one of those feckless figures who wandered the heartland at the turn of

BORN Dec. 5, 1901, in Chicago	1928 Launches Mickey Mouse, an instant sensation, in the first talking cartoon	1937 Premiers *Snow White*, first full-length animated film		1964 Conceives EPCOT, which opens in Orlando, Fla., in 1971
1901				**1966**
	1923 Opens cartoon studio in Hollywood	1932 Wins first of a record 32 personal Oscars	1955 Opens Disneyland	DIES in Los Angeles

Disney in 1944, three years after a labor dispute roiled his fantasy factory

the century seeking success in many occupations but always finding sour failure. Embittered, he spared his children affection, but never the rod. They all fled him at the earliest possible moment.

BEFORE LEAVING HOME AT 16 TO JOIN THE RED Cross Ambulance Corps during World War I, Walt, the youngest son, had discovered he could escape Dad's—and life's—meanness in art classes. In the service he kept drawing, and when he was mustered out, he set up shop as a commercial artist in Kansas City, Mo. There he discovered animation, a new field, wide open to an ambitious young man determined to escape his father's sorry fate. Animation was as well a form that placed a premium on technical problem solving, which was absorbing but not emotionally demanding. Best of all, an animated cartoon constituted a little world all its own—something that, unlike life, a man could utterly control. "If he didn't like an actor, he could just tear him up," an envious Alfred Hitchcock would later remark.

Reduced to living in his studio and eating cold beans out of a can, Disney endured the hard times any worthwhile success story demands. It was not until he moved to Los Angeles and partnered with his shrewd and kindly older brother Roy, who took care of business for him, that he began to prosper modestly. Even so, his first commercially viable creation, Oswald the Rabbit, was stolen from him. That, naturally, reinforced his impulse to control.

It also opened the way for the mouse that soared. Cocky, and in his earliest incarnations sometimes cruelly mischievous but always an inventive problem solver, Mickey would become a symbol of the unconquerably chipper American spirit in the depths of the Depression. Mickey owed a lot of his initial success, however, to Disney's technological acuity. For Disney was the first to add a music and effects track to a cartoon, and that breakthrough, coupled with anarchically inventive animation, wowed audiences, especially in the early days of sound, when live-action films were hobbled to immobile microphones.

Artistically, the 1930s were Disney's best years. He

Animation pioneer Disney filmed natural models for his artists to copy. Here, around 1930, he records behavior for *Peculiar Penguins*

Kids celebrate the opening day of Disney's masterwork, Disneyland, in 1955

embraced Technicolor as readily as he had sound, and, though he was a poor animator, he proved to be a first-class gag man and story editor, a sometimes collegial, sometimes bullying, but always hands-on boss, driving his growing team of youthfully enthusiastic artists to ever greater sophistication of technique and expression.

When Disney risked everything on his first feature, *Snow White and the Seven Dwarfs*, it turned out to be no risk at all, so breathlessly was his work embraced. Even the intellectual and artistic communities saw in it a kind of populist authenticity—naive and sentimental, courageous and life affirming.

But they misread Disney. In his dark and brilliant *Pinocchio* and the hugely ambitious *Fantasia*, he would stretch technique to the limits. But the latter film, rich as it was in unforgettable animation, is also full of banalities. It exposed the fact that, as film historian David Thomson says, "his prettiness had no core or heart."

Artistically Disney strove for realism; intellectually, for a bland celebration of tradition. There had been an Edenic moment in his childhood when the family settled on a farm outside little Marceline, Mo., and he used his work to celebrate the uncomplicated sweetness of the small-town life and values he had only briefly tasted.

His insistence on the upbeat also possibly served as an anodyne for the bitterness he felt when an ugly 1941 labor dispute ended his dream of managing his studio on a communitarian basis with himself as its benign patriarch.

Commercially, this worked out beautifully for him. Most people prefer their entertainments to embrace the comfortably cute rather than the disturbingly acute—especially when they're bringing the kids. Movie critics started ignoring him, and social critics began hectoring him, because his work ground off the rough, emotionally instructive edges of the folk- and fairy-tale tradition on which it largely drew,

robbing it of "the pulse of life under the skin of events," as one critic put it.

Disney didn't give a mouse's tail about all that. As far as he was concerned, the whole vexing issue of content was solved, and though he enjoyed being a hero to the culturally conservative, he was free to focus on what had always mattered most to him, which was not old pieties but new technologies.

Predictably, he became the first Hollywood mogul to embrace television. The show with him as host for more than a decade became not just a profit center for his company but also a promotional engine for all its works. These included chuckleheaded live-action comedies, nature documentaries that ceaselessly anthropomorphized their subjects, and, of course, Disneyland, which attracted his compulsive attention in the '50s and '60s.

Disneyland was another bet-the-farm risk, and Disney threw himself obsessively into the park's design, which anticipated many of the best features of modern urban planning, and into the "imagineering" by which the simulacrums of exotic, even dangerous creatures, places, fantasies could be unthreateningly reproduced.

THESE ATTRACTIONS WERE BETTER THAN ANY MOVIE in his eyes—three dimensional and without narrative problems. They were, indeed, better than life, for they offered false but momentarily thrilling experiences in a sterile, totally controlled environment from which dirt, rudeness, mischance (and anything approaching authentic emotion) had been totally eliminated. All his other enterprises had to be delivered into the possibly uncomprehending world. When Disneyland opened in 1955, that changed: he now had his own small world, which people had to experience on his terms.

Before he was felled by cancer at 65, it is possible to imagine that he was happy. He had at last devised a machine with which he could endlessly tinker. The little boy, envious of the placid small-town life from which he was shut out, had become mayor—no, absolute dictator—of a land where he could impose his ideals on everyone. The restless, hungry young entrepreneur had achieved undreamed-of wealth, power and honor. Asked late in life what he was proudest of, he did not mention smiling children or the promulgation of family values. "The whole damn thing," he snapped, "the fact that I was able to build an organization and hold it." These were not the sentiments of anyone's uncle—except perhaps Scrooge McDuck. And their consequences—many of them unintended and often enough unexplored—persist, subtly but surely affecting the ways we all live, think and dream. ∎

Richard Schickel, a TIME *film critic, wrote* The Disney Version: The Life, Times, Art and Commerce of Walt Disney.

Juan Trippe

Bringing the glamour of aviation to the masses, Pan Am's founder got Everyman flying everywhere

By RICHARD BRANSON

BY BUSINESS SCHOOL STANDARDS, JUAN TRIPPE WAS not a model chief executive. He didn't delegate well. He made big deals without telling his top managers. He almost single-handedly built a world airline, Pan American, but often acted as if he owned the world. He also had a vision that would change it, at least as regards airline travel. While his Pan Am does not survive today, his vision does.

He graduated from Yale in 1921 and worked briefly on Wall Street but got thoroughly bored. Planes fascinated him, though. Trippe was convinced that the future of travel was in the air. With an inheritance, he began a business with Long Island Airways in New York, a taxi service for the well-heeled. When that failed, he raised money from some wealthy Yale pals and joined Colonial Air Transport, which won the first U.S. airmail contract, between New York City and Boston. That same crowd liked to play in the Caribbean (excellent choice), where he created Pan American Airways Inc. from a merger of three groups. Trippe began service with a flight from Key West, Fla., to Havana, Cuba, on Oct. 28, 1927.

What characterized Trippe thereafter was an uncanny ability to pace his airline's growth with the range of the airliner as it slowly evolved: first crawling from island to island across the Caribbean and into Mexico, then extending to Central and South America. It was Trippe's backing of the flying boat, the first Pan Am Flying Clippers, that pioneered transoceanic aviation: first across the Pacific and, in the late 1930s, across the Atlantic. By the end of World War II, Trippe had in place a route system that was truly global.

Before anyone else, he believed in airline travel as something to be enjoyed by ordinary mortals, not just a globetrotting élite. In 1945 other airlines didn't think or act that way. Trippe decided to introduce a "tourist class" fare from New York to London. He cut the round-trip fare more than half, to $275 ($1,684 in today's dollars, which makes current pricing a bargain, right?). This went over like a lead

BRUCE McCALL

BORN
June 27,
1899, in Sea
Bright, N.J.

**1927 Starts Pan Am
with first international
mail contract, between
Florida and Cuba**

**1952 Tourist-class fares
across the Atlantic
become widely available**

**1968 Resigns
as head of
Pan Am**

1899

U.S. MAIL

SOARING Left, Trippe at a
1920 airplane meet. Right, he
cheers the first New York–to-
Boston airmail run in 1927

**1935 "China
Clipper" service
begins to Asia**

**1958 Launches
Boeing 707 jet
service between
New York and Paris**

1981

DIES
April 3
in New
York City

" The average man's holiday has been the prisoner of two grim keepers, money and time. "

JUAN TRIPPE, in a 1944 speech that presaged his strategy

balloon in the industry, where air fares were fixed by a cartel, the International Air Transport Association; it didn't want to hear about the tourist class. Incredibly, Britain closed its airports to Pan Am flights that had tourist seats. Pan Am was forced to switch to remote Shannon, Ireland. The industry's aversion to competition and making travel affordable was to have a long life, as Sir Freddie Laker would discover in the 1970s and as I would learn with my airline, Virgin Atlantic, nearly a decade later.

Trippe managed to find one route where the cartel could not thwart him: New York to San Juan, Puerto Rico. Pan Am's one-way fare was $75, and the flights were packed. Finally, in 1952, Trippe's relentless attacks on the I.A.T.A. forced all airlines to accept the inevitability of tourist class. But by then his vision had taken off for its next destination.

Flying the oceans was still mostly for the rich and famous. For millions of others, it was just a dream or a once-in-a-lifetime binge. Trippe saw that the jets being introduced by Boeing and Douglas could mark the end of that, and he ordered plenty of them. In October 1958, a Pan Am Boeing 707 left New York for its first scheduled flight to Paris.

A stewardess serves snacks aboard a Pan Am 707 in 1958, its first year in operation

THE JET AGE HAD BEGUN, and the transformation was dramatic. The 707 flew almost twice as fast, at 605 m.p.h., as the propeller-driven Stratocruiser it had replaced. The 707 carried about twice as many people. And for the first time, it flew mostly "over" the weather: typically at 32,000 ft., much higher than the Stratocruiser, a civilian version of the B-29 bomber. But those were not the numbers that intrigued Trippe. While he brilliantly exploited the glamour of his first jet-set passengers—celebrities and VIPs—he was calculating the new math of what we call in our business "bums on seats"—the seat-mile cost.

The first 707s were flying with five-abreast seating, two on one side of the aisle, three on the other. Trippe switched to six abreast and cut fares, making flying "the pond" far more accessible. As traffic soared, the relentless Trippe had a big idea: he reasoned that mass air travel could come to the international routes only with a larger airplane—a much larger airplane. He put the notion to his old friend Bill Allen, the boss of Boeing, saying he wanted a jet 2½ times the size of the 707. It was a staggering request given the development cost of the 707. And Trippe didn't stop there. Pam Am was operating the 707 with a seat-mile cost, at best, of 6.6¢. Trippe set for Boeing the goal of reducing that 30%.

"If you build it," said Trippe, "I'll buy it." "If you buy it," said Allen, "I'll build it." My kind of guys. Trippe said he would buy 25 airplanes. The price: $450 million, in those days big money. Pan Am under Trippe always rode shotgun with any new airplane it ordered. Trippe hired Charles Lindbergh to ride his airplanes incognito, and Lindbergh's ideas helped shape the cabin of the first jets. Pan Am engineers crawled all over Boeing as the company conceived the outline for the new jet, the 747.

By pure chance, it was Trippe himself who gave the jumbo its signature bulge. In a rare lapse of vision, Trippe thought the 747 would be superseded by a big supersonic jet, as cheap to run as a subsonic jet. Some hope. He therefore decreed that on the 747, pilots should sit above the flight deck so the nose could be opened up and take cargo. The 747's ultimate fate, he thought, would be as a flying Mack truck. Boeing showed him a wooden mock-up of the 747's flight deck, in the hump above the nose. He foraged around and came upon the space behind the flight deck, the rest of the hump. "What is this for?" he asked. "A crew rest area," said a Boeing engineer. "Rest area?" barked Trippe. "This is going to be reserved for passengers."

And so as co-creator of the 747, Trippe gave us the world's traveling machine. I launched Virgin Atlantic in June 1984 with the 747 at the point when it was really shrinking the world and air travel was truly democratized, as Trippe intended. Sadly, the 747 also sank Pan Am, which bought too many of the giant jets in the early 1970s. A world oil crisis hit airline travel hard, and Pan Am's business never recovered. Boeing itself almost went belly-up because of the cost of launching the 747.

Trippe had been a continuous innovator, but the sad irony is that he failed to re-invent his company for the leaner, far more competitive age he had done so much to shape: the age of travel for Everyman. A decade after his death, his airline, substantially dismembered, finally expired in 1991.

Throughout his career, Juan Trippe had been driven by the great American instinct for seeing a market before it happened—and then making it happen. In a real sense, he fathered the international airline business we know today. To get that job done, he took on the entire airline industry, and risked his company to see his vision through. You've got to admire a guy like that. ∎

Richard Branson, founder of Virgin Atlantic and occasional balloonist, knows a bit about airline renegades.

Lucky
Luciano

He downsized,
he restructured,
and he resorted
to Standard &
Poor's as much
as Smith &
Wesson to
become the
first CEO of
organized crime

By **EDNA BUCHANAN**

N.Y.C. POLICE.
7 2 3 2 1
4 18 36

**Despite his busy
criminal career,
Luciano was
jailed by the
feds only as a
pimp in 1936**

This 1949 photo of Luciano was taken, fittingly, in an unknown location—most likely Sicily

HE WAS BORN AND DIED IN ITALY, YET THE influence on America of a grubby street urchin named Salvatore Lucania ranged from the lights of Broadway to every level of law enforcement, from national politics to the world economy. First, he reinvented himself as Charles ("Lucky") Luciano. Then he reinvented the Mafia.

His story was Horatio Alger with a gun, an ice pick and a dark vision of Big Business. He was nine when the family immigrated from Sicily, where his father had labored in the sulphur pits, to New York City. He took to the streets early, was busted almost at once for shoplifting, later for delivering drugs. Luciano was a tough teenage hoodlum on the Lower East Side when his gang targeted a skinny Jewish kid whose bold defiance won their respect. The encounter led to a merger of Jewish and Italian gangs and a lifelong friendship. When Luciano rebuilt the Mob, Meyer Lansky was the architect. A ruthless natural ability enabled them to

rise through the ranks of their chosen profession. Sometimes they simply eliminated the ranks. When they downsized colleagues, it was permanent.

Taking advantage of Prohibition in 1920, Luciano and Lansky supplied booze to Manhattan speakeasies. While others used small boats to offload mother ships, their contacts enabled them to dock ships in New York Harbor.

An upwardly mobile member of New York's largest Mafia family, run by Giuseppe ("Joe the Boss") Masseria, Luciano grew impatient at the Castellammarese war in the late 1920s, a long and bloody power struggle between Masseria and Salvatore Maranzano. Lucky offered to eliminate his boss and end the violence, which he saw as disruptive to business. At an Italian restaurant, Joe the Boss ate lead. Lucky assumed control of the dead man's lottery business, while Maranzano seized his bootlegging turf.

Lucky's vision of replacing traditional Sicilian strongarm methods with a corporate structure, a board of direc-

BORN
Nov. 11, 1897, in Sicily

1906 Immigrates to New York City, lives in slums

1929 Survives rubout attempt on Staten Island

1936 Jailed on charges of running a prostitution ring

DEPORTEE Luciano, on left, in Capri in 1951, after he left the U.S.

1897 — 1962

1911 Drops out of school in fifth grade

1931 Becomes crime CEO after masterminding murders of two big bosses

1946 Wins prison release for wartime assistance, and is deported to Italy

DIES Jan. 26 in the Naples, Italy, airport

> ## "The vice industry, since Luciano took over, is highly organized and operates with businesslike precision."

THOMAS E. DEWEY, New York City special prosecutor

tors and systematic infiltration of legitimate enterprise failed to impress Maranzano. An ancient-history aficionado and would-be Julius Caesar, Maranzano aspired to be boss of all bosses. Most of all, he wanted to avoid Caesar's fatal miscalculation. He came to believe Lucky was too ambitious, too enterprising, too dangerous.

But Maranzano was too late. He was killed by police impersonators, hit men provided by Lansky and mutual friend Benjamin ("Bugsy") Siegel. More rubouts followed, in a well-orchestrated cutback of old-time Sicilian gangsters. Yet Luciano's management style would be far different from that of his Chicago counterpart Al Capone, who spent more time killing than doing business.

The FBI describes Luciano's ascendancy as the watershed event in the history of organized crime. After his hostile takeover, Luciano organized organized crime. He modernized the Mafia, shaping it into a smoothly run national crime syndicate focused on the bottom line. The enterprise was operated by two dozen family bosses who controlled bootlegging, numbers, narcotics, prostitution, the waterfront, the unions, food marts, bakeries and the garment trade, their influence and tentacles ever expanding, infiltrating and corrupting legitimate business, politics and law enforcement.

Luciano also led the trend in gangster chic. He lived large, in a suite at the Waldorf Astoria. Expensive and elegant suits, silk shirts, handmade shoes, cashmere topcoats and fedoras enhanced his executive image. There was always a beautiful woman, a showgirl or a nightclub singer on his arm. Frank Sinatra and actor George Raft were pals.

The good life began to go bad in 1935. Thomas E. Dewey was appointed New York City special prosecutor to crack down on the rackets. He targeted Luciano, calling him "the czar of organized crime in this city," and charged him with multiple counts of compulsory prostitution. The trial was sensational. Tabloids went wild. Lucky vehemently denied being a pimp. "It's a bum rap," he said, a lament echoed down the years to modern Miami, where a few aging mobsters remember the man. "Nobody had anything bad to say about Charlie," one of them told me. "He's the one who put it all together. A gentleman. He'd give a girl $100 just for smiling at him. That pimp charge was a frame just to get him off the streets." Convicted on 62 counts in June 1936, Luciano got 30 to 50 years in prison.

It took Hitler to win Lucky his freedom. After Pearl Harbor, German U-boats off the U.S. coast were sinking merchant ships regularly. U.S. intelligence suspected they were aided by spies or Nazi sympathizers. Then the *Normandie*, a French liner being retrofitted into a troop ship, sank in the Hudson River, sparking fears of sabotage.

Luciano does the "perp walk" on his way to Sing Sing prison to await deportation to Italy in 1946

STYMIED INTELLIGENCE AGENTS TURNED TO THE underworld for help. Lansky, virulently anti-Nazi, acted as liaison to Luciano. Lucky put the word out to cooperate, and formerly mute dockworkers, fishermen and hoodlums became the eyes and ears of naval intelligence. Soon eight German spies, who had landed by U-boat, were arrested, and explosives, maps and blueprints for sabotage were seized.

When the invasion of Italy was planned, the Allies needed intelligence for the landing at Sicily. Lucky for them, again. On V-E day in 1945, Luciano's lawyer petitioned for clemency, citing his war efforts. Eventually, a deal was reached that included deportation—Luciano had never become a citizen—and he was sent to Italy in February 1946. He surfaced months later in sunny Cuba. Lansky, Sinatra and other pals paid visits—so many, in fact, that the press took note, and in February 1947 the U.S. Bureau of Narcotics learned of his reappearance. U.S. authorities claimed that he planned to base a worldwide drug-smuggling operation in Cuba. Lucky was again packed off to Italy.

He died there, in homesick exile, on Jan. 26, 1962. Unlike so many of his peers, he expired from a coronary—an occupational hazard common to hard-driving execs. Or maybe he was just fortunate. Italian and U.S. officials quickly said they had been about to arrest him as a player in a major heroin ring.

Lucky Luciano excited the American imagination, always captivated by bad guys. A reporter who tracked him down in the twilight of his life asked if he would do it all again. "I'd do it legal," Lucky replied. "I learned too late that you need just as good a brain to make a crooked million as an honest million. These days you apply for a license to steal from the public. If I had my time again, I'd make sure I got that license first." ∎

Novelist and reporter Edna Buchanan's Garden of Evil *will be published next year. She won the Pulitzer Prize in 1986.*

William Levitt

His answer to a postwar housing crisis created a new kind of home life and culture: suburbia

By RICHARD LACAYO

SO LONG AS YOU DON'T COUNT SEX AND VIOLENCE, there's no human impulse older than the urge to find a nice, affordable house, something outside of town but not too far. In *Crabgrass Frontier*, the essential history of suburbanization, Kenneth T. Jackson quotes a letter to the King of Persia, inscribed on a clay tablet and dated 539 B.C., that describes the pleasures of the Ur-suburb. (Literally. It was in Ur.) "Our property ... is so close to Babylon that we enjoy all the advantages of the city, and yet when we come home we are away from all the noise and dust."

Ur shriveled. But the inclination to get out of town survived. Ancient Rome had its surrounding settlements. Chaucer mentions the 'burbs in *The Canterbury Tales*. All

the same, it wasn't until the later 20th century that suburbia was imagined as the ideal human habitation, an arrangement of houses and lives so fundamental that it was taken for granted the Flintstones lived there.

Suburbia required cars, highways and government-guaranteed mortgages. It also required William Levitt, who first applied a full panoply of assembly-line techniques to housing construction. That insight enabled him, and the many builders who copied him, to put up houses fast and cheap. Levitt's houses were so cheap (but still reasonably sturdy) that bus drivers, music teachers and boilermakers could afford them. And the first place he offered them was Levittown, N.Y., a town that is as much an achievement of its cultural moment as Venice or Jerusalem.

That moment came right after World War II. When the servicemen and -women headed home, there wasn't much home for them to come to. Wartime shortages of everything had crippled the housing industry. Returning veterans, their libidos fully charged with the ambitions that would create the baby boom, found themselves doubled up with parents and in-laws. To publicize their search for an apartment, one New York City couple camped out for two days in a department-store window.

In those years, the American housing industry was not so much an industry as a loose affiliation of local builders, any one of whom completed an average of four houses a year. What Levitt had in mind was 30 to 40 a day. Before the war, Levitt and his brother Alfred had built a few houses on land their father owned in Manhasset, N.Y. And in 1941 the Levitts won a government contract to provide 2,350 housing units for defense workers in Norfolk, Va. Once the fighting ended, they brought the lessons of that experience to 1,000 acres of potato farms on New York's Long Island,

Levitt sold out for $92 million but later lost most of it

25 miles east of Manhattan. On July 1, 1947, Levitt, then 40, broke ground on the first of what would be 17,000 homes.

He could build fast because he had divvied up the construction process into 27 operations, then mustered specialized teams to repeat each operation at each site. Twenty acres were set aside as an assembly point, where cement was mixed and lumber cut. Trucks would deliver materials to homesites placed at 60-ft. intervals. Then the carpenters, tilers, painters and roofers arrived, each in his turn. There was a team for white paint, another for red. One worker's sole daily task was to bolt washing machines to floors.

Levitt liked to compare himself to General Motors. "We channel labor and materials to a stationary outdoor assembly line instead of bringing them together inside a factory." To keep down lumber costs, the Levitts bought their own forests and built a sawmill in Oregon. They purchased appliances direct from the manufacturer, cutting out the distributor's markup. They even made their own nails. Their methods kept costs so low that in the first years the houses, which typically sat on a seventh-of-an-acre lot, could sell for just $7,990, a price that still allowed the Levitts a profit of about $1,000. ('90s price: $150,000+.)

Yet however much it may have been a triumph of free enterprise, Levittown depended on massive government assistance. The Federal Housing Administration guaranteed the loans that banks made to builders. Then the Veterans Administration gave buyers low-interest mortgages to purchase those houses. Thus the risk to the lenders was small, and so were the houses: 750 sq. ft., two bedrooms, living room and kitchen, with an unfinished second floor and no garage. All the same, compared with the cramped arrangements of the cities, even a place that size seemed

BORN Feb. 11, 1907, in Brooklyn, N.Y.

1924 Enters N.Y.U., staying until his junior year

1927 Takes a job in his father's law firm

1929 Levitt & Sons starts work on its first house

1941 With brother Alfred, builds housing for defense workers in Norfolk, Va.

1947 Starts transforming farmland on New York's Long Island into Levittown

1968 Sells his company to ITT for $92 million

FAMILY Bill sold; brother Al, right, designed; father Abe opined

1907

1994

DIES Jan. 28 in Manhasset, N.Y.

Some assembly required: the components of a single Levitt house in 1948

literal way. Unlike the automobile or the radio, the home was an ancient possession, a thing too intimate to be mass-produced without offending notions of Yankee individuality that were already under intense pressure from modernity. And as Levittown matured, suburbia itself began to look like humanity at room temperature, a place where the true countryside was denatured, while the true civilization of the cities collapsed into strip malls and dinner theater.

Within that context, Levittown became the anti-Williamsburg: not a re-creation of some idealized past but a living glimpse of the ticky-tacky future. The social critic Lewis Mumford called it "a low-grade uniform environment from which escape is impossible." Levittown was also tainted by the offhand racism of midcentury America. Though Levittown is racially mixed today, for years Levitt's sales contracts barred resale to African Americans. He once offered to build a separate development for blacks but refused to integrate his white Levitt developments. "We can solve a housing problem, or we can try to solve a racial problem," he once said. "But we can't combine the two." In 1963 his all-white policies led to civil rights protests at a Levitt subdivision in Bowie, Md.

Building modest homes made Levitt rich. In 1968, after his company had built more than 140,000 houses around the world, Levitt & Sons was sold to ITT Corp. for $92 million in stock, most of which went to him. That fortune bought, among other things, a 237-ft. yacht, *La Belle Simone*, named for his third wife, and a 30-room mansion in Mill Neck, N.Y. But the deal barred him from the domestic construction business for 10 years. Within four years, the ITT stock, which he had been using as collateral to build subdivisions in places like Iran, Venezuela and Nigeria, lost 90% of its value. When those foreign projects foundered, his indebtedness reached into the millions of dollars.

His legacy is Levittown, a utopia for working stiffs rather than a visionary product of high design. It was what you get when a canny businessman sees a massive public appetite and applies capital and logistics in a timely fashion. No major architect went near the place—or imposed uniform standards on it. Levitt homes were made to be customized. The avid householders of Levittown got busy, adding porches, dormers and new wings, the outcroppings of anybody's headlong life. The line on their town used to be that Levitt houses were indistinguishable from one another, and the people would be too. But the place is now, as a town is supposed to be, a work in progress, a setting that can be held to the light at any angle. And William Levitt, a man who just about never read a novel, turned out to be the author of an entire world. ∎

Richard Lacayo, who writes about politics and culture for TIME, *grew up in Levittown.*

sumptuous and full of potential. Levitt understood this well enough to see himself as more than a builder. He was a prime facilitator of the American Dream in its cold war formulation. "No man who owns his own house and lot can be a communist," he once said. "He has too much to do."

THE LEVITT MEN WERE A TYPICAL FAMILY. THEY loved each other. They were also a cocoon of misfits who drove each other crazy. Father Abe was a onetime Brooklyn lawyer and would-be philosopher who eventually became Levittown's unofficial landscape theorist. He could face a reporter with a fistful of dahlias and tell him, with a straight face, "Every man has a right to flowers!" Brother Alfred designed the houses and grumbled about how credit always went to Bill, the idea man, organizer and salesman.

On Saturdays, in a lordly mood that can only be imagined by anyone who has not fathered his own town, Levitt would drive his black Cadillac convertible through the streets, checking out what the citizens were doing across the abundant stage he had built for them, his ears attuned to local gossip, his eyes to lawn care. (In the early days, homeowners who didn't mow their grass would find Levitt gardeners sent to do it and a bill for the job in their mailbox.) He was the consummate marketing guy, unmoved by books, paintings or music. His first wife once complained that she had dragged him to see *Death of a Salesman* but couldn't get him to identify with the title character.

In the larger culture, Levitt's achievement was contested ground. Levittown entered 20th century folklore as the place where democratic equality edged into an unnerving conformity. By stamping whole townships onto old farmland, Levitt brought the machine into the garden in a very

After consolidating control of the U.A.W. in 1947, Reuther won improved benefits for union members

Walter
Reuther

He built the benefits package that workers now take for granted, from health care to pensions. But his agenda was bigger than unionism

By IRVING BLUESTONE

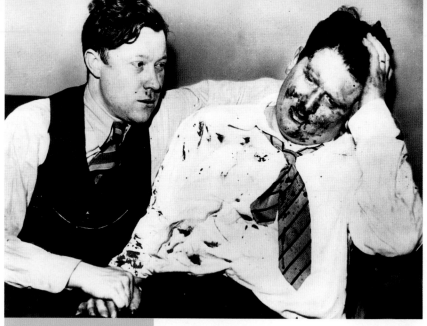

MEN WITH QUEASY STOMachs had no place one afternoon last week on the overpass at the No. 4 gate of Henry Ford's great River Rouge plant." So began TIME's account of the Battle of the Overpass, the confrontation that made May 26, 1937, a red-letter day in labor history and brought to national attention a young United Auto Workers official named Walter P. Reuther.

When Ford's goons bloodied Reuther, left, and Richard Frankensteen, the photos turned the public their way

Reuther and his colleagues suspected the day's events could escalate into something historic as they prepared to hand out organizing leaflets (slogan: "Unionism, Not Fordism") to Ford's workers. That morning Reuther had put on his Sunday suit, complete with vest, gold watch and chain. He had invited newspapermen, priests and local officials to be witnesses.

When Reuther and three other officials arrived at the gate, Ford company police charged at them and delivered a brutal, prolonged beating. Pictures of the battered victims were published across the U.S., a huge p.r. victory that would slowly but surely lead, several years later, to U.A.W. organization at the plant.

The pictures, ironically, capture the wrong image of Walter Reuther. While he arrived on the national scene as a scuffler with blood on his face, he would evolve into one of labor's most dynamic and innovative leaders, as well as a humanitarian whose impact ranged well beyond his field. His achievements were guided by his oft expressed philosophy of human endeavor: "There is no greater calling than to serve your fellow men. There is no greater contribution than to help the weak. There is no greater satisfaction than to have done it well." Reuther believed it wholeheartedly and, as they say, walked the talk.

He was nurtured to a devoted commitment to unionism. His father, a brewery-wagon driver and union leader in Wheeling, W.Va., had the family regularly discuss the role of unions, as well as social and economic issues. Like thousands of others born in poor regions, Walter and two of his brothers, Roy and Victor, migrated to the Detroit area to find jobs in the auto industry. Not surprisingly, they became

actively involved in the budding United Automobile, Aircraft and Agricultural Implement Workers Union.

Reuther was 29 in 1936, when he became president of Local 174. It was a tumultuous period in labor history, as the U.A.W. literally fought for survival. Reuther became one of the union's generals, directing a series of sit-down strikes and other guerrilla tactics to organize auto plants. He soon gained national prominence and even entry into President Roosevelt's White House. He and his wife May also became great friends of Eleanor Roosevelt's. It's not difficult to see why he was welcome. In 1940, a year before Pearl Harbor, he proposed converting available capacity in auto plants to military production. Echoing F.D.R.'s "Arsenal of Democracy" stance, he urged that the industry turn out "500 planes a day." His plan was harshly criticized by the corporations, which were unwilling to give up any part of their profitable business. When the Japanese attacked Pearl Harbor, the rapid conversion to military production validated Reuther's vision.

At the 1946 U.A.W. convention, Reuther won the presidency in a close race, on a platform against Soviet-communist "outside interference" and for a new, more socially conscious approach to collective bargaining. He pledged to work for "a labor movement whose philosophy demands that it fight for the welfare of the public at large … We won the war. The task now is to win the peace." Two years later, a would-be assassin, for reasons still unknown, fired shots through Reuther's kitchen window, shattering his right arm.

During the postwar boom, Reuther campaigned for wage increases, winning a major victory in a 1948 settlement with General Motors that established the concept of an annual

BORN Sept. 1, 1907, in Wheeling, W.Va.

1936 Leads first major auto strike in Detroit

1946 Elected president of United Auto Workers

1955 Helps engineer a merger of AFL and CIO unions

1907

1970

BEATEN On May 26, 1937, Reuther, in vest, and crew tried to stage a rally at Ford, but company thugs turned it into a battle

1941-45 Acts as informal government adviser during World War II

1948-55 Secures key benefits, including pensions and health care

UNITY With Cesar Chavez, 1965

DIES Killed May 9 in plane crash in Pellston, Mich.

> ## There is no greater calling than to serve your fellow men ... no greater contribution than to help the weak.
>
> **WALTER REUTHER, as president of the U.A.W.**

wage increase (annual improvement factor) tied to a quarterly cost of living allowance. The AIF-COLA formula has, over the years, been a pillar of progress in enhancing workers' living standards and ensuring protection of the purchasing power of the earned dollar against the impact of inflation.

After his breakthroughs on wages, Reuther pressed for improved benefits. He had a penchant for slogans, and they often became rallying cries for the union's programs. "Too Old to Work—Too Young to Die" was one, used to negotiate pension plans. "Thirty and Out" was aimed at a contract clause permitting retirement after 30 years of service, regardless of age. "We Live by the Year—We Should Be Paid by the Year" was behind the demand for a guaranteed annual wage. The ultimate bargaining victory was the Supplementary Unemployment Benefit, which now mandates a 95% replacement of wages in the event of layoffs.

Reuther kept fighting for new and better benefits, and over time, the union won the reforms that employees today take for granted: comprehensive health-care programs, tuition-refund programs, life insurance, profit sharing, severance pay, bereavement pay, jury-duty pay—plus improvements in vacations, holidays and rest time. The negotiation of decent working, health and safety conditions, coupled with a sound grievance procedure, added immeasurably to the personal sense of dignity and self-respect of the worker.

Reuther's activism wasn't limited to the collective-bargaining arena. He fought the despoiling of Lake Erie, a dying body of water that has been substantially revived by the cleanup effort he supported. He was actively involved in developing low-cost housing units in Detroit's inner city.

Long before medical costs became a national issue, Reuther was advocating universal health care. He organized the Committee of One Hundred to put the issue on the national agenda and set the stage for congressional action. At the same time, he helped establish one of the early HMOs, an association that eventually became the Health Alliance Plan, a major health-care provider in the metropolitan Detroit area. Whether testifying before Congress or elsewhere, Reuther threw his weight behind the public issues of the day. He called for a Citizens Crusade Against Poverty, federal aid in housing and education, the peaceful use of atomic energy and a national minimum wage.

Trade unions have a mixed record in civil rights—but from early on, Reuther was an ardent advocate of the cause. He organized the Citizens Committee for Equal Opportunity and worked closely with Martin Luther King Jr. Reuther was one of the few non–African Americans invited to speak at the March on Washington in 1963. A favorite anecdote concerned his introduction to the crowd. Standing close to the podium were two elderly women. As he was introduced, one of the women was overheard asking her friend, "Who is Walter Reuther?" The response: "Walter Reuther? He's the white Martin Luther King."

IN 1955, AS PRESIDENT OF THE CONGRESS OF INDUStrial Organizations, Reuther negotiated a historic merger with the American Federation of Labor, whose leader was George Meany. Reuther then headed up the AFL-CIO's Industrial Union Department, but 13 years later, sharp differences over policy and programs led to the U.A.W.'s withdrawal from the organization—it would stay out until reaffiliating in 1981.

For Reuther, unionism was not confined simply to improving life at the workplace. He viewed the union as a social movement aimed at uplifting the community within the guarantees of democratic values. After his untimely death, with May, in a plane crash in 1970, waves of downsizing devastated cities and created problems for labor that still exist today. You can just imagine him wading into the fight against those who destroy jobs to prop up corporate profits. One of his favorite slogans was "Progress with the Community—Not at the Expense of the Community." Reuther's works fulfilled that philosophy. ■

Irving Bluestone, retired U.A.W. vice president, is professor of labor studies at Wayne State University.

As 20,000 workers rally below, sit-down strikers hoist their banner on the roof of an occcuped Dodge plant, 1937

A Bestiary of Bosses: The Good, the Bad And the Ugly

You're the top! Will you inspire through example, lead by following—or just try to command respect by scaring the hell out of your cowering troops?

GOOD Jack Welch

After taking the helm of General Electric in the early 1980s, Welch earned the title "Neutron Jack" by closing plants and laying off workers. But the incisive, farsighted manager led a reorganization that simplified GE into a company with dominant positions in carefully chosen fields—and that challenged and inspired its employees.

GOOD Alfred Sloan

He literally wrote the book on managing large companies— *My Years with General Motors*. No large firm is untouched by his concept of decentralized management. Sloan came into a GM that was chaotic and nearly bankrupt and gave it discipline, definition—and a way to multiply sales by segmenting markets and keeping products fresh.

GOOD Konosuke Matsushita

The genius behind Panasonic built a bigger empire than Ford, Kroc or Walton by constantly innovating, paying attention to the consumer and striving to increase demand and reduce prices. A philosopher, he followed the Japanese way, honoring his employees above all—even profits.

BAD **Armand Hammer**

Occidental Petroleum's boss learned from pal V.I. Lenin; he required board member/ employees to give him signed, undated resignation letters to ensure they'd vote his way. His subordinates formed a club whose emblem was a cowering mouse on a red carpet.

BAD **Leona Helmsley**

Dubbed the Queen of Mean by New York City's brash tabloids, Leona played evil stepmom to the employees of her husband, real estate mogul Harry. The "tough bitch" (her own lawyer's term) fired her terrified workers on a whim before landing in jail for tax evasion.

UGLY **J. Paul Getty**

The get-rich-quick oil business yielded a gusher of eccentrics, including the stingy H.L. Hunt and the even tighter Getty, who kicked back in palatial style on a country estate in England—equipped with a pay phone for the convenience of his guests.

UGLY **Howard Hughes**

His fetishes have entered folklore, and today this successful industrialist-aviator-moviemaker is remembered less for his business genius than for having become a prisoner of his fears, isolated behind Mormon bodyguards and hoarding his own urine.

Leo
Burnett

He launched advertising's visual assault on the senses by arguing that images, not words, generated impact. TV proved him right

By STUART EWEN

H E WAS NOT THE ADMAN'S ADMAN. HE WASN'T A hipster like William Bernbach, who tapped into youthcult with the "Think Small" campaign for Volkswagen. He wasn't an elegant rationalist like David Ogilvy, whose ads famously advised the rich that a Rolls-Royce was the sensible car to buy. He didn't even work on Madison Avenue, but in Chicago's Loop instead. Yet Leo Burnett, the jowly genius of the heartland subconscious, is the man most responsible for the blizzard of visual imagery that assaults us today.

In a career that spanned five decades, his aptitude for inventing evocative, easily recognizable corporate identities spawned the Jolly Green Giant, the Marlboro Man, the Pillsbury Doughboy and Tony the Tiger, among other familiar icons of commerce. By the late 1950s Burnett had emerged as a prime mover in advertising's creative revolution, which grew in the glow of television's ascent as America's consummate commercial medium. By 1960 Burnett's roster of clients had grown exponentially; at the time of his death the agency's billings exceeded $400 million annually. By 1997 that figure approached $6 billion.

Burnett's creativity was in stark contrast to that of some of his contemporaries, who built advertising companies around research and marketing expertise. Burnett forged his reputation around the idea that "share of market" could only be built on "share of mind," the capacity to stimulate consumers' basic desires and beliefs. To achieve this goal, Burnett moved beyond standard industry practice. Early advertising schemes were based primarily on a foundation of carefully worded argument focused on the purported qualities of the product being sold. Images were mere decoration for the argument.

The industry was already changing when Burnett joined the Homer McGee agency in Indianapolis, Ind., in 1919, after a brief stint as a newspaperman. Product claims were giving way to elaborate narratives—imaginary stories of consumers whose purchase had been rewarded with popularity, success, romance.

Burnett moved the image to center stage. Visual eloquence, he was convinced, was far more persuasive, more poignant, than labored narratives, verbose logic or empty promises. Visuals appealed to the "basic emotions and primitive instincts" of consumers. Advertising does its best work, he argued in 1956, by impression, and he spent much of his career encouraging his staff to identify those symbols, those visual archetypes, that would leave consumers with a "brand picture engraved on their consciousness."

Burnett did not originate this conceit. In his classic 1922 study *Public Opinion*, journalist Walter Lippmann maintained that pictures are "the surest way of conveying an idea. A leader or an interest that can make itself master of current symbols is master of the current situation."

Burnett was exactly that. Creativity, he advised, called for an intuitive ability to identify the inherent drama that resided within a product through the conscious use of "earthy vernacular" imagery. To explain his concept of

		1955 **The Marlboro Man first smokes filters**		
BORN Oct. 21, 1891, in St. Johns, Mich.	**1935 Founds his own agency in Chicago**	**1951 Tony the Tiger endorses Frosted Flakes**		**1968 Keebler elves bake busily and Morris the cat finds a food he will eat**

1891   **1971**

	1919 Goes to work for Indianapolis ad agency Homer McGee		**1965 Pillsbury's Doughboy cooked up**	**DIES at age 79 in Lake Zurich, Ill.**

inherent drama, Burnett repeatedly cited a 1945 print campaign for the American Meat Institute. After careful consideration, he related, "we convinced ourselves that the image of meat should be a virile one, best expressed in red meat." At the time it was highly unusual, even distasteful, to portray uncooked meat in advertisements. Enthusiastically breaking the code, Burnett produced full-page ads depicting thick chops of raw red meat against a bright-red background. "Red against red was a trick," he explained, "but it was a natural thing to do. It just intensified the red concept and the virility and everything else we were trying to express. This was inherent drama in its purest form."

Burnett, center, leads a team working on campaigns for new client Kellogg in 1949

REVIEWING HIS AGENCY'S WORK, ONE IS STRUCK BY Burnett's penchant for employing a range of masculine archetypes. Some were designed to appeal to female consumers. With the Jolly Green Giant, he resurrected a pagan harvest god to monumentalize "the bounty of the good earth"—and to sell peas. Years later, with the creation of the Doughboy, Burnett employed a cuddly endomorph to symbolize the friendly bounce of Pillsbury home-baking products. Aiming at male audiences in the '50s, a time when filter cigarettes were viewed as effeminate, Burnett introduced a tough and silent tattooed cowboy on horseback, "the most masculine type of man," he explained, to transform the image of Marlboro cigarettes. For better or worse, the Marlboro Man is one of the most enduring advertising icons ever devised.

Like many other persuasion professionals of his generation—most notably Edward Bernays, the patriarch of public relations—Burnett was obsessed with finding visual triggers that could circumvent consumers' critical thought. Though

an advertising message might be rejected consciously, he maintained, it was accepted subliminally. Through the "thought force" of symbols, he said, "we absorb it through our pores, without knowing we do so. By osmosis."

With the arrival of television in the late '40s—an electronic salesroom going into nearly every American home—Burnett believed merchandisers had found the Holy Grail. "Television," he asserted, "is the strongest drug we've ever had to dish out." It marked the moment when graphic representation arrived as the lingua franca of commerce.

Evaluating Leo Burnett's contribution nearly 30 years after his death, one is of two minds. There is something both old-fashioned and timeless in the slightly homoerotic repertoire of corporate images he fathered. Born during the springtime of American consumer culture, when sales pitches were infused with an unfettered sense of optimism, a booming-voiced tiger like Tony and a benevolent Green Giant today come across as quaint throwbacks to the time when sugared breakfast cereals could still claim to provide an ideal start to the perfect day, and when mushy canned peas nestled alongside a piece of fat-marbled beef represented a healthy diet. Though Burnett's corporate talismans endure, they occupy a world where consumers are increasingly caustic about the products they purchase. The effort by marketers to capitalize on the cynical mind-set of an MTV generation has overwhelmed the quest for universal human archetypes. Jadedness and sarcasm are becoming the dominant argot of advertising.

Yet the central principles that guided Burnett's practice remain prescient. His celebration of nonlinear advertising strategies, characterized by visual entreaties to the unconscious, continues to inform the strategies of adcult. In advertising copy, the conspicuous triumph of typography over text, of catchphrase over explanation, reflects Burnett's admonition that—to the public mind—visual form is more persuasive than carefully reasoned argument.

Burnett's thinking has come to define much of our mental environment beyond advertising. He saw advertising as the "fun" side of business, but the historical repercussions of his wisdom can be disquieting. Amid the present-day flood of images—each designed to rally emotions for a social, political or commercial goal—the notion of an informed public, once a cherished cornerstone of democracy, may be passing into oblivion. ∎

Stuart Ewen, professor of film and media studies at Hunter College, is the author of PR!, *a social history of spin.*

Brought to You By...

What becomes a pitchman most? An understanding of the consumer instinct, as evidenced by the careers, contributions and legacies of four men who helped define the industry

Edward Bernays

The father of public relations was instrumental in the use of polls and spokesfolk. Bernays grasped the power of public opinion and staged events to shape it. He threw "green" parties to make the color of Lucky Strikes' packaging fashionable to women and, to lighten Calvin Coolidge's grim image, sent Al Jolson to the White House.

William Bernbach

Dismissing such sacred conventions as repetition and the hard sell, Bernbach led a velvet revolution in advertising at Doyle Dane Bernbach in the '60s by relying on creativity, sly humor and instinct. Characteristically clever campaigns included "Hey Mikey" for Life cereal and Avis' "We try harder."

George Gallup

The creator of the public opinion poll exerted an influence that would extend far beyond advertising—just ask today's politicians, who are often accused of having forsaken principle for statistical sampling. The inquisitive Iowan began the Gallup Poll in 1935, after he was hired to do research for the New York City ad agency Young & Rubicam.

David Ogilvy

The urbane Brit's early job with Gallup informed his famed dogma: trust research, stick to the facts, relish words (but avoid adjectives). Ogilvy only took on clients whose products he admired; he established enduring brand images like the eye-patched Hathaway shirt man.

Thomas
Watson Jr.

The man who built IBM into a computer giant found motivation at home, in his fears that he could never fill his father's shoes

By JOHN GREENWALD

AS THE ELDEST SON OF THE PRESIDENT OF INTER-national Business Machines, Thomas Watson Jr. grew up tortured by self-doubt. He suffered bouts of depression; when he was 12, he burst into tears over the thought that his formidable father wanted him to join IBM and eventually run what was already a significant company. "I can't do it," he wailed to his mother. "I can't go to work for IBM."

Yet Watson succeeded his father 26 years later—and eventually surpassed him. IBM is now synonymous with computers, even though the company did not invent the device that would change our life, nor had it shipped a single computer before Tom Jr. took over.

But he boldly took IBM—and the world—into the computer age, and in the process developed a company whose dark-suited culture and awesome sales and service savvy stood for everything good and bad about corporate America. No wonder the Justice Department eventually sought (unsuccessfully) to break it up.

Under Tom Jr., Big Blue put its logo on 70% of the world's computers and so thoroughly dominated the industry that even rivals like Univac—which built the first large commercial computer—were dismissed as merely part of "the Bunch." And while newcomers such as Compaq and Microsoft brought the company to its knees in the 1980s, the colossus that Watson inherited and reinvented in the 1950s and '60s stands strong again: in 1998 it was the sixth largest company in America.

Not a bad legacy for someone who spent his youth "convinced that I had something missing" inside. A perpetually failing student, "Terrible Tommy" Watson vented his frustration by pulling pranks and tangling with authority. He needed six years and three schools to get through high school, and managed to graduate from Brown University only through the forbearance of a sympathetic dean. The young playboy rated the pleasures of drinking and dancing far above those of learning.

Watson enrolled in IBM sales school after college and hated that as well. He devoted more time to indulging his passions for flying airplanes by day and partying by night than to calling on clients. Even so, Watson filled his entire sales quota for 1940 on the first day of that year—but only because the company had thrown the boss's son a big account to make him look good.

World War II liberated Tom Watson Jr. from his demons. His success in promoting the use of flight simulators earned him a job as aide and pilot for Major General Follett Bradley, the Army Air Forces' inspector general. Watson flew throughout Asia, Africa and the Pacific, displaying steel nerves and shrewd foresight and planning skills. He was set to fly for United Air Lines after the war when a chance conversation with Bradley changed his course. Informed of Watson's job plans, the general said, "Really? I always thought you'd go back and run the IBM company." A stunned Watson asked Bradley if he really thought his former aide up to the job. The general replied, "Of course."

BORN Jan. 8, 1914, in Dayton, Ohio

1937 Joins IBM

1940-45 Serves in U.S. Army Air Forces

1952 Becomes company president

1956 Becomes chairman

1971 Retires from IBM

1979-81 Serves as U.S. ambassador to Russia

1914 — 1993

WITH DAD Tom Jr. was not his father's favorite child. His sister Jane claimed that honor

1946 Rejoins IBM

1953 First IBM computer introduced

1964 Revolutionary System/360 introduced

DIES in Connecticut

> # I wanted all the executives of IBM to feel the urgency I felt; whatever they did, it was never enough.

THOMAS J. WATSON JR., writing in *Father, Son & Co.*

The IBM that Watson went home to was an American icon. It was the outgrowth of a debt-ridden maker of scales, time clocks and accounting machines that his father had taken charge of in 1914, the year Tom Jr. was born. The elder Watson created a fanatically loyal work force at IBM—the company's name since 1924—hanging THINK signs everywhere, leading employee sing-alongs (corporate anthem: *Hail to IBM*) and dictating everything from office attire (white shirt, dark suit) to policies on smoking and drinking (forbidden on the job and strongly discouraged off it). IBM dominated the market for punch-card tabulators—forerunners of computers that performed such tasks as running payrolls and collating census data.

Back from the war, Tom Jr. saw IBM afresh and quickly realized that its future lay in computers, not a 19th century information technology like tabulators. Even the first primitive vacuum-tube machines could calculate 10 times as fast as IBM's tabulators. Many people, however, including Watson's father, couldn't believe the company's core products were headed for extinction. But Tom Jr., who became IBM president in 1952, never retreated. He recruited electronics

In 1965 IBM's mainframe computers were so massive they required their own rooms

experts and brought in luminaries like computer pioneer John von Neumann to teach the company's engineers and scientists. By 1963, IBM had grabbed an 8-to-1 lead in revenues over Sperry Rand, the manufacturer of Univac.

Watson, who shared his father's volcanic temper, was just warming up. Fearful of falling behind in the fast-changing industry, Watson promoted "scratchy, harsh" individuals and pressured them to think ahead. (When IBM engineers complained that transistors were unreliable, Watson handed out transistor radios and challenged the critics to wear them out.) He never backed away from

conflict, not even what he called "savage, primal and unstoppable" fights with his father over issues like finance. He installed a "contention" system that encouraged IBM managers to challenge one another. Watson was paternal with rank-and-file employees, but he was murder on his lieutenants, in accordance with his dictum that "the higher the monkey climbs, the more he shows his ass."

WITH IBM CLEARLY ON TOP IN THE EARLY '60s, Watson took one of the biggest gambles in corporate history. He proposed spending more than $5 billion—about three times IBM's revenues at the time—to develop a new line of computers that would make the company's existing machines obsolete. The goal was to replace specialized units with a family of compatible computers that could fill every data-processing need. Customers could start with small computers and move up as their demands increased, taking their old software along with them. This "circle" of flexibility inspired the name System/360.

The strategy nearly failed when software problems created delivery delays. Panic raced through IBM's top echelons as rivals closed in. A desperate Watson ousted his younger brother Dick as head of engineering and manufacturing for the System/360 project, derailing the younger man's career and filling Watson with shame. Yet System/360 ultimately proved to be wildly successful, revolutionizing the industry. IBM's base of installed computers jumped from 11,000 in early 1964 to 35,000 in 1970, and its revenues more than doubled, to $7.5 billion. At the same time, IBM's market value soared from about $14 billion to more than $36 billion.

A heart attack forced Watson to retire at age 57 in 1971, leaving him plenty of time for such adventures as retracing a flight across Siberia that he had made during the war. A lifelong Democrat (his father had been a Franklin Roosevelt confidant), Watson served for two years as Jimmy Carter's ambassador to Moscow. But perhaps his proudest achievement was to emerge from the shadow of his legendary, demanding father. In his first five years as chairman, the younger Watson observed the anniversary of his father's death in 1956 with a ritual. He quietly took stock of what IBM had achieved since his father died, and then said to his wife, "That's another year I've made it in his absence." ∎

TIME *senior writer John Greenwald wrote his first cover story for the magazine in 1982. The subject: IBM.*

Screen Saviors

A new breed—the tycoon-as-geek—drove a revolution that made the computer today's essential tool (and toy)

Steve Jobs

He's the anti-Gates: a master of hardware, not software; a trailblazer, not a follower; a creator, not a cloner. Jobs started Apple Computer in the 1970s, launching the personal computer revolution. But Microsoft prevailed, and Jobs was forced out of the lagging company. In the late '90s he returned, reviving Apple with the snazzy iMac machine.

Larry Ellison

A poster boy for Billionaire Chic (fast cars, exotic Japanese-style homes, jets and yachts), he is politically active—and he hates Microsoft. In two decades the tough, mercurial software baron built Oracle into the leader in database management.

Scott McNealy

A tireless promoter of network computing and the Java software that is its calling card (check the T shirt), the Sun Microsystems CEO took a humdrum builder of computers for engineers and turned it into the dominant maker of the intranet machines that corpo- rations love. The user- friendly Java is touted as the software that may finally humble Microsoft.

Jerry Yang & David Filo

In the '90s land rush to stake claims on the Web, these youngsters were cyber-sooners, turning Yang's casual guide to his favorite sites into a search-engine powerhouse. As Web use soared, so did Yahoo stock. Bingo—billionaires!

Kroc saw more potential in the McDonald's system than its founding brothers, who sold out for $2.7 million

Ray
Kroc

McDonald's begat an industry because a 52-year-old mixer salesman understood that we don't dine—we eat and run

By JACQUES PÉPIN

AMONG THE ARMY OF BURGER FLIPPERS AT WORK across America in the 1960s was a French chef putting his training to use at Howard Johnson's in New York City. I worked for HoJo's from the summer of 1960 to the spring of 1970, doing my American apprenticeship, learning about mass production and marketing. The company had been started in 1925 in Massachusetts by Howard Deering Johnson, and by the mid-'60s its sales exceeded that of Burger King, Kentucky Fried Chicken and McDonald's combined. There would be more than 1,000 Howard Johnson restaurants and 500 motor lodges. Yet after Johnson's death in 1972, the company lost its raison d'être. The restaurants became obsolete; the food quality deteriorated. You underestimate the clientele at your peril. The late restaurateur Joe Baum used to say, "There is no victory over a customer."

As the Howard Johnson Co. went to pieces, Ray Kroc's obsession with Quality, Service, Cleanliness and Value—the unwavering mission of McDonald's—was gaining momentum. Kroc was perceptive in identifying popular trends. He sensed that America was a nation of people who ate out, as opposed to the Old World tradition of eating at home. Yet he also knew that people here wanted something different. Instead of a structured, ritualistic restaurant with codes and routine, he gave them a simple, casual and identifiable venue with friendly service, low prices, no waiting and no reservations. The system eulogized the sandwich—no tableware to wash. One goes to McDonald's to eat, not to dine.

Kroc gave people what they wanted or, maybe, what he wanted. As he said, "The definition of salesmanship is the gentle art of letting the customer have it your way." He would remain the ultimate salesman, serving as a chairman of McDonald's Corp., the largest restaurant company in the world, from 1968 until his death in 1984.

In 1917, Ray Kroc was a brash 15-year-old who lied about his age to join the Red Cross as an ambulance driver. Sent to Connecticut for training, he never left for Europe because the war ended. So the teen had to find work, which he did, first as a piano player and then, in 1922, as a salesman for the Lily Tulip Cup Co.

Although he sold paper cups by day and played the piano for a radio station at night, Kroc's ears were better tuned to the rhythms of commerce. In the course of selling paper cups he encountered Earl Prince, who had invented a five-spindle multimixer and was buying Lily cups by the truckload. Fascinated by the speed and efficiency of the machine, Kroc obtained exclusive marketing rights from Prince. Indefatigable, for the next 17 years he crisscrossed the country peddling the mixer.

On his travels he picked up the beat of a remarkable restaurant in San Bernardino, Calif., owned by two brothers, Dick and Mac McDonald, who had ordered eight mixers and had them churning away all day. Kroc saw the restaurant in 1954 and was entranced by the effectiveness of the operation. It was a hamburger restaurant, though not of the drive-in variety popular at the time. People had to

BORN Oct. 5, 1902, in Oak Park, Ill.

1955 Kroc opens his first McDonald's unit in Des Plaines, Ill.

1968 The company opens its 1,000th restaurant

1971 McDonald's opens in Europe and Australia

1902

1922 Begins work as a salesman for Lily Tulip Cup Co. Moonlights as a piano player

1948 Brothers Dick and Mac McDonald open their first restaurant

1961 Buys out the McDonald brothers

DIES on Jan. 14 in San Diego

1984

> # "This is rat eat rat, dog eat dog. I'll kill 'em, and I'm going to kill 'em before they kill me."
>
> **RAY KROC, speaking of competition in the fast-food industry**

Kroc got mixed up with McDonald's by selling blenders to the brothers

get out of their cars to be served. The brothers had produced a very limited menu, concentrating on just a few items: hamburgers, cheeseburgers, french fries, soft drinks and milk shakes, all at the lowest possible prices.

Kroc, ever the instigator, started thinking about building McDonald's stores all over the U.S.—each of them equipped with eight multimixers whirring away, spinning off a steady stream of cash. The following day he pitched the idea of opening several restaurants to the brothers. They asked, "Who could we get to open them for us?" Kroc was ready: "Well, what about me?"

THE WOULD-BE GREAT WAR VETERAN BECAME RICH serving the children of World War II vets. His confidence in what he had seen was unshakable. As he noted later, "I was 52 years old. I had diabetes and incipient arthritis. I had lost my gall bladder and most of my thyroid gland in earlier campaigns, but I was convinced that the best was ahead of me." He was even more convinced than the McDonalds; he cajoled them into selling out to him in 1961 for a paltry $2.7 million.

He was now free to run the business his way, but he never changed the brothers' fundamental format. Kroc added his own wrinkles, certainly. He was a demon for cleanliness. From the overall appearance to the parking lot, the kitchen floor and the uniforms, cleanliness was foremost and essential. "If you have time to lean, you have time to clean," was a favorite axiom. He was dead on, of course. The first impression you get from a restaurant, through the eyes and nose, often determines whether you'll go back.

By 1963 more than 1 billion hamburgers had been sold, a statistic that was displayed on a neon sign in front of each restaurant. That same year, the 500th McDonald's restaurant opened and the famous clown, Ronald McDonald, made his debut. He soon became known to children throughout the country, and kids were critical in deciding where the family ate. According to John Mariani in his fine book *America Eats Out,* "Within six years of airing [in] his first national TV ad in 1965, the Ronald McDonald character was familiar to 96% of American children, far more than knew the name of the President of the United States."

Being a baby-boom company, McDonald's has found maturity a bit difficult. Its food today is as consistent as ever. But Americans are different, much surer of their tastes. They no longer need the security McDonald's provides. So the same assets that had made the restaurants so great started to turn against the company, especially after Kroc died in 1984. People looked at uniformity as boring, insipid and controlling, the Golden Arches as a symbol of junk food. Franchisees began to feel alienated from top management, especially in its aggressive expansion policies.

Ironically, no adjustments are needed outside the U.S. With restaurants in more than 114 countries, McDonald's still represents Americana. When I return to France, my niece's children, who are wild about what they call "Macdo," clamor to go there. It has a snobbish appeal for the young, who are enamored of the American life-style.

Still, it's likely Ray Kroc would have moved on to something else if he had found a better idea. Even after McDonald's was well established, Kroc still tried, often with dismal results, to launch upscale hamburger restaurants, Germantavern restaurants, pie shops and even theme parks, like Disneyland. He always had a keen sense of the power of novelty and a strong belief in himself and his vision.

Like many of America's great entrepreneurs, Kroc was not a creator—convenience food already existed in many forms, from Howard Johnson's to White Castle—but he had the cunning ability to grasp a concept with all its complexities and implement it in the best possible way. And that's as American as a cheeseburger. ∎

Jacques Pépin is a chef, author and host of the PBS TV series Jacques Pépin's Kitchen: Cooking with Claudine.

At 80, Lauder strikes a pose befitting the monarch of an empire of beauty

Estée
Lauder

She turned cosmetics into a big business by making the experience at the sales counter a personal one

By GRACE MIRABELLA

Lauder promoted multiple sales by using elegant displays that linked the products

become the shipping or billing department as needed.

You more or less know the Estée Lauder story because it's a chapter from the book of American business folklore. In short, Josephine Esther Mentzer, daughter of immigrants, lived above her father's hardware store in Corona, a section of Queens in New York City. She started her enterprise by selling skin creams concocted by her uncle, a chemist, in beauty shops, beach clubs and resorts.

No doubt the potions were good—Estée Lauder was a quality fanatic—but the saleslady was better. Much better. And she simply outworked everyone else in the cosmetics industry. She stalked the bosses of New York City department stores until she got some counter space at Saks Fifth Avenue in 1948. And once in that space, she utilized a personal selling approach that proved as potent as the promise of her skin regimens and perfumes.

"Ambition." Ask Leonard for one defining word about his mother, and that's his choice. Even after 40 years in business, Estée Lauder would attend every launch of a new shop or cosmetics counter—even in Moscow and other East European cities. On Saturdays she might go to her grandson's Origins store in Manhattan's hip SoHo district and say, "Let me teach you how to sell." Only declining health halted those visits.

In her prime, Lauder never stopped selling. She would give her famous friends small samples of her products for their handbags; she wanted her brand in the hands of people who were known for having "the best." Early in my career at *Vogue* she invited me to lunch. Before the meal was finished, she made sure to give me three recipes to help me interest the man I hoped to marry. (And did.)

She personified the mantra of "think globally, act locally." You can't get any more local than Estée Lauder's turning up

EONARD LAUDER, THE CHIEF EXECUTIVE OF THE company his mother founded, says she always thought she "was growing a nice little business." And that it is. A little business that controls 45% of the cosmetics market in U.S. department stores. A little business that sells in 118 countries and by 1997 had grown to be $3.6 billion big in sales. The Lauder family's shares are worth more than $6 billion.

But early on, there wasn't a burgeoning business; there weren't houses in New York City, Palm Beach, Fla., or the south of France. It is said that at one point there was one person to answer the telephones who changed her voice to

BORN July 1, around 1910, in New York City

1930 Marries Joseph Lauter (later changed)

1944 Opens first office in New York

1957 Prices Re-Nutriv cream at $115 per lb.

1979 Prescriptives brand skin-care products debut

1910

FIRST MATE Joseph Lauder probably didn't dream that one day he would help his wife build a dynasty

1953 Launches her first scent, Youth Dew

1968 Introduces Clinique, allergy-tested cosmetics

1982 Son Leonard succeeds her as CEO

at Saks on a Saturday, showing the sales staff how to give customers personal attention and a free gift (a pioneering promotional breakthrough of utter genius). Now an army of young women and men, exquisitely turned out and properly trained, do the same in every department store that's worthy of the brands.

Estée embodied the glamour she sold to women

THE GLOBAL ENTERPRISE OF THE ESTÉE LAUDER COS. is centered on the 40th floor of the General Motors Building in Manhattan. Here the realm of very Big Business meets the world of Estée Lauder. Intensely refined, it is every woman's dream office. It has been the office of a businesswoman and mother, where work and family mingled seamlessly for decades in a major corporation—the Holy Grail of many working women today (her grandchildren are in key positions). Carol Phillips, who founded the company's Clinique line, describes Lauder's management style as highly creative and notes that she conducted business in subtly elegant comfort. "Her conference room was like a dining room, and everything was perfect. In the office were all the pleasant things that go with running a household."

And what households. Estée Lauder loved to "entertain," as giving large dinner parties was once called. She enjoyed "beautiful people"—celebrities, the rich and famous—and invited them to dine with her at a table that could seat 30 without extensions. The food and the wines, lovely. She learned as she grew up. She watched; she enjoyed her world; she focused intently on the world around her and on all women, wherever they might be. She "liked to think about beauty and was determined to give women the opportunity to feel beautiful," says Leonard.

Beautiful didn't necessarily mean fashionable. I've edited two leading women's magazines over the past 25 years, but I'm hard pressed to think of a trend that Lauder started. The company never made any effort to be the makeup choice in the fashion shows. What you had with Estée Lauder was the quality of her view, of her demand for an ultrafeminine portrayal of the product. Every woman in every ad was the essence of femininity. Is that the kind of women we are talking about now? I'm not sure, but women know who Lauder is. Hers is a product with a focus—it's not MTV.

You will recognize the brand names, and what they stand for, as you would a friend's name: Estée Lauder, Prescriptives, Clinique, Origins and Aramis. The company has even bought hot new lines such as M.A.C., Bobbi Brown Essentials and Tommy Hilfiger fragrances. Lauder's company may not be able to set trends, but it is never going to be left behind by them. The boss—and her son after her—would never allow it. Says the company's vice chairman Jeanette Wagner: "No matter how she aged in years, she was still the youngest thinker in the room." ∎

Grace Mirabella, who was editor in chief of Vogue *magazine for 17 years, is the founder of* Mirabella *magazine.*

Cracking the Ceiling

It's overdue—but thanks to pioneers like these, business is no longer a boys' club

C.J. Walker

Born on a Louisiana cotton plantation, she tapped into the racial aesthetic that favored Caucasian features, selling products that straightened hair—and building an empire that came to number 20,000 "agents." An activist and philanthropist, she unveiled U.S. blacks' vast economic potential.

Katherine Graham

Plunged into the role of publisher of the Washington *Post* when her husband Philip committed suicide in 1963, the shy Graham struggled at first. But soon she was battling with unions and taking on the government by publishing portions of the secret Pentagon papers. Then she faced down Richard Nixon, backing the Watergate duo of Carl Bernstein, left, and Bob Woodward.

Jean Nidetch

It's a classic before-and-after tale: in 1961 Nidetch was an overweight, unhappy Queens, N.Y., housewife. She formed a support group of other dieting women, lost 70 pounds—and incorporated her idea. While its members kept slimming down, Weight Watchers International just kept growing. She sold out to H.J. Heinz in 1978 for $71 million.

Ruth Handler

Her legacy is controversial. In 1945 she co-founded the company that became toy giant Mattel (sales in the 1990s: $2 billion a year). But critics say her signature product—the curvaceous Barbie doll she named after her daughter—projects a dangerously unrealistic body image to the young girls who play with it.

Linda Wachner

For many years she was the only woman to head a FORTUNE 500 company: Warnaco Group, a maker of intimate apparel for women. Intense and focused, the former Macy's buyer revels in her tough-gal image.

Martha Stewart

She plays along when David Letterman makes fun of her Queen of Homemakers persona. But the former Connecticut caterer is an imaginative, no-nonsense entrepreneur who nurtured her magazine into a multimedia colossus. Its name reveals her dream: Martha Stewart Omnimedia.

Geraldine Laybourne

A legend in the cable industry, she built Nickelodeon from a blip on the TV-ratings chart in 1980 to the top channel for kids by the time she left in 1996. After a brief stint at ABC/Disney Cable Networks, she is rolling up her sleeves again with Oxygen Media, a new venture that will combine TV and websites for a female audience.

Rozelle on the sidelines in 1967, the year one of his great creations—the Super Bowl—was first played

Pete
Rozelle

He hooked us on football as show biz and gave Sundays (and Mondays) a new kind of religious significance

By MICHAEL LEWIS

WHEN MOST PEOPLE THINK OF PETE ROZELLE, if they think at all of Pete Rozelle, they probably recall a genial fellow with a balding pate and the ready smile of a car salesman who popped up at the end of the Super Bowl. Rozelle was the commissioner of the National Football League, of course, but what did that really mean? The players played, the coaches coached, the owners owned, the fans stomped and hollered, but what the hell does a commissioner do? Commission?

Until his death in 1996, Rozelle was dwarfed in every way by owners, coaches and players, and it was possible for those innocent of the inner workings of pro sports to regard him as little more than a functionary. The hired help. The guy whose job it was to order the stuffed mushrooms for the party after the game.

Those a bit closer to the game had another opinion of Rozelle: as a shrewd promoter of his sport. He invented the Super Bowl, for example, and sold the rights to the first game to two networks (NBC and CBS), which forced them to compete for viewers. With ABC Sports chief Roone Arledge, he invented *Monday Night Football*, which is the second longest running prime-time show on American television, after *60 Minutes*. He exhibited a taste for kitsch and spectacle unrivaled in professional sports. He loved floats and glitter and marching bands. His idea of beauty was a balloon drop. (He did not, however, like the name Super Bowl. It was coined by the son of Kansas City Chiefs owner

Lamar Hunt, whose imagination had been captured by the newly invented Super Ball.) It is now commonplace for a regular-season football game to attract ratings that surpass the playoff games in other sports. And the reason for that is Pete Rozelle.

But there is a third view of Rozelle espoused by those who watched him work: he was an iron-willed tycoon who created the business model for all of professional sports. In addition, he figured out a way to make the NFL far more valuable than other sports, including the national pastime, baseball. Rozelle recognized that a sporting event was more than a game—it was a valuable piece of programming. Such media moguls as Ted Turner and Rupert Murdoch have used that strategy to build entire networks. Rozelle, however, did them one better. In the long-winded discussions about the money sloshing around professional sports, the structure of the businesses receives little attention. But the structure, as designed by Rozelle, has been largely responsible for the money. That structure, in a word, was a cartel.

The football league Rozelle inherited in 1960 was a fragmented collection of 12 franchises, each run more or less as a stand-alone business. The squabbling owners faced serious competition from the newly formed American Football League, bankrolled by one of the richest men in America, Lamar Hunt. Rozelle's first trick, one that Rockefeller would have admired, was to put an end to the unprofitable competition. In 1962 he traveled to Washington and persuaded Congress to grant the NFL the first of two exemp-

BORN March 1, 1926, in Los Angeles

1926

ATHLETE At 14, Rozelle, No. 8 in front, played hoops

1960 Elected NFL commissioner

1960-62 Persuades teams to forgo individual TV deals for league-wide contract

1962-64 NFL broadcast rights triple, to $14 million

1967 Presides over first Super Bowl

1970 Creates *Monday Night Football*

1987 NFL inks $2.1 billion TV contract

1996

DIES in Rancho Santa Fe, Calif.

tions to the Sherman Anti-Trust Act, enabling him to fold the two leagues into a single, albeit fragmented, business.

Rozelle's next big move was to weld the owners of the new, expanded league into a cartel. This too required an exemption from the antitrust laws, which Congress granted in 1966. One morning the three major television networks woke up and found not a collection of individual teams competing with one another to sell their TV rights, but a single entity with a growing sense of its value.

The result was potent new bargaining power— and new revenues to promote the game and help it grab an ever greater slice of the entertainment business. "When the networks put up as much money as they did for the rights, they felt they had to promote the game," says NFL spokesman Joe Browne. "And by promoting the game, the game grew."

Back in 1960, when the 33-year-old Rozelle accepted the job as NFL commissioner, the combined revenues of the NFL and the franchises were less than $20 million;

Rozelle's 1970 merger of the two pro leagues turned the NFL into a powerful sports cartel

by 1998 the NFL was projecting combined revenues of nearly $4 billion. Similarly, the Dallas Cowboys and the Minnesota Vikings were each sold for about $1 million in Rozelle's rookie year. The newest NFL franchise, in Cleveland, was auctioned for $530 million in 1997.

I N HIS EULOGY OF ROZELLE IN JANUARY 1997, ARLEDGE said that a president of a sports division negotiating with Pete Rozelle and the NFL had "about as much clout as the Dalai Lama has dealing with the Chinese army." What he failed to mention was that Rozelle had created the army.

In retrospect, the whole thing looks like an outrageous violation of old-fashioned American free-market principles. But in 1966 virtually no one but Rozelle was thinking of pro sports as a seriously big business. The notion of pro football's "bargaining power" was patently absurd. Having formed his cartel, however, Rozelle managed it in much the same way the Japanese manage their cartels—with a view to market share (read: global domination).

He understood, somewhat ironically, that the key to attracting fans was fierce competition on the field, and that the key to fierce competition was every team's having roughly the same amount of money to spend on players. To

that end Rozelle persuaded NFL owners—two dozen raving megalomaniacs—to share their television spoils equally. While there still remains a discrepancy between the richest franchise (Dallas) and the poorest (Indianapolis), the difference is a fraction of that in other pro sports.

Probably it helped that unlike so many would-be power brokers, Rozelle did not look like a man who wished to wield power. Of course the gifts required to pull this off aren't the ones normally associated with empire building: they are the gifts of a diplomat. Diplomat in this case is another word for a man with a talent for dealing with megalomaniacs. Each year that Rozelle presided over the NFL, another owner published an autobiography explaining how he was the visionary behind the rise of pro football. Each year Rozelle laughed and let him enjoy his press. Rozelle seems to have been the sort of spectral tycoon who took his satisfaction in managing other people without their knowing it.

Rozelle's career was built on his talent for 1) persuading rich men who were accustomed to having everything they wanted to take less than they deserved, and 2) preventing full-scale revolt the minute the stakes became high. The subsequent pressures on Rozelle are familiar to anyone who has ever built a successful cartel—and cartels by and large fail. A member is more inclined to cheat the group the more successfully the group drives up his price. When Jerry Jones of the Dallas Cowboys cut a side deal with Pepsi to become the official drink of Texas Stadium, thus violating at least the spirit of the lucrative agreement the NFL had cut with Coca-Cola, he was playing the same game as the renegade Libyan oil industry.

By today's standards, Pete Rozelle was vastly undercompensated, given the wealth he created. He was a special case: the business giant who didn't lust for financial fortune and overt personal dominance. But if the measure of business success is the creation of new enterprise, then Rozelle was one of the greats. Once, late in his career, the commissioner was asked by a reporter if he had an ego. He replied that if you took all the egos in pro sports—the players', the coaches', the owners'—and averaged them out, his ego was just above the average. It might have been true, but no one ever knew it. That was his genius. ∎

Michael Lewis is the author of Liar's Poker *and* Trail Fever.

Milestones of TV Sports

The marriage of television and pro sports gave birth to a host of unforgettable images

1967 The Ice Bowl

The NFL's Green Bay Packers under coaching legend Vince Lombardi snatch the championship from the Dallas Cowboys in the tense final seconds of the "Ice Bowl." Suddenly, American men wake up to the joys of pro football on TV—and the value of the NFL's broadcast rights jumps.

1975
The Thrilla In Manilla

Muhammad Ali outfoxes power-punching Joe Frazier in the Thrilla in Manilla— and the era of the big made-for-TV fight is born. Boxing's only problem: coming up with new fighters with the moves— and the mouth— of the colorful Ali.

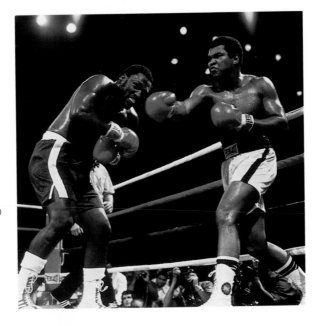

1996 Jordan's Triumph

After his father's murder, Michael Jordan leads the Chicago Bulls to the NBA title, then collapses in tears.

1980
Olympic Hockey Upset

At Lake Placid in upstate New York, an amateur U.S. hockey team beats the seasoned Soviets 4-3 in one of the Olympics' greatest upsets. The fan waving the flag completes the moment.

Akio
Morita

He made Sony a trusted name everywhere, because a company without borders is a company without limits

By KENICHI OHMAE

WHILE PLAYING A GAME OF TABLE TENNIS in 1993, Akio Morita—Mr. Sony—fell to the ground. The co-founder and chairman of the board had suffered a stroke. He has since been in a wheelchair. This is particularly sad, as Morita had never been able to sit still and relax. At 72, he was playing tennis at 7 a.m. each Tuesday. I know this well because I would practice on the court next to him. My tennis, however, was very different from his. I played with an instructor, and if I was tired, I would just take a break. Not him. He challenged everybody, including young athletes.

This was in keeping with a man who created one of the first global corporations. He saw long before his contemporaries that a shrinking world could present enormous opportunities for a company that could think beyond any border, whether physical or psychological. And he pursued that strategy with relentless energy in every market, particularly the U.S. It is notable that in 1998, according to a Harris survey, Sony was rated the No. 1 brand name by American consumers, ahead of Coca-Cola and General Electric.

The best way to describe Morita's extraordinary drive is to scan his schedule for the two-month period immediately preceding his stroke. He took trips from his home base in Tokyo to New Jersey, Washington, Chicago, San Francisco, Los Angeles, San Antonio, Dallas, Britain, Barcelona and Paris. During that time he met with Queen Elizabeth II, General Electric chief Jack Welch, future French President Jacques Chirac, Isaac Stern and many other politicians, bureaucrats and business associates. He attended two concerts and a movie; took four trips within Japan; appeared at eight receptions; played nine rounds of golf; was guest of honor at a wedding ceremony; and went to work as usual for 17 days at Sony headquarters. Morita's schedule had been set more than a year in advance. Whenever there was a small opening, he would immediately arrange a meeting with someone he wanted to get to know or catch up with. Unlike so many executives who remove themselves from the rest of the corporate pyramid, he was always in the middle of the action.

Morita had been groomed since the third grade to become the successor of a 14-generation family business: a prominent sake-brewing company in Nagoya. With true entrepreneurial spirit, however, he traded this life of comfort and privilege for the uncertainties of a start-up called Tokyo Telecommunications Engineering, Inc., launched in the rubble of postwar Japan.

From the outset, Morita's marketing concept was brand-name identification: the name would instantly communicate high product quality. This marketing concept is common today, but at that time most companies in Japan were producing under other brand names. Pentax, for example, was making products for Honeywell, Ricoh for Savin and Sanyo for Sears.

BORN Jan. 26, 1921, in Nagoya, Japan

1921

BOY With his father Kyazaemon in 1922

1946 Co-founds company with Masaru Ibuka

1955 Introduces pocket-size transistor radio

1958 Company name changed to Sony

1963 Moves family to U.S. to study American market

1970 Sony is first Japanese firm on N.Y.S.E.

1976 Named chairman and CEO of Sony Corp.

1979 Walkman tape player hits the streets

1993 Incapacitated by a stroke

Complementing Morita's unusual focus on brand identity were the talents of company co-founder, Masaru Ibuka, the engineering and product-design force behind Sony's inventions. The two sought to provide the best available technology and quality to the consumer. One of Sony's first products was a transistor radio. While the transistor was developed by Bell Labs in 1947 and produced by Western Electric, it was Sony that first used it for a small pocket radio, in 1955, creating a new market in the bargain.

The radio's success led to more firsts in transistorized products, such as an 8-in. television and a videotape recorder. Sony's technological achievements in product design, manufacturing and marketing helped change the image of MADE IN JAPAN from a sign of cheap imitations to one associated with superior quality. In Morita's own words, they made Sony the Cadillac of electronics.

The creation of the name Sony highlights Morita's intuition and determination to communicate globally. He wanted a name recognizable everywhere: creative, Roman letters, short and catchy. He and Ibuka pored over dictionaries and found the word *sonus*, which in Latin means sound. In addition, the word sonny was part of the pop vernacular

> # He seems to be making snap judgments—until you realize that he anticipated your question months ago.
>
> **RAY STEINER, Sony executive**

Moving beyond hardware, Sony bought U.S. music and film companies

in America at the time, and they thought it suggested a company made up of young people with abundant energy. The combination of the two formed Sony.

Sony's globalization began in the U.S., where Morita moved his entire family in 1963 in order to understand Americans, their market, customs and regulations and thereby increase the chances of his company's success. It was a brilliant decision. Not many businessmen in those days possessed such a passionate and determined vision. In the U.S., Morita settled into a large Fifth Avenue apartment in Manhattan. He built a solid and valuable network by continually socializing and giving parties during the week, a habit he maintained throughout his career.

Morita was a workaholic, but he was also a playaholic. He followed art and music, and was a sports fanatic. In his 60s he took up wind surfing and scuba diving and started skiing to ensure good exercise through the winter. He loved to water-ski and even crafted a water-resistant microphone on a handle, connected by a wire on the ski rope to a speaker on the boat so he could relay instructions to his wife Yoshiko. He was so proud of this invention. To simply have a good time, he would invent and perfect such a product.

The Walkman is just such an invention. Morita watched as his children and their friends played music from morning until night. He noticed people listening to music in their cars and carrying large stereos to the beach and the park. Some in Sony's engineering department opposed the concept of a tape player without a recording function (it would be added later), but Morita would not be denied. He insisted on a product that sounded like a high-quality car stereo yet was portable and allowed the user to listen while doing something else—thus the name Walkman.

Sony America considered that bad English and changed it to Soundabout; it became Freestyle for Sweden and Stowaway for Britain. Morita was leery of using a different name for each country, and when sales were less than rewarding, he changed the name universally to Sony Walkman. Subse-

quently, the Walkman became a worldwide hit, and the name now appear in major dictionaries.

Yet the man who put Sony on the global radar also had a nationalist side. This you can sense in reading his best seller, *Made in Japan*. When I would complain about the ambivalence, he'd grin and say, "Ohmae-san, it is the generation gap." A navy veteran, he returned from service to a Japanese economy that had been destroyed by the war, so for a long time he maintained a Japan-first frame of mind. His initial intentions were simply to make a contribution toward rebuilding his country from the ashes of the war.

But he eventually adopted a more international point of view; in the 1960s he began to speak of issues, such as encouraging free trade by reducing tariffs and other barriers, that many Japanese businessmen had been reluctant to discuss for decades. He represented, very vocally, the business community of Japan, a country that had during the 1970s become the No. 2 economy in the world and could no longer be ignored by the major economic players. But as Sony grew internationally, Morita expanded his vision. Now it was "Think globally, act locally"—that is, have a common value system that transcends national objectives; serve international customers, shareholders and employees, regardless of the origin of the company.

IN 1993, MORITA WAS ASKED BY GAISHI HIRAIWA, THEN chairman of Keidanren, the most prestigious business association in Japan, to be his successor. Until this time, Morita had never really been accepted by the Japanese establishment, for Sony was a relatively small company and didn't come from the traditional strong houses of steelmaking, public utilities and heavy industry. As it turned out, the day of Morita's stroke was the day the succession announcement was to have taken place.

Morita's ascent would have been a wonderful thing for Japan in 1993, when it was about to collapse into sustained recession. Already thinking about reforming Japan, he had convened groups of politicians, business people and bureaucrats to discuss what would be needed. Japan's economic situation in the '90s might have been very different if someone like Morita had been in a position to speak on behalf of its entrepreneurs and in favor of the dynamics of business, as opposed to those who beg the government to rescue industry after industry. The great tragedy is that Japan does not have another like him.

Akio Morita achieved more than most could imagine in one lifetime. If he had been able to read that Sony was the No. 1 consumer brand in the U.S., he would have smiled from his beachside mansion in Oahu and said, "Of course! I told you so! After all, Sony was made in the U.S.A.!" ■

Kenichi Ohmae, author of The Borderless World, *is a management consultant and founder of a satellite-TV channel.*

High Tech, Big Bucks

These gizmos laid golden eggs, while they changed the way we work, play and learn

Television

A Russian-born American scientist, Vladimir K. Zworykin, demonstrated the first practical television in 1929. But it was another 10 years before RCA, which owned NBC, made the first national broadcast and began producing sets. Then the war intervened. In 1951 (the year *I Love Lucy* debuted) the networks extended broadcasting from the Northeast to the whole country.

Brownie Box Camera

In 1900 George Eastman's Kodak introduced the camera that popularized amateur photography. The price: $1 (and a six-exposure packet of film cost 15¢). Some of the century's great photographers, such as Ansel Adams, began with a Brownie.

Compact Disc

In the early '80s, digitally stored music displaced the LP. Philips created and marketed the CD, Sony introduced the player—and record companies prospered by selling the same music to consumers they had already bought once before.

Transistor Radio

The transistor, which changed the face of electronics, was invented by three Americans in 1947, but it took Japan's Sony Corp. to see its possibilities for the consumer. Handy, fun and inexpensive, the radio hit shelves in 1955, ushering in Japan's long reign in pop electronics.

Cell Phone

The first cellular telephone was developed in 1973 by Martin Cooper at Motorola, and testing of 1,000 such phones followed in Chicago. The Federal Communications Commission authorized cellular service in 1982, and we haven't shut up since. More than a third of all households in the U.S. subscribe.

Sam
Walton

Big deal! Bringing low prices to small cities, Wal-Mart changed U.S. retailing, while its creator changed the way Big Business is run

By JOHN HUEY

N O ONE BETTER PERSONIFIED THE VITALITY OF the American Dream in the second half of the 20th century than Sam Walton. A scrappy, sharp-eyed bantam rooster of a boy, Walton grew up in the Depression dust bowl of Oklahoma and Missouri, where he showed early signs of powerful ambition: Eagle Scout at an improbably young age and quarterback of the Missouri state-champion high school football team. He earned money to help his struggling family by throwing newspapers and selling milk from the cow. After graduating from the University of Missouri, he served in the Army during World War II. Then, like millions of others, he returned home in 1945 to earn a living and raise a family in an uncertain peacetime economy.

Over the decades that followed, the way America worked and lived changed profoundly, and Walton found himself at the center of much of that change. He possessed a gift for anticipating where things were headed, and he probably understood the implications of the social and demographic currents that were sweeping the country—especially outside its cities—better than anyone else in business. That acumen hastened his rise from humble proprietor of a variety store in the little Delta cotton town of Newport, Ark., to largest retailer in the world and richest man in America.

When Sam Walton died in 1992, with a family net worth approaching $25 billion, he left behind a broad and important legacy in American business as well as a corporate monument: in 1998 Wal-Mart was the No. 4 company in

the FORTUNE 500, behind only General Motors, Ford and Exxon, with annual sales of close to $120 billion,

The easiest way to grasp the essence of what Sam Walton meant to America is to read his ad slogan emblazoned on all those Wal-Mart trucks you see barreling down U.S. highways: WE SELL FOR LESS, ALWAYS. Walton didn't invent discount retailing, just as Henry Ford didn't invent the automobile. But even as Ford and his cars revolutionized America's industrial model, Walton's extraordinary pursuit of discounting revolutionized the country's service economy. Walton not only altered the way much of America shopped; he changed the philosophy of much of American business, instigating the shift of power from manufacturer to consumer that has become prevalent in industry after industry.

Though it's hard to believe today, discount retailing was a controversial idea when it began to gain ground in the '50s at stores such as Ann & Hope, which opened in a reclaimed mill in Cumberland, R.I. Traditional retailers hated it, and so did manufacturers; it threatened their control of the marketplace. Most states had restrictions on the practice.

When the business began to emerge in the early '60s, Walton was a fairly rich merchant in his 40s, operating some 15 variety stores spread mostly around Arkansas, Missouri and Oklahoma. They were traditional small-town stores with relatively high price markups. Walton was an active student of retailing—all family vacations included store visits—so by the time a barber named Herb Gibson from Berryville, Ark., began opening discount stores

BORN March 29, 1918, in Kingfisher, Okla.

1918

GRIT Whether cranking ice cream or his own business during college, young Sam was spectacularly ambitious

1945 Gets franchise for Ben Franklin store in Newport, Ark.

1962 Opens his first Wal-Mart discount store in Rogers, Ark., after Ben Franklin spurns his plans for discounting

1985 The value of his Wal-Mart stock makes him the wealthiest American

1991 Wal-Mart passes Sears to become the country's biggest retailer

1992

DIES in Little Rock, April 5

Sam's down-home rep was no act. A good ole boy, he liked people, pickup trucks and dogs

outside towns where Sam ran variety stores, Walton saw what was coming. On July 2, 1962, at the age of 44, he opened his first Wal-Mart store, in Rogers, Ark. That same year, S.S. Kresge launched K Mart, F.W. Woolworth started Woolco and Dayton Hudson began its Target chain. Discounting had hit America in a big way. At that time, Walton was too far off the beaten path to attract the attention of competitors or suppliers, much less Wall Street.

Once committed to discounting, Walton began a crusade that lasted the rest of his life: to drive costs out of the merchandising system wherever they lay—in the stores, in the manufacturers' profit margins and with the middleman—all in the service of driving prices down, down, down.

Using that formula, which cut his margins to the bone, it was imperative that Wal-Mart grow sales at a relentless pace. It did, of course, and Walton hit the road to open stores wherever he saw opportunity. He would buzz towns in his low-flying airplane, studying the lay of the land. When he had triangulated the proper intersection between a few small towns, he would touch down, buy a piece of farmland at that intersection and order up another Wal-Mart store, which his troops could roll out like a rug.

As the chain began to take off, Walton always seemed to see ahead. As early as 1966, when he had 20 stores, he attended an IBM school in upstate New York. His goal: to hire the smartest guy in the class to come down to Bentonville, Ark., and computerize his operations. He realized that he could not grow at the pace he desired without computerizing merchandise controls. He was right, of course, and Wal-Mart went on to become the icon of just-in-time inventory control and sophisticated logistics—the ultimate user of information as a competitive advantage. Today Wal-Mart's computer database is second only to the Pentagon's in capacity, and though he is rarely remembered that way, Walton may have been the first true information-age CEO.

To his great delight, Walton spent much of his career largely unnoticed by the public or the press. In fact, hardly anyone had ever heard of him when, in 1985, *Forbes* magazine determined that his 39% ownership of Wal-Mart's stock made him the richest man in America. After that, the first wave of attention focused on Walton as populist retailer: his preference for pickup trucks over limos and for the company of bird dogs over that of investment bankers. His extraordinary charisma had motivated hundreds of thousands of employees to believe in what Wal-Mart could accomplish, and many of them had ridden the company's stock to wealth. It was the American Dream.

AS WAL-MART'S INFLUENCE GREW, HOWEVER, AND passed that of competitors K Mart and Sears, Walton began to be villainized, especially by beleaguered small-town merchants. They rallied a nostalgic national press, which—from its perch in Manhattan—waxed eloquent on the lost graces of small-town America, blaming that loss squarely on him.

Walton viewed all these arguments as utter foolishness. He had been a small-town merchant. And he had seen the future. He had chosen to eat rather than be eaten. And anyway, he believed that small-town merchants could compete—if they would make major changes to adapt. As it turned out, of course, the consumer voted with Walton. He gave America what it really wanted—low prices every day.

Yes, Sam Walton cluttered the landscape of the American countryside, and he forced a lot of people to change the way they made a living. But he merely hastened inevitable changes. His empowering management methods were widely copied; his harnessing of information technology to cut costs quickly traveled upstream to all kinds of companies; his pioneering retailing concepts paved the way for a new breed of "category killer" store. Low-overhead, low-inventory selling keeps accelerating: the Internet is its latest iteration. One can only wonder what a young cyber Sam would accomplish if he were just getting started. ∎

Rallying the troops: Sam reveled in waving the flag for Wal-Mart—and the U.S.A.

John Huey, managing editor of FORTUNE, *co-wrote* Sam Walton: Made in America.

The Customer Is King
Retailers wooed buyers with lower prices, bigger stores and more convenient shopping

First Self-Serve Grocery
Breaking down old barriers, Piggly Wiggly empowered the customer in 1916 by inviting consumers into the once-forbidden stock shelves to make hands-on selections.

First Shopping Center
The Country Club Plaza opened in 1929 in Kansas City, Mo. The archetypal suburban strip mall, it housed a clutch of retailers anchored by an S.S. Kresge five-and-ten and yoked to a parking lot.

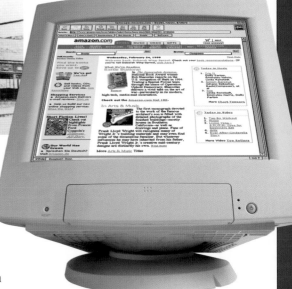

First Supermarket
A "monstrous" store, King Kullen debuted in 1930 in New York City. The self-serve food palace was four times the size of a typical grocery of the day but a tenth the size of today's 60,000-sq.-ft. superstores.

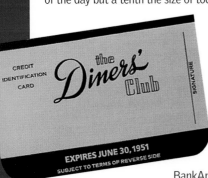

First Credit Card
In 1950, executive Frank McNamara dreamed up Diners Club after coming up short when treating clients to dinner. By the mid-'50s, computers accelerated billing and accounting. In 1958 Bank of America launched the first widely used bank credit card, BankAmericard, which became Visa. Another entrant that year: American Express. In 1998 140 million U.S. cardholders charged more than $1 trillion.

First Online Shopping
Amazon.com rocketed retail into the cyber age in July 1995 with its bookstall-on-the-Web. By 1998 the total number of online buyers had soared from 3 million to 16 million, and Internet stocks were booming.

Bill
Gates

He controls something
the world's PCs can't live
without. But he's neither as
good nor as bad as the hype

By **DAVID GELERNTER**

IF WE ARE TALKING CREATIVITY AND IDEAS, BILL GATES IS AN American unoriginal. He is Microsoft's chief and co-founder, he is the world's richest man, and his career delivers this message: It can be wiser to follow than to lead. Let the innovators hit the beaches and take the losses; if you hold back and follow, you can clean up in peace and quiet.

Gates is the Bing Crosby of American technology, borrowing a tune here and a tune there and turning them all into great boffo hits—by dint of heroic feats of repackaging and sheer Herculean blandness. Granted, he is (to put it delicately) an unusually hard-driving and successful businessman, but the Bill Gates of our imagination is absurdly overblown.

Yet we have also been unfair to him. Few living Americans have been so resented, envied and vilified, but in certain ways his career is distinguished by decency—and he hasn't got much credit for it. Technology confuses us, throws us off the scent. Where Gates is concerned, we have barked up a lot of wrong trees.

The 1968 photo on the next page shows Bill as a rapt young teenager, watching his friend Paul Allen type at a computer terminal. Allen became a co-founder of Microsoft. The child Gates has neat hair and an eager, pleasant smile; every last detail says "pat me on the head." He entered Harvard but dropped out to found Microsoft in 1975. Microsoft's first product was a version of the programming language BASIC for the Altair 8800, arguably the world's first personal computer. BASIC was someone else's idea. So was the Altair. Gates merely plugged one into the other, cream-cheesed the waiting bagel and came up with a giant hit.

By 1980, IBM had decided to build personal computers and needed a PC operating system. (Computers are born naked; they need operating systems to be presentable.) Mammoth, blue-chip IBM employed thousands of capable software builders, and didn't trust a single one of them; IBM hired Microsoft to build its operating system. Microsoft bought Q-DOS from a company called Seattle Computer Products and retailored it for the PC.

The PC was released in August 1981 and was followed into the market by huge flocks of honking, beeping clones. Microsoft's DOS was one of three official PC operating systems but quickly beat out the other two. DOS was clunky and primitive, but despite (or maybe because of) its stodginess, it established itself as the school uniform of computing. It was homely but essential. Once again, Gates had brokered a marriage between other people's ideas and come up with a hit. DOS was even bigger than BASIC. Gates had it made.

Apple released the Macintosh in January 1984: a tony, sophisticated computer was now available to the masses. Henceforth DOS was not merely homely, it was obsolete. But it continued to rake in money, so what if the critics hated it? In May 1990, Microsoft finally perfected its own version of Apple windows and called it Microsoft Windows 3.0—another huge hit. Now Gates really (I mean really) had it made.

By the early '90s, e-mail and the Internet were big. Technophiles enthused about the "information superhighway." The World Wide Web emerged in 1994, making browsers necessary, and Netscape was founded. Sun Microsystems developed Java, the Internet programming language. Gates hung back. It wasn't until 1996 that Microsoft finally, according to Gates, "embraced the Internet wholeheartedly."

> ## He's relentless, Darwinian. Success is defined as flattening competition, not creating excellence.
>
> ROB GLASER, a former Microsoft executive, on Gates

Why lead when you can follow? Microsoft's first browser, Internet Explorer 1.0, was licensed from a company called Spyglass. It was an afterthought, available off the shelf as part of a $45 CD-ROM crammed with random tidbits, software antipasto, odds and ends you could live without—one of which was Explorer. Today Microsoft is the world's most powerful supplier of Web browsers, and Gates *really* has it made. As this book goes to press, the U.S. Justice Department is suing Microsoft for throwing its weight around illegally, hitting companies like Netscape below the belt. Whoever wins, Gates will still be the No. 1 man in the industry.

And yet in sizing up Gates, we tend to overlook his basic decency. He has repeatedly been offered a starring role in the circus freak show of American Celebrity, Julius Caesar being offered the Emperor's crown by clamorous sycophants. He has turned it down. He does not make a habit of going on TV to pontificate, free-associate or share his feelings. His wife and young child are largely invisible to the public, which represents a deliberate decision on the part of Mr. and Mrs.

The baby face that launched a million PCs—Gates as a teenager with fellow geek Paul Allen in 1968

If postwar America of the 1950s and '60s democratized middle-classness, Gates has democratized filthy-richness—or has at least started to. Get the right job offer from Microsoft, work hard, get rich; no miracle required. Key Microsoft employees pushed Gates in this direction, but he was willing to go, and the industry followed. The Gates Road to Wealth is still a one-laner, and traffic is limited. But the idea that a successful corporation should enrich not merely its executives and stockholders but also a fair number of ordinary line employees is (while not unique to Microsoft) potentially revolutionary. Wealth is good. Gates has created lots and he's been willing to share.

Today Gates, grown very powerful and great, sits at the center of world technology like an immense frog eyeing insect life on the pond surface, now and then consuming a tasty company with one quick dart of the tongue. But the Microsoft Windows world view is dead in the water, and Gates has nothing to offer in its place. Windows is a relic of the ancient days when e-mail didn't matter, when the Internet and the Web didn't matter, when most computer users had only a relative handful of files to manage. Big changes are in the works that will demote computers and their operating systems to the status of TV sets. You can walk up to any television set and tune in CBS; in a few years you will be able to walk up to any computer and tune in your own files, your electronic life. The questions of the moment are, What will the screen look like? How will the controls work? What exactly will they do? and Who will profit from it?

Microsoft? Maybe. However, being the biggest, toughest frog in the pond doesn't help if you're in the wrong pond. Some people have the idea that Microsoft is fated to dominate technology forever. They had this same idea about IBM, once admired and feared just as Microsoft is today. They had essentially the same idea about Japan's technology sector back in the 1980s and early '90s. It isn't quite fair to compare Microsoft to a large country yet. But Japan looked invincible—once. (Or, if you go back to Pearl Harbor, twice.)

As for Gates himself, he is no visionary; he is a technology groupie with a genius for showing up, for being at the right place at the right time. His secret is revealed in that old photo with Paul Allen just above. Gates is a man who likes computers very much. Not their intellectual underpinnings, not the physics or electronics, not the art or philosophy or mathematics of software—just plain computers. He's crazy about them. It seems like an odd passion, but after all, some people are crazy about Pop-Tarts. And Gates will be remembered alongside Pop-Tarts, in the long run, as vintage Americana, a sign of the times. A little on the bland side perhaps, unexciting, not awfully deep, not to everyone's taste, but not all that bad. ■

David Gelernter is a professor of computer science at Yale University and author most recently of Machine Beauty.

BORN Oct. 28, 1955, in Seattle	1975 Drops out of Harvard to co-found Microsoft with Paul Allen	1980 Licenses MS-DOS to IBM for its inaugural PC	1990 Releases Windows 3.0, a hit, a user-friendly answer to the Mac OS	1998 Justice Department files antitrust suit against Microsoft

1955

1977 Gates after a minor run-in with the law—not as potentially costly as the antitrust rap he later fought

1986 Becomes billionaire at 31 with company IPO

1995-96 Debuts Windows 95 and Internet Explorer browser for the Net age

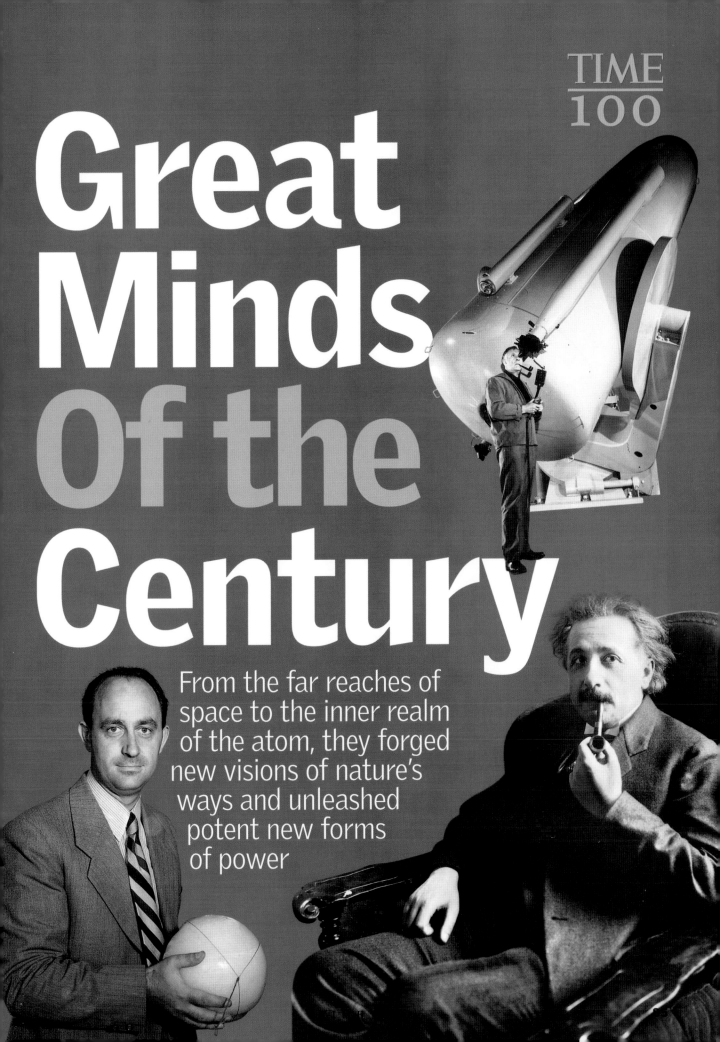

Great Minds Of the Century

From the far reaches of space to the inner realm of the atom, they forged new visions of nature's ways and unleashed potent new forms of power

Faust's Pact

This was the century that split the atom, probed the psyche, spliced genes and cloned a sheep. It invented plastic, the Pill and the silicon chip. It built airplanes, space ships, televisions, computers and atom bombs. It overthrew our inherited ideas about logic, learning, language, mathematics, economics and even space and time. And behind each of these great insights, inventions and discoveries is, in most cases, a single extraordinary human mind.

THE SCIENTIST
Luba Lukova

THIS FOURTH SECTION OF THE TIME 100 SERIES CELEBRATES those great minds—the scientists, philosophers and inventors who shaped a century that was dominated more than any other by science and technology.

Of course the great minds of the previous century had every reason to believe that *theirs* was the triumphant era of scientific advancement. Indeed, the industrialized world at the end of the 19th century fairly hummed with applied science. Steam engines—their inner workings elegantly captured by the laws of thermodynamics—moved mountains, reshaped cities and put the world on a predictable timetable. Giant dynamos turned coal into electrical power, pumping J.J. Thomson's newly discovered electrons though telegraph, telephone and power cables. No sooner had Darwin divined the laws of natural selection than some of his followers began trying to apply them to the human population, looking for ways to encourage "good" births and discourage "bad."

There were, to be sure, lingering uncertainties, even among Darwin's true believers: about what lay beyond the Milky Way that marked the limit of the known universe; about the age of the sun, the earth and the life upon it; about strange discrepancies that were turning up in Newton's billiard-ball laws of celestial mechanics; about X rays and bizarre radiation effects that didn't fit Thomson's cozy model of the atom as a sphere of matter in which electrons were embedded "like raisins in a pudding."

Still, science at the turn of the century was on a roll, and the prevailing mood was one of exuberant optimism. This was the spirit in which Russell and Whitehead and their followers set out to construct a logical foundation for all of human knowledge, starting with mathematics. And in which Henry Adams, visiting the Great Hall of Dynamos at the Exposition of 1900, described a technological epiphany. "As he grew accustomed to the great gallery of machines," Adams wrote in *The Education of Henry Adams*, "he began to feel the 40-foot dynamos as a moral force, much as the early Christians felt the Cross ... The dynamo became a symbol of infinity. Before the end, one began to pray to it."

Within a few decades, all that had changed. A series of rapid-fire scientific revolutions toppled assumptions that had held sway for hundreds, even thousands of years.

Freud, himself a devout logical positivist, tried to apply a scientist's rigor to the study of the human mind and discovered, to everyone's dismay, a roiling snake pit of unconscious lust, rage and repression. Wittgenstein, Russell's most brilliant acolyte, lost faith in the power of pure reason, sensing the futility of trying to capture knowledge in one grand logical system—an effort that Gödel and Turing would later prove was, in fact, impossible.

But it was Einstein's theory of relativity that sparked the most excitement, confusion and dismay. Space, the world learned to its shock, could be warped and buckled by gravity. And time, which seemed so uniform and constant, turned out to be as elastic as an India rubber band.

It got worse. According to the emerging theories of

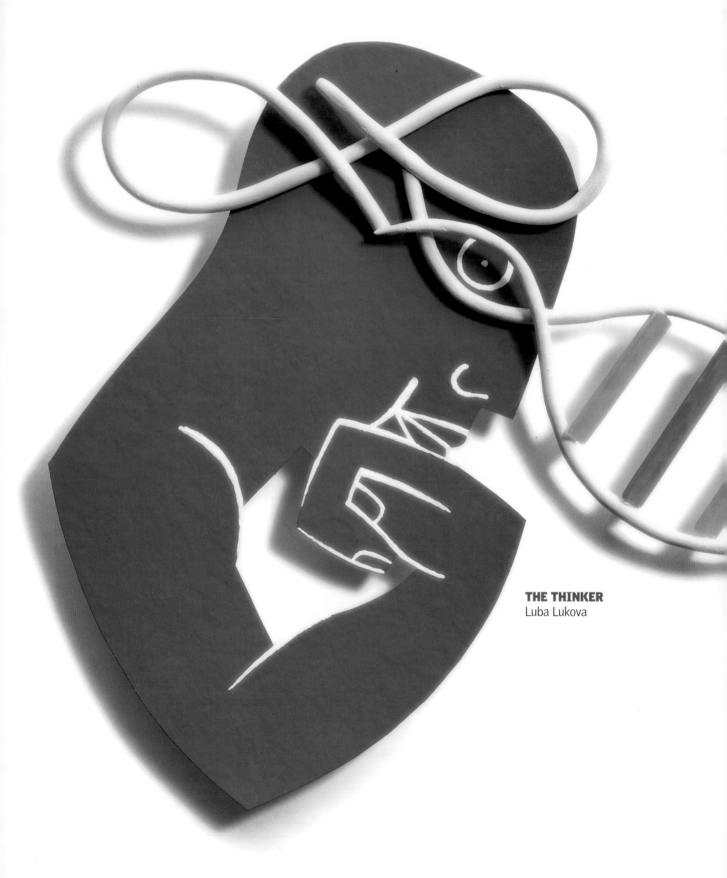

THE THINKER
Luba Lukova

quantum physics, even the laws of cause and effect were suspect. Matter was energy, and energy could turn into matter. Light was neither a particle nor a wave, but could be both, or either, depending on how you looked at it. Subatomic particles popped in and out of existence for no apparent reason, moving from place to place without seeming to occupy the space in between. And though these particles could not be pinned down—so greatly were they disturbed by the very act of observation—they could dictate in an instant the state of matter on the other side of the universe.

That universe, meanwhile, was discovered to be infinitely more vast and strange than anyone could have imagined. The Milky Way that filled the night sky turned out to be only one of billions of distant galaxies, and those galaxies in turn were flying away from each other at ever increasing speeds. Plotting backward, it all seemed to have been created in a single explosive moment—the very start of time—when the entire universe was contained in something the size of a marble, or an atom, or even smaller, if you can imagine that. Is this possible? If so, then what came before the Big Bang? And into what, exactly, is this rapidly inflating universe expanding? Even Einstein couldn't wrap his mind around that.

It's hard to overstate the cumulative effect of these shocks, coming one after another, in the first decades of the century. The scientific mind boggled. It was comparable, in its way, to the effect of the horrors of World War I on the political and cultural life of Europe. It may be no accident that Einstein proposed his general theory of relativity the same year as the Battle of Verdun, or that Wittgenstein completed his *Tractatus* while serving in

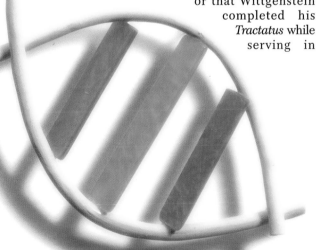

the Austrian artillery. Nothing was as it seemed. Everything was falling apart. The center, as Yeats put it, could not hold.

Not that everybody noticed. As far as most people were concerned, science and technology were marching bravely on, and even flourishing. Men were flying. Rockets were soaring. Radio was celebrating its golden age, and television would soon be blinking into life. Penicillin was discov-

ered, and before long humanity's average life span had nearly doubled. Nobody seemed to know or care that cause and effect had been suspended, or that matter could be transformed into energy.

Until the Bomb. And then suddenly it was clear to anyone who didn't already suspect it that the century had made a Faustian bargain with science. The price of understanding how the world worked—at its deepest level—was the very real possibility that the world itself would be destroyed.

AFTERWARD, IT WAS HARD TO LOOK AT ANY TECHnological advance without weighing its costs. The automobile gave us great freedom of movement but it also brought pollution, oil dependence and the traffic jam. The birth control pill freed women from the servitude of unwanted pregnancies, but it also undermined the family and helped spread venereal disease, including AIDS. The green revolution postponed Malthusian famines but it also gave us monocultures, phosphate run-offs and DDT. No wonder the first electronic computer was greeted about as warmly as George Orwell's Big Brother, or that the breakthrough discovery of the structure of DNA was seen as ushering in Aldous Huxley's *Brave New World*.

In that context, it's hard to believe that the electronic computer (a quintessential wartime invention) and the transistor (a bit of applied quantum mechanics) could give rise to the microchip and soon after to the personal computer—an invention so democratic and empowering to the individual as to make Orwell seem delusional. And it seems little short of miraculous that a command-and-control network designed to survive a nuclear holocaust could give rise to the Internet and the World Wide Web. The very technologies that were going to blow the world to smithereens seem to be stitching it back together.

As the 20th century draws to a close, the great scientific enterprise to keep your eye on is molecular genetics, best symbolized by the multinational effort known as the Human Genome Project. In the year 2000, scientists hope to have a rough draft of the biochemical code of the 100,000 or so genes that determine every physical characteristic of the human body. By 2003, they plan to make the finished map freely available on the Web. The idea is to encourage scientists around the world to use that map to establish a precise chemical explanation for every medical malfunction, from heart disease to cancer. And eventually, for all of life.

Once again, science is on a roll. The prevailing mood is one of exuberant optimism. The postindustrial world fairly hums with electronic information. We have every reason to believe that *ours* is the triumphant era of scientific advancement. In another 100 years, our grandchildren will know if we were right. ∎

Philip Elmer-DeWitt, an assistant managing editor of TIME, *supervised the Great Minds of the Century project.*

The Wright Brot

**ers** A pair of self-taught engineers working in a bicycle shop, they made the world a forever smaller place

By **BILL GATES**

In France, huge crowds flocked to see Wilbur fly a new two-seater in 1908

WILBUR AND ORVILLE WRIGHT WERE TWO brothers from the heartland of America with a vision as sweeping as the sky and a practicality as down-to-earth as the Wright Cycle Co., the bicycle business they founded in Dayton, Ohio, in 1892. But while there were countless bicycle shops in turn-of-the-century America, in only one were wings being built as well as wheels.

When the Wright brothers finally realized their vision of powered human flight in 1903, they made the world a forever smaller place. I've been to Kitty Hawk, N.C., and seen where the brothers imagined the future, and then literally flew across its high frontier. It was an inspiration to be there, and to soak up the amazing perseverance and creativity of these two pioneers.

The Wright brothers had been fascinated by the idea of flight from an early age. In 1878 their father, a bishop in the Church of the United Brethren in Christ, gave them a flying toy made of cork and bamboo. It had a paper body and was powered by rubber bands. The young boys soon broke the fragile toy, but the memory of its faltering flight across their living room stayed with them. By the mid-1890s Wilbur was reading every book and paper he could find on the still

earthbound science of human flight. And four years before they made history at Kitty Hawk, the brothers built their first, scaled-down flying machine—a pilotless "kite" with a 5-ft. wingspan, and made of wood, wire and cloth. Wilbur was convinced by that experiment that he could build an aircraft that would be "capable of sustaining a man."

While the brothers' bicycle business paid the bills, it was Wilbur's abiding dream of building a full-size flying machine that inspired their work. For many years, he once said, he had been "afflicted with the belief that flight is possible."

The reality of that obsession was a lonely quest for the brothers in the workroom behind their bike shop, plotting to defy gravity and conquer the wind. Yet that obsessive kind of world-changing belief is a force that drives you to solve a problem, to find the breakthrough— a force that drives you to bet everything on a fragile wing or a new idea. It was a force that led the Wright brothers to invent, single-handedly, each of the technologies they needed to pursue their dream.

When published aeronautical data turned out to be unreliable, the Wright brothers built their own wind tunnel to test airfoils and measure empirically how to lift a flying machine into the sky. They were the first to discover that a long, narrow wing shape was the ideal architecture of flight. They figured out how to move the vehicle freely, not just across land, but up and down on a cushion of air. They built a forward elevator to control the pitch of their craft as it nosed up and down. They fashioned a pair of twin rudders in back to control its tendency to yaw from side to side. They devised a pulley system that warped the shape of the wings in midflight to turn the plane and to stop it from rolling laterally in air.

Recognizing that a propeller isn't like a ship's screw, but becomes, in effect, a rotating wing, they used the data from their wind-tunnel experiments to design the first effective airplane props—a pair of 8-ft. propellers, carved out of laminated spruce, that turned in opposite directions to offset the twisting effect on the machine's structure. And when they discovered that a lightweight gas-powered engine did

BORN Wilbur: April 16, 1867, Millville, Ind.
BORN Orville: Aug. 19, 1871, Dayton, Ohio

1892 Open bike shop

1903 Pilot first manned, powered flights of heavier-than-air craft

1908 Contract to make planes for U.S. Army

1915 Orville sells interest in airplane factory

1867/1871

1948

1899-1902 Build and test kites and gliders

1906 Establish patents on airplane-control system

FAME The brothers, 1909

DIES Orville suffers heart attack

1912 Wilbur dies of typhoid

Imagine a locomotive that ... is climbing up in the air ... without any wheels ... but with white wings instead.

A.R. ROOT, an Ohio merchant, watching the Wrights in flight in 1904

not exist, they decided to design and build their own. It produced 12 horsepower and weighed only 152 lbs.

The genius of Leonardo da Vinci imagined a flying machine, but it took the methodical application of science by these two American bicycle mechanics to create it. The unmanned gliders spawned by their first efforts flew erratically and were at the mercy of any strong gust of wind. But with help from their wind tunnel, the brothers amassed more data on wing design than anyone before them, compiling tables of computations that are still valid today. And with guidance from this scientific study, they developed the powered 1903 Flyer, a skeletal flying machine of spruce, ash and muslin, with a wingspan of 40 ft. and an unmanned weight of just over 600 lbs.

On Dec. 17, 1903, with Orville at the controls, the Flyer lifted off shakily from Kitty Hawk and flew 120 ft.—a distance little more than half the wingspan of a Boeing 747-400. That 12-sec. flight changed the world, lifting it to new heights of freedom and giving mankind access to places it had never before dreamed of reaching. Although the Wright brothers' feat was to transform life in the 20th century, the next day only four newspapers in the U.S. carried news of their achievement—news that was widely dismissed as exaggerated.

The Wright brothers gave us a tool, but it was up to individuals and nations to put it to use, and use it we have. The airplane revolutionized both peace and war. It brought families together: once, when a child or other close relatives left the old country for America, family and friends mourned for someone they would never see again. Today, the grandchild of that immigrant can return again and again across a vast ocean in just half a turn of the clock. But the airplane also helped tear families apart, by making international warfare an effortless reality.

The Wrights created one of the greatest cultural forces since the development of writing, for their invention effectively became the World Wide Web of that era, bringing people, languages, ideas and values together. It also ushered in an age of globalization, as the world's flight paths became the superhighways of an emerging international economy. Those superhighways of the sky not only revolutionized international business; they also opened up isolated economies, carried the cause of democracy around the world and broke down every kind of political barrier. And they set travelers on a path that would eventually lead beyond Earth's atmosphere into outer space.

The Wright brothers and their invention, then, sparked a revolution as far-reaching as the industrial and digital revolutions. But that revolution did not come about by luck or accident. It was vision, quiet resolve and the application of scientific methodology that enabled Orville and Wilbur to carry the human race skyward. Their example reminds us that genius doesn't have a pedigree, and that you don't discover new worlds by plying safe, conventional waters. Recalling their experiments with 10 years of hindsight, even Orville admitted that "I look with amazement upon our audacity in attempting flights with a new and untried machine."

Now, at the dawn of another century, who knows where the next Wright brothers will be found, in what grade of school they're studying, or in what garage they're inventing the next Flyer of the information age. Our mission is to make sure that wherever they are, they have the chance to run their own course, to persevere and follow their own inspiration. We have to understand that engineering breakthroughs are not just mechanical or scientific—they are liberating forces that can continually improve people's lives.

By 1911, Orville (between crack-ups) had set a glider record of nearly 10 minutes aloft

Who would have thought, as the 20th century opened, that one of its greatest contributions would come from two obscure, fresh-faced young Americans who pursued the utmost bounds of human thought and gave us all, for the first time, the power literally to sail beyond the sunset?

The 20th century has been the American Century in large part because of great inventors such as the Wright brothers. May we follow their flight paths and blaze our own in the 21st century. ∎

Bill Gates is the chairman and CEO of Microsoft.

Albert
Einstein

From space travel to the Bomb, from electronics to quantum physics, we live in a universe he first charted—in his mind

By **JAMES GLEICK**

THE NAME ECHOES THROUGH THE LANGUAGE: IT doesn't take an Einstein. A poor man's Einstein. He's no Einstein. In this busy century, dominated like no other by science—and exalting, among the human virtues, braininess, IQ, the ideal of pure intelligence—he stands alone as our emblem of intellectual power. We talk as though humanity could be divided into two groups: Albert Einstein and everybody else. He discovered, just by thinking about it, the essential structure of the cosmos. The scientific touchstones of our age—the Bomb, space travel, electronics—all bear his fingerprints.

We may as well join him in 1905, when he was a patent-office clerk in Bern, Switzerland—not the revered white-haloed icon of a thousand photographs, but a confident 26-year-old with wavy black hair and droll, wide eyes. That year, in his spare time, he produced three world-shattering papers for a single volume (now priceless) of the premier journal *Annalen der Physik*. They were "blazing rockets which in the dark of the night suddenly cast a brief but powerful illumination over an immense unknown region," as the physicist Louis de Broglie said.

One offered the startling view that light comes as much in particles as in waves—setting the stage for generations of tension between granularity and smoothness in physicists' view of energy and matter. The second discussed, imaginatively, the microscopic motion of molecules in a liquid—making it possible to find their exact size and incidentally proving their very reality (many scientists, as the century

began, still doubted that atoms existed). And the third—well, as Einstein said in a letter to a friend, it "modifies the theory of space and time." Ah, yes. Relativity.

The time had come. The Newtonian world view was fraying. The 19th century had pressed its understanding of space and time to the very limit. Everyone believed in the ether, that mysterious background substance of the whole universe through which light waves supposedly traveled, but where was the experimental evidence for it? Nowhere, as Einstein realized. He found it more productive to think in terms of utterly abstract frames of reference—because these could move along with a moving observer. Meanwhile, a few imaginative people were already speaking of time in terms of a fourth dimension—H.G. Wells, for example, in his time-obsessed science fiction. Humanity was standing on a brink, ready to see something new.

It was Einstein who saw it. Space and time were not apples and oranges, he realized, but mates—joined, homologous, inseparable. "Henceforth space by itself and time by itself are doomed to fade away into mere shadows," said Hermann Minkowski, a teacher of Einstein's and one of relativity's first champions, "and only a kind of union of the two will preserve an independent reality." Well, we all know that now. "Space-time" we knowingly call it. Likewise energy and matter: two faces of one creature. $E=mc^2$, as Einstein memorably announced.

All this was shocking and revolutionary and yet strangely attractive, to the public as well as to scientists. The speed of

BORN March 14 in Ulm, Germany

1905 Publishes three seminal papers on theoretical physics, including the special theory of relativity

1922 Wins Nobel Prize in Physics

1939 Urges F.D.R. to develop atom bomb

1879

1955

DAY DREAMER
A poor student at 14, by 26 he had reshaped both time and space

1902 Begins work at Swiss patent office

1916 Proposes general theory of relativity; is proved correct three years later

1933 Emigrates to Princeton, N.J.

DIES in his sleep on April 18

Standing room only: the century's most influential physicist lectures in Paris

person in his circle not trying to win a $5,000 *Scientific American* prize for the best 3,000-word summary ("I don't believe I could do it").

The very name relativity fueled the fervor, for accidental and wholly unscientific reasons. In this new age, recovering from a horrible war, looking everywhere for originality and modernity, people could see that absolutism was no good. Everything had to be looked at relative to everything else. Everything—for humanity's field of vision was expanding rapidly outward, to planets, stars, galaxies.

Einstein had conjured the whole business, it seemed. He did not invent the "thought experiment," but he raised it to high art: *Imagine twins, wearing identical watches; one stays home, while the other rides in a spaceship near the speed of light …* Little wonder that Einstein remains the world's most famous scientist.

light; the shifting perspective of the observer—it was heady fare. A solar eclipse in 1919 gave English astronomer Arthur Eddington the opportunity to prove a key prediction of relativity: that starlight would swerve measurably as it passed through the heavy gravity of the sun, a dimple in the fabric of the universe. Light has mass. Newspapers and popular magazines went wild. More than 100 books on relativity appeared within a year. Einstein claimed to be the only

In his native Germany he became a target for hatred. As a Jew, a liberal, a humanist, an internationalist, he attracted the enmity of nationalists and anti-Semites, abetted by a few jealous physicists—an all too vigorous faction that Einstein called, while it was still possible to find this amusing, "the Antirelativity Theory Co. Ltd." His was now a powerful voice, widely heard, always attended to, especially after he

EINSTEIN'S THEORY OF RELATIVITY

Relativity asserts that light always moves in a straight line through empty space, and always at the same speed in a vacuum, no matter what your vantage point. From these simple claims follow bizarre consequences that challenge common sense and our perception of reality– but have been verified repeatedly by experiments.

TIME Graphics by Ed Gabel

Sources: World Book Encyclopedia; Einstein for Beginners

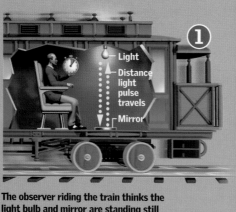

The observer riding the train thinks the light bulb and mirror are standing still

Relativity and Time

A moving clock runs slower than a stationary one from the perspective of a stationary observer

① A man riding a moving train is timing a light beam that travels from ceiling to floor and back again. From his point of view, the light moves straight down and straight up.

② Watching from trackside, Einstein sees the man, bulb and mirror moving sideways; the light traces a diagonal path as it goes. From Einstein's viewpoint, the light travels farther. But since the speed of light is always the same, that means the same event measured on his clock takes more time.

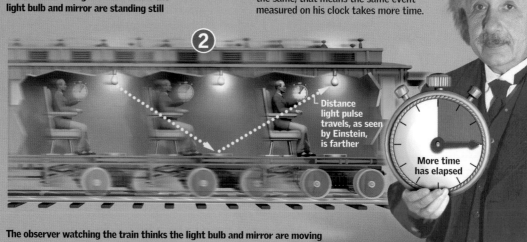

The observer watching the train thinks the light bulb and mirror are moving

> # "To punish me for my contempt for authority, Fate made me an authority myself."
>
> **EINSTEIN, on his rebelliousness**

moved to the U.S. He used it to promote Zionism, pacifism and, in his secret 1939 letter to Franklin D. Roosevelt, the construction of a uranium bomb.

Meanwhile, like any demigod, he accreted bits of legend: that he flunked math in school (not true). That he opened a book and found an uncashed $1,500 check he had left as a bookmark (maybe—he was absentminded about everyday affairs). That he was careless about socks, collars, slippers … that he couldn't work out the correct change for the bus … that he couldn't even remember his address: 112 Mercer Street in Princeton, N.J., where he finally settled, conferring an aura of scientific brilliance on the town, the university and the Institute for Advanced Study.

H E DIED THERE IN 1955. HE HAD NEVER ACCEPTED the strangest paradoxes of quantum mechanics *(see box)*. He found "intolerable" the idea that subatomic particles would not obey the laws of cause and effect, or that the act of observing one particle could instantly determine the nature of another halfway across the universe. He had never achieved what he considered a complete, unified field theory. Indeed, for some years he had watched the growth of physics into the most powerful and expensive branch of the sciences from a slight remove. He had lived, he said, "in that solitude which is painful in youth but delicious in the years of maturity."

Following his death Einstein was cremated, but his brain remained, soaking for decades in a jar of formaldehyde belonging to Dr. Thomas Harvey, the Princeton Hospital pathologist. No one had bothered to dissect the brain of Freud, Stravinsky or Joyce, but in the 1980s, bits of Einsteinian gray matter were making the rounds of certain neurobiologists, who thus learned … absolutely nothing. It was just a brain—the brain that dreamed a plastic fourth dimension, that banished the ether, that released the pins binding us to absolute space and time, that refused to believe God played dice, that finally declared itself "satisfied with the mystery of life's eternity and with a knowledge, a sense, of the marvelous structure of existence."

In embracing Einstein, our century took leave of a prior universe and an erstwhile God. The new versions were not so rigid and deterministic as the old Newtonian world. Einstein's God was no clockmaker, but he was the embodiment of reason in nature—"subtle but malicious he is not." This God did not control our actions or even sit in judgment on them. ("Einstein, stop telling God what to do," Niels Bohr retorted.) This God seemed kindly and absentminded, as a matter of fact. Physics was freer, and we too are freer, in the Einstein universe. Which is where we live. ∎

James Gleick is the author of Chaos *and the award-winning biography of physicist Richard Feynman,* Genius.

Relativity and Length

A moving object appears to shrink in the direction of motion, as seen by a stationary observer

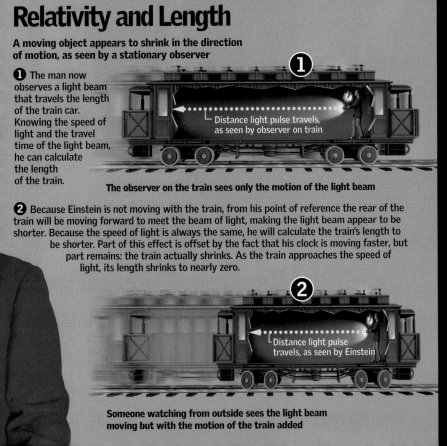

1 The man now observes a light beam that travels the length of the train car. Knowing the speed of light and the travel time of the light beam, he can calculate the length of the train.

Distance light pulse travels, as seen by observer on train

The observer on the train sees only the motion of the light beam

2 Because Einstein is not moving with the train, from his point of reference the rear of the train will be moving forward to meet the beam of light, making the light beam appear to be shorter. Because the speed of light is always the same, he will calculate the train's length to be shorter. Part of this effect is offset by the fact that his clock is moving faster, but part remains: the train actually shrinks. As the train approaches the speed of light, its length shrinks to nearly zero.

Distance light pulse travels, as seen by Einstein

Someone watching from outside sees the light beam moving but with the motion of the train added

Space-Time Distortion

In general relativity, time is considered a dimension like height, width and depth, creating a four-dimensional universe called space-time. Einstein argued that gravity is really a warping of space-time, with the greatest distortions near the most massive objects. Because light travels in a straight line through the contours of space-time, a light beam will curve where space-time curves. This curving was first measured in 1919, vindicating Einstein's theory.

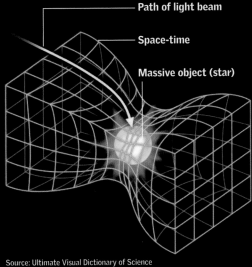

Path of light beam

Space-time

Massive object (star)

Source: Ultimate Visual Dictionary of Science

Particle Pioneers

Quantum theory suggests that the only thing certain about nature—is its uncertainty

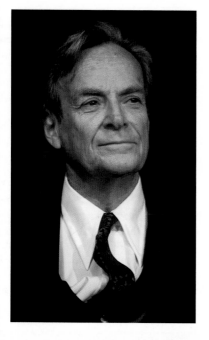

Richard Feynman

Perhaps the greatest physicist of the mid-20th century, free-spirit Feynman retooled quantum mechanics, turning it into a practical mathematical tool, but he also played bongos, cracked safes and picked up women in bars. Solving the mystery of why the *Challenger* blew up, he was part genius, part showman and thus pure Feynman.

Werner Heisenberg

Heisenberg explained and calculated the quantum behavior of particles. His uncertainty principle says that the act of observing nature at its most fundamental level changes that which is observed.

Niels Bohr

The first to apply quantum principles to the structure of the atom, Bohr argued that electrons near a nucleus could occupy only certain positions and change position through "quantum leaps," moving without seeming to traverse the space between.

Max Planck

In what he called "an act of desperation," the German physicist suggested that energy could be absorbed and emitted by matter only in tiny chunks, or "quanta," not in a continuous stream.

Ludwig
Wittgenstein

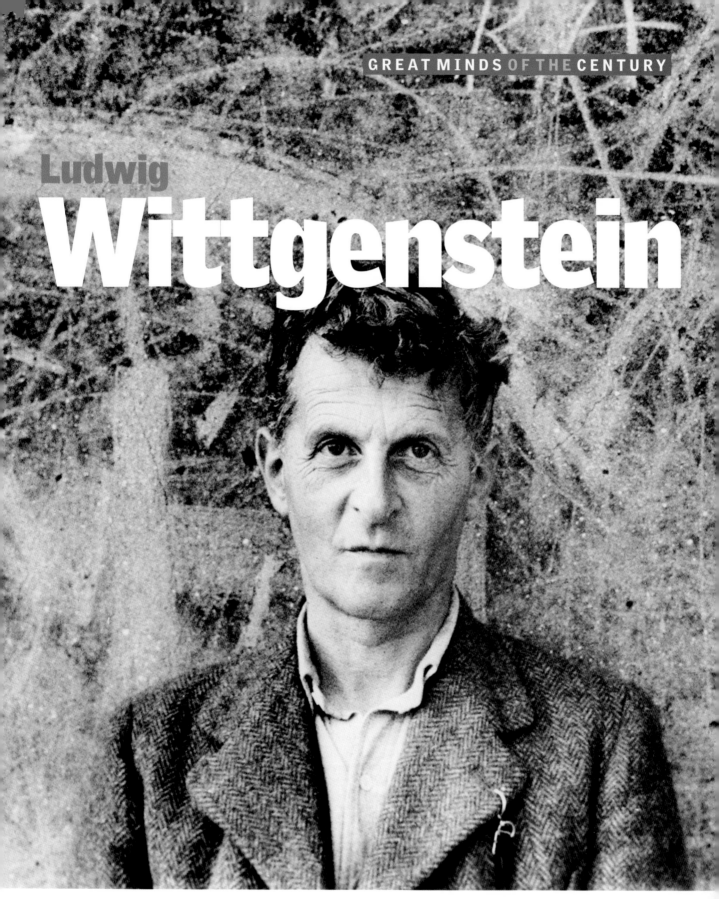

Chalk it up as irony: he began by trying to reduce all mathematics to logic and ended by finding most metaphysics to be nonsense

By DANIEL DENNETT

The soldier, right, visits his wealthy family on leave in 1918

IF YOU WOULD LIKE TO WATCH PHILOSOPHERS SQUIRM— and who wouldn't?—pose this tough question: Suppose you may either a) solve a major philosophical problem so conclusively that there is nothing left to say (thanks to you, part of the field closes down forever, and you get a footnote in history); or b) write a book of such tantalizing perplexity and controversy that it stays on the required-reading list for centuries. Which would you choose? Many philosophers will reluctantly admit that they would go for option b): they would rather be read than right. The Austrian philosopher Ludwig Wittgenstein tried brilliantly to go for a) and ended up with b).

The revolution in mathematical logic early in the 20th century opened up a delicious prospect: a rigorous science of meanings. Just as the atomic theory in physics had begun to break matter down into its constituent parts and show how they fit together to produce all the effects in nature, logic held out the promise of accounting for all meaningful texts and utterances—from philosophy and geometrical proofs to history and legislation—by breaking them into their logical atoms and showing how those parts fit together (in an ideal language) to compose all the meanings there could be.

As a young engineering student in England, Wittgenstein saw the hope of the new mathematical logic, and rushed to Cambridge to become the protégé of Bertrand Russell, whose monumental *Principia Mathematica* (1913), written with Alfred North Whitehead, was an attempt to reduce all mathematics to logic. Wittgenstein's first book, published in England in 1922, the even more grandly titled *Tractatus Logico-philosophicus*, went even further, and was thought by him, and by some of his admirers, to have brought philosophy to an end, its key problems definitively solved once and for all. Some "philosophical" propositions could be readily expressed and evaluated within his system; those that couldn't—among them, metaphysical riddles that had bedeviled philosophers for centuries—were nonsense.

Wittgenstein returned to Austria to teach school. But the worm of doubt soon gnawed, and he returned to England in 1929 to declare dramatically that he had got it all wrong the first time. The "later Wittgenstein" spent the next 18 years agonizing in front of a small Cambridge seminar of devoted and transfixed students, who posed curious questions that he then answered—or pointedly did not answer— with wonderfully austere if often enigmatic aphorisms. An obsessive perfectionist, Wittgenstein worked and reworked his notes and left his second masterpiece, *Philosophical Investigations,* for posthumous publication in 1953. Both books will be required reading as far into the future as any philosopher could claim to see.

The family into which Wittgenstein was born in 1889 was one of the wealthiest in Vienna, and young Ludwig grew up in a hothouse atmosphere of high culture and privilege; Brahms and Mahler were frequent visitors to the palatial family home. It was during the war that Ludwig, a volunteer in the Austrian artillery, completed the *Tractatus* shortly before he was captured and taken prisoner. Always an ascetic, he gave away his inheritance, relying on the generosity of his Cambridge champions, Russell and John Maynard Keynes, to secure academic employment for him. He lived frugally and in later life was cared for by his disciples.

You know from the moment you open the *Tractatus* that it is something special. Each left-hand page is in German, facing its English translation on the right, and the sentences are numbered in the hierarchical system of a formal proof. The book begins straightforwardly enough: "1. The world is everything that is the case." (In German, it makes a memorable rhyming couplet: *Die Welt ist alles, was der Fall ist.*) And it ends with an ending to end all endings: "7. Whereof one cannot speak, thereof one must be silent."

BORN April 26 in Vienna

1889

THE THINKER A portrait at age 21

1912 Moves to Cambridge to study with Bertrand Russell

1918 Completes the *Tractatus* during active service in World War I

1920 Works first as a schoolteacher, then as a gardener

1929 Returns to Cambridge as a lecturer and begins work on *Philosophical Investigations*

1951

DIES in Cambridge

> # "I asked him to admit that there was not a rhinoceros in the room, but he wouldn't.
>
> BERTRAND RUSSELL, on Wittgenstein's refusal to believe his own eyes

In between, there is some tough sledding. Wittgenstein draws a distinction between what can be said, using words, and what can only be shown, and this raises the inevitable question: Does the *Tractatus*, as a text, say things that can't be said? Maybe. The next-to-last proposition is a famous shocker: "6.54. My propositions are elucidatory in this way: he who understands me finally recognizes them as senseless, when he has climbed out through them, on them, over them. (He must so to speak throw away the ladder, after he has climbed up on it.) He must surmount these propositions; then he sees the world rightly."

Did this mean that the wonderful dream of logical atomism—a science of meanings—was hopeless? Or that there was much less to be said than one might have thought? Or what? When Wittgenstein returned to philosophy in 1929, it was with the message that the rigorous methods of pure logic could get no grip on the problems of philosophy: "We have got on to slippery ice where there is no friction and so in a certain sense the conditions are ideal, but also, just because of that, we are unable to walk. We want to walk: so we need friction. Back to the rough ground!"

Where before he had favored explicit logical rules, now he spoke of language games, governed by tacit mutual understanding, and he proposed to replace the sharp boundaries of set theory with what he called family resemblances. "Philosophy is a battle against the bewitchment of our intelligence by means of language," he claimed, and language bewitches us by enticing us to concoct "theories" to solve philosophical problems that arise only "when language goes on holiday."

Wittgenstein set out in particular to subvert the seductive theories about mind and consciousness that philosophers since Descartes had puzzled and battled over. Again and again in *Philosophical Investigations*, he catches his interlocutors in the act of being suckered by their overconfident intuitions about what their words mean—what their words must mean, they think—when they talk about what's going on in their own minds. As he says, "The decisive moment in the conjuring trick has been made, and it was the very one that we thought quite innocent." (Today's neuroscientists fall into these same traps with stunning regularity, in exploring consciousness. Unfortunately, Wittgenstein's work has not been appreciated by many scientists.) But didn't his own antidote to such theories constitute a theory of the mind? That is just one of many quandaries and paradoxes he has left behind for posterity.

In 1939, Wittgenstein's Cambridge seminar on the foundations of mathematics included the brilliant young Alan Turing, who was giving his own course that term on the same topic. Turing too had been excited by the promise of mathematical logic and, like Wittgenstein, had seen its limitations. But in the course of Turing's formal proof that the dream of turning all mathematics into logic was strictly impossible, he had invented a purely conceptual device—now known as a Universal Turing Machine—that provided the logical basis for the digital computer. And whereas Wittgenstein's dream of a universal ideal language for expressing all meanings had been shattered, Turing's device actually achieved a somewhat different sort of universality: it could compute all computable mathematical functions.

Some of Wittgenstein's disciples took verbatim notes, so we can catch a rare glimpse of two great minds addressing a central problem from opposite points of view: the problem of contradiction in a formal system. For Turing, the problem is a practical one: if you design a bridge using a system that contains a contradiction, "the bridge may fall down." For Wittgenstein, the problem was about the social context in which human beings can be said to "follow the rules" of a mathematical system. What Turing saw, and Wittgenstein did not, was the importance of the fact that a computer doesn't need to understand rules to follow them. Who "won"? Turing comes off as a bit flatfooted and naive, but he left us with the computer, while Wittgenstein left us ... Wittgenstein.

Like any other charismatic thinker, Wittgenstein continues to attract fanatics who devote their life to disagreeing with one another (and, presumably, with my brief summary) about the ultimate meaning of his words. These disciples cling myopically to their Wittgenstein, not realizing that there are many great Wittgensteins to choose from. My hero is the one who showed us new ways of being suspicious of our own convictions. The fact remains that one's first exposure to either the *Tractatus* or *Philosophical Investigations* is a liberating and exhilarating experience. Here is a model of thinking so intense, so pure, so self-critical that even its mistakes are gifts. ■

Philosopher Daniel Dennett is the author of eight books, most recently Brainchildren: A Collection of Essays 1984-1996.

TIME 100

101

Sigmund
Freud

He opened a window on the unconscious—where, he said, lust, rage and repression contend—and changed the way we view ourselves

By PETER GAY

THERE ARE NO NEUTRALS IN THE FREUD WARS. Admiration, even downright adulation, on one side; skepticism, even downright disdain, on the other. This is not hyperbole. A psychoanalyst who tries to enshrine Freud in the pantheon of cultural heroes today must contend with a relentless critic who devotes his days to exposing Freud as a charlatan. But on one thing the dueling parties agree: for good or ill, Sigmund Freud, more than any other explorer of the psyche, has shaped the mind of the 20th century. The very fierceness and persistence of his detractors are a wry tribute to the staying power of his ideas.

Such embittered confrontations have dogged Freud's footsteps since he first developed the cluster of theories he would give the name of psychoanalysis. His fundamental idea—that all humans are endowed with an unconscious mind in which potent sexual and aggressive drives, and defenses against them, struggle for supremacy, as it were, behind a person's back—has struck many as a romantic, scientifically unprovable notion. His contention that the catalog of neurotic ailments to which humans are susceptible is nearly always the work of sexual maladjustments, and that erotic desire starts not in puberty but in infancy, seemed to

Sofa of the century: Freud's couch

the respectable nothing less than obscene. His dramatic evocation of a universal Oedipus complex, in which (to put a complicated issue too simply) the little boy loves his mother and hates his father, seems more like a literary conceit than a thesis worthy of a scientifically minded psychologist.

Freud first used the term psychoanalysis in 1896, when he was already 40. He had been driven by ambition from his earliest days and encouraged by his doting parents to think highly of himself. The firstborn of an impecunious Jewish family in the Moravian hamlet of Freiberg (now Pribor in the Czech Republic), he moved with the rest of a growing brood to Vienna. In recognition of his brilliance, his parents privileged him over his siblings by giving him a room to himself, to study in peace. He did not disappoint them. After an impressive career in school, he matriculated in 1873 in the University of Vienna and drifted from one philosophical subject to another until he hit on medicine. His choice was less that of a dedicated healer than of an inquisitive explorer eager to solve some of nature's riddles.

As he pursued his medical researches, he came to the conclusion that the most intriguing mysteries lay concealed in the complex operations of the mind. By the early 1890s,

BORN May 6 in Freiberg, Moravia	1885 Receives appointment as lecturer in neuropathology, University of Vienna	PIONEER Freud in 1891		1938 Emigrates from Vienna to London
1856				**1939**
	1881 Earns medical degree	1886 Marries and begins private practice in Vienna	1900 Publishes *The Interpretation of Dreams* 1910 Establishes International Psychoanalytic Association	1939 Dies Sept. 23 in London

Freud's daughter Anna, here at 17 with her father, became a famous analyst in her own right, specializing in children

he was specializing in "neurasthenics" (mainly severe hysterics); they taught him much, including the art of patient listening. He began to write down his dreams, convinced that they might offer clues to the workings of the unconscious, a notion he borrowed from the Romantics. He saw himself as a scientist taking material both from his patients and from himself, through introspection. By the mid-1890s, he was launched on a full-blown self-analysis, an enterprise for which he had no guidelines and no predecessors.

THE BOOK THAT MADE HIS REPUTATION—ALTHOUGH IT sold poorly—was *The Interpretation of Dreams* (1900), an indefinable masterpiece—part dream analysis, part autobiography, part theory of the mind, part history of contemporary Vienna. Its underlying principle was that mental experiences and entities, like physical ones, are part of nature. Thus there were no mere accidents in mental procedures. The most nonsensical notion, the most casual slip of the tongue, the most fantastic dream, must have a meaning and can be used to unriddle the often incomprehensible maneuvers we call thinking.

Although the second pillar of Freud's psychoanalytic structure, *Three Essays on the Theory of Sexuality* (1905), further alienated him from the mainstream of contemporary psychiatry, he found loyal recruits. They met weekly to hash out case histories, converting themselves into the Vienna Psychoanalytic Society in 1908. Working on the frontiers of mental science, these often eccentric pioneers

had their quarrels. The two best known "defectors" were Alfred Adler and Carl Jung. Adler, a Viennese physician and socialist, developed a psychology that stressed the aggression with which those people lacking in a quality they desire—say, manliness—express their discontent by acting out. "Inferiority complex," a much abused term, is Adlerian. Freud did not regret losing Adler, but Jung was something else. Freud was aware that most of his acolytes were Jews, and he did not want to turn psychoanalysis into a "Jewish science." Jung, from a Swiss Protestant background, struck Freud as his successor, his "crown prince." The two men were close for several years, but Jung's ambition, and his growing interest in religion and mysticism—most unwelcome to Freud, an aggressive atheist—finally drove them apart.

Freud was intent not merely on originating a sweeping theory of mental functioning and malfunctioning. He also wanted to develop the rules of psychoanalytic therapy and expand his picture of human nature to encompass not just the couch but the whole culture. As to the first, he created the largely silent listener who encourages the analysand to say whatever comes to mind, no matter how foolish, repetitive or outrageous, and who intervenes occasionally to interpret what the patient on the couch is struggling to say. While some adventurous early psychoanalysts thought they could quantify just what proportion of their analysands went away cured, improved or untouched by analytic therapy, such confident enumerations have more recently shown themselves untenable. The efficacy of analysis remains a matter of controversy, though the possibility of mixing psychoanalysis and drug therapy is gaining support.

Freud's ventures into culture—history, anthropology, literature, art, sociology, the study of religion—have proved little less controversial; they retain their fascination and plausibility and continue to enjoy a widespread reputation. Freud drew a sharp distinction between religious faith (which is not checkable or correctable) and scientific inquiry (which is both). For himself, this meant the denial of truth-value to any religion, including Judaism. As for politics, in his late—and still best known—essay, *Civilization and Its Discontents* (1930), he noted that the human animal, with its insatiable needs, must always remain an enemy to organized society, which exists largely to tamp down sexual and aggressive desires. At best, civilized living is a compromise between wishes and repression—an uncomfortable doctrine. It ensures that Freud, taken straight, will never become popular, even if today we all speak Freud.

In mid-March 1938, when Freud was 81, the Nazis took over Austria, and after some reluctance, he immigrated to England with his wife and his favorite daughter and colleague Anna "to die in freedom." He got his wish, dying not long after the Nazis invaded Poland. Listening to an idealistic broadcaster proclaiming this to be the last war, Freud, his stoical humor intact, commented wryly, "*My* last war." ∎

Yale historian Peter Gay is the author of 22 books, among them the biographical study Freud: A Life for Our Times.

Magellans of the Mind

Other psychologists continued the work that Freud began, though not always in ways that he would have approved

Benjamin Spock

One of the first pediatricians to utilize psychoanalytic training, Dr. Spock formed commonsense principles of child rearing that helped shape the baby-boom generation. Since 1946 his book on baby and child care has sold 50 million copies.

B.F. Skinner

A strict behaviorist who avoided all reference to internal mental states, Skinner believed that behavior can best be shaped through positive reinforcement. Contrary to popular misconception, he did not raise his daughter in the "Skinner box" that he used to train pigeons.

Carl Jung

A former disciple of Freud's, Jung shared his mentor's enthusiasm for dreams but not his obsession with the sex drive. Jung believed humans are endowed with a "collective unconscious" from which myths, fairy tales and other archetypes spring.

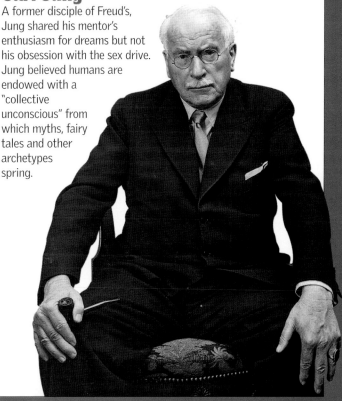

Alfred Kinsey

A biologist who knew little about sex and less about statistics, Kinsey nonetheless led the first large-scale empirical study of sexual behavior. His mid-century reports shocked readers by documenting high rates of masturbation and extramarital and homosexual sex.

Leo
Baekeland

Setting out to make an insulator, he invented the first true plastic and transformed the world

By IVAN AMATO

IN THE OPENING SCENE OF *THE GRADUATE*, BENJAMIN Braddock (played by a young Dustin Hoffman) is awkwardly working an affluent Southern California crowd at a graduation party arranged for him by his parents when a family friend offers one of the century's most famous pieces of cinematic advice: "I just want to say one word to you. Just one word: plastics."

Millions of moviegoers winced and smiled. The scene neatly captured their own late-'60s ambivalence toward the ever more synthetic landscape of their times. They loved their cheap, easy-to-clean Formica countertops but envied— and longed for—the authentic touch and timelessness of marble and wood. The chord struck by that line in *The Graduate* underscored how much had happened in the six decades since the summer of 1907, when Leo Hendrik Baekeland made the laboratory breakthrough that would change the stuff our world is made of.

A Belgian-born chemist-entrepreneur, Baekeland had a knack for spotting profitable opportunities. He scored his first success in the 1890s with his invention of Velox, an improved photographic paper that freed photographers from having to use sunlight for developing images. With Velox, they could rely on artificial light, which at the time usually meant gaslight but soon came to mean electric. It

Plastic dice, circa 1945

was a far more dependable and convenient way to work. In 1899 George Eastman, whose cameras and developing services would make photography a household activity, bought full rights to Velox for the then astonishing sum of $1 million. With that windfall, Baekeland, his wife Celine and two children moved to Snug Rock, a palatial estate outside Yonkers, N.Y., overlooking the Hudson River. There, in a barn he converted into a lab, he began foraging for his next big hit. It wasn't long before the burgeoning electrical industry seemed to say just one word to him: insulators.

The initial lure for Baekeland—"Doc Baekeland" to many—was the rising cost of shellac. For centuries, the resinous secretions that *Laccifer lacca* beetles deposited on trees had provided a cottage industry in southern Asia, where peasants heated and filtered it to produce a varnish for coating and preserving wood products. Shellac also happened to be an effective electrical insulator. Early electrical workers used it as a coating to insulate coils, and molded it into stand-alone insulators by pressing together layers of shellac-impregnated paper. When electrification began in earnest in the first years of the century, demand for shellac soon outstripped supply. Baekeland recognized the possibility of a killer app when he saw one. If only he could come up with a synthetic substitute for shellac.

WATCH circa 1938

BORN in Ghent, Belgium	1899 Sells rights to Velox to George Eastman for $1 million	1907 Develops the first all-artificial plastic, which he calls Bakelite		
1863				**1944**
	1889 Moves to U.S.	1904 Sets out to find a synthetic substitute for shellac	1909 Introduces Bakelite at a chemical conference and founds the General Bakelite Corp.	DIES in Beacon, N.Y., at 80

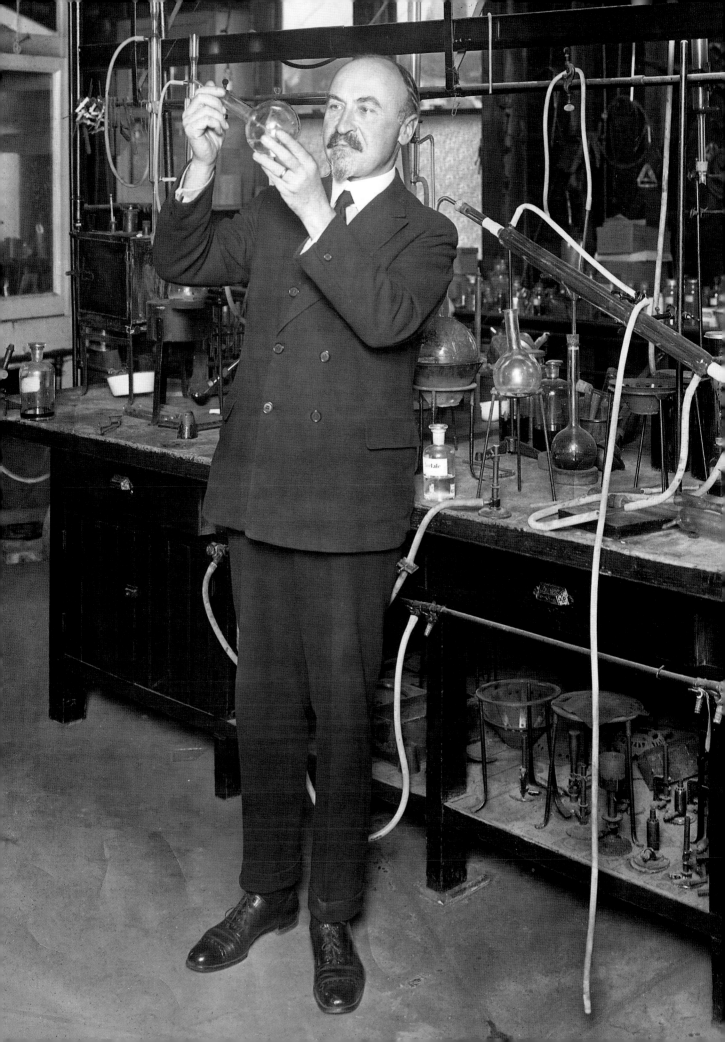

> # "I just want to say one word to you. Just one word: plastics. There's a great future in plastics."
>
> **MR. MCGUIRE,** *The Graduate*

Others nearly beat him to it. As early as 1872, German chemist Adolf von Baeyer was investigating the recalcitrant residue that gathered in the bottom of glassware that had been host to reactions between phenol (a turpentine-like solvent distilled from coal tar, which the gas-lighting industry produced in bulk) and formaldehyde (an embalming fluid distilled from wood alcohol). Von Baeyer set his sights on new synthetic dyes, however, not insulators. To him, the ugly, insoluble gunk in his glassware was a sign of a dead end.

TO BAEKELAND AND OTHERS AIMING TO FIND commercial opportunities in the nascent electrical industry, that gunk was a signpost pointing toward something great. The challenge was to find some set of conditions—some slippery ratio of ingredients and heat and pressure—that would yield a more workable, shellac-like substance. Ideally it would be something that would dissolve in solvents to make insulating varnishes and yet be as moldable as rubber.

Starting around 1904, Baekeland and an assistant began their search. Three years later, after filling laboratory books with pages of failed experiments, Baekeland developed a material that he dubbed in his notebooks "Bakelite." The key turned out to be his "bakelizer," a heavy iron vessel—part pressure cooker, part basement boiler—that let him control the formaldehyde-phenol reaction with more finesse than had anyone before him.

Initial heating of the phenol and formaldehyde (in the presence of an acid or base to get the reaction going) produced a shellac-like liquid good for coating surfaces like a varnish. Further heating turned the liquid into a pasty, gummier goo. And when Baekeland put this stuff into the bakelizer, he was rewarded with a hard, translucent, infinitely moldable substance. In a word: plastic.

He filed patent applications and soon began leaking word of his invention to other chemists. In 1909 Baekeland unveiled the world's first fully synthetic plastic at a meeting of the New York chapter of the American Chemical Society. Would-be customers discovered it could be fashioned into molded insulation, valve parts, pipe stems, billiard balls, knobs, buttons, knife handles and all manner of items.

It was 20th century alchemy. From something as vile as coal tar came a remarkably versatile substance. It wasn't the first plastic, however. Celluloid had been used by manufacturers for decades as a substitute for tortoise-shell, horn, bone and other materials. But celluloid, which had developed a reputation as a cheap mimic of better traditional materials, was derived from chemically treated cotton and other cellulose-containing vegetable matter. Bakelite was lab-made through and through. It was 100% synthetic.

Baekeland founded the General Bakelite Corp. to both make and license the formula for Bakelite. Competitors soon marketed knock-offs—most notably Redmanol and Condensite, which Thomas Edison used in a failed attempt to dominate the nascent recording industry with "unbreakable" phonograph disks. The proliferation of inauthentic Bakelite products led to an early 20th century version of the "Intel Inside" logo. Items made with the real thing carried a "tag of genuineness" bearing the Bakelite name. Following drawn-out patent wars, Baekeland finally negotiated a merger with his rivals that put him at the helm of a veritable Bakelite empire.

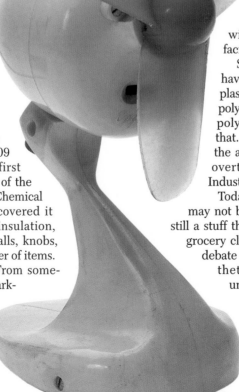

Above: A Bakelite camera, 1934. Below: all-plastic fan, 1950

Bakelite became so visible in so many places that the company advertised it as "the material of a thousand uses." It became the stuff of everything from cigar holders and rosary beads to radio housings, distributor caps and telephone casings. A 1924 TIME cover story on Baekeland predicted that "in a few years [Bakelite] will be embodied in every mechanical facility of modern civilization."

Since Bakelite's heyday, researchers have churned out a polysyllabic catalog of plastics: Plexiglas, polyesters, polyethylene, polyvinyl chloride (PVC, a.k.a. vinyl), nylon polymers, polyurethane, poly-this, poly-that. In 1979, 12 years after *The Graduate*, the annual volume of plastic manufactured overtook that of steel, the symbol of the Industrial Revolution.

Today plastic is everywhere, and while it may not be as vilified now as it was in 1967, it's still a stuff that people love and hate. Every time a grocery clerk asks, "Paper or plastic?", the great debate between old and new, natural and synthetic, biodegradable and not, silently unfolds in a shopper's breast. ∎

NPR science correspondent Ivan Amato is author of Stuff: The Materials the World Is Made Of.

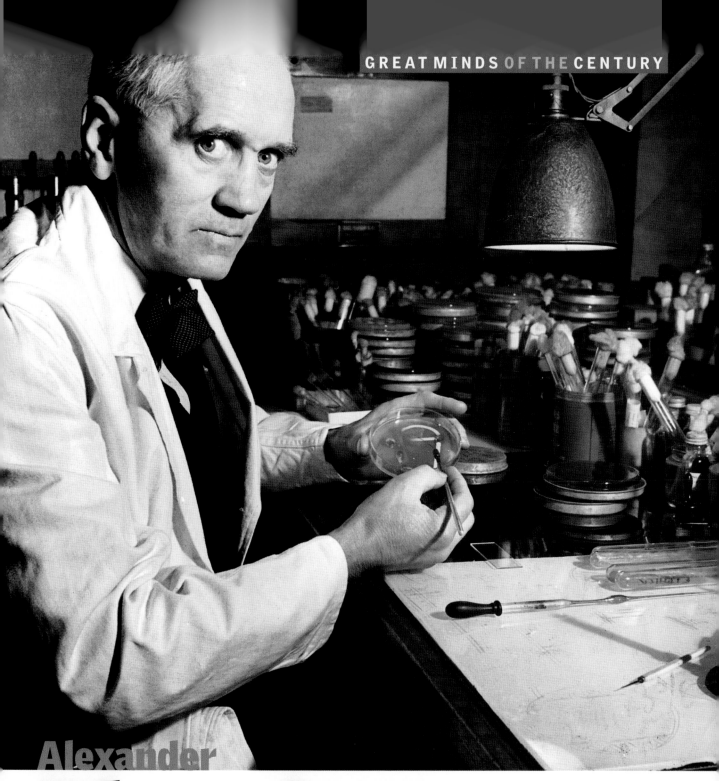

Alexander

Fleming

A spore that drifted into his lab and took root on a culture dish started a chain of events that altered forever the treatment of bacterial infections

By DR. DAVID HO

THE IMPROBABLE CHAIN OF EVENTS THAT led Alexander Fleming to discover penicillin in 1928 is the stuff of which scientific myths are made. Fleming, a young Scottish research scientist with a profitable side practice treating the syphilis infections of prominent London artists, was pursuing his pet theory—that his own nasal mucus had antibacterial effects—when he left a culture plate smeared with *Staphylococcus* bacteria on his lab bench while he went on a two-week holiday.

When he returned, he noticed a clear halo surrounding the yellow-green growth of a mold that had accidentally contaminated the plate. Unknown to him, a spore of a rare variant called *Penicillium notatum* had drifted in from a mycology lab one floor below. Luck would have it that Fleming had decided not to store his culture in a warm incubator, and that London was then hit by a cold spell, giving the mold a chance to grow. Later, as the temperature rose, the *Staphylococcus* bacteria grew like a lawn, covering the entire plate—except for the area surrounding the moldy contaminant. Seeing that halo was Fleming's "Eureka!" moment, an instant of great personal insight and deductive reasoning. He correctly deduced that the mold must have released a substance that inhibited the growth of the bacteria.

It was a discovery that would change the course of history. The active ingredient in that mold, which Fleming named penicillin, turned out to be an infection-fighting agent of enormous potency. When it was finally recognized for what it was—the most efficacious life-saving drug in the world—penicillin would alter forever the treatment of bacterial infections. By the middle of the century, Fleming's discovery had spawned a huge pharmaceutical industry, churning out synthetic penicillins that would fight some of mankind's most ancient scourges, including syphilis, gangrene and tuberculosis.

Fleming was born to a Scottish sheep-farming family in 1881. He excelled in school and entered St. Mary's Hospital in London to study medicine. He was a short man, usually clad in a bow tie, who even in his celebrity never mastered

By the 1940s, penicillin was being mass-produced in labs like this one in New Jersey

the conventions of polite society. Fleming probably would have remained a quiet bacteriologist had serendipity not come calling that fateful September in 1928.

In fact, Fleming was not even the first to describe the antibacterial properties of *Penicillium*. John Tyndall had done so in 1875 and, likewise, D.A. Gratia in 1925. However, unlike his predecessors, Fleming recognized the importance of his findings. He would later say, "My only merit is that I did not neglect the observation and that I pursued the subject as a bacteriologist." Although he went on to perform additional experiments, he never conducted the one that would have been key: injecting penicillin into infected mice. Fleming's initial work was reported in 1929 in the *British Journal of Experi-*

BORN Aug. 6, 1881, in Ayrshire, Scotland

1881

1901 Enters medical school at St. Mary's Hospital in London

1928 Identifies penicillin

EUREKA! At top left, a *Penicillium* mold

1939 Provides penicillin indirectly to Howard Florey and Ernst Chain

1929 Publishes his first report on penicillin's antibacterial properties

1945 Shares Nobel Prize for Medicine with Florey and Chain

1955

1944 Knighted by King George VI

DIES of a heart attack March 11 in London

> # People have called it a miracle. For once in my life as a scientist, I agree. It is a miracle, and it will save lives by thousands. "
>
> SIR ALEXANDER FLEMING, on the life-saving potential of penicillin

mental Pathology, but his discovery would remain in relative obscurity for a decade.

By 1932, Fleming had abandoned his work on penicillin. He would have no further role in the subsequent development of this or any other antibiotic, aside from happily providing other researchers with samples of his mold. It is said that he lacked both the chemical expertise to purify penicillin and the conviction that drugs could cure serious infections. However, he did safeguard his unusual strain of *Penicillium notatum* for posterity. The baton of antibiotic development was passed to others.

In 1939 a specimen of Fleming's mold made its way into the hands of a team of scientists at Oxford University led by Howard Florey, an Australian-born physiologist. This team had technical talent, especially in a chemist named Ernst Boris Chain, who had fled Nazi Germany. Armed with funds from the Rockefeller Foundation, these scientists made it their objective to identify and isolate substances from molds that could kill bacteria. The mission was inspired by the earlier work of Gerhard Domagk, who in 1935 showed that the injection of a simple compound, Prontosil, cured systemic streptococcal infections. This breakthrough demonstrated that invading bacteria could be killed with a drug and led to a fevered search in the late 1930s for similar compounds. Fleming's *Penicillium notatum* became a convenient starting point for Florey's team at Oxford.

In a scientific tour de force, Florey, Chain and their colleagues rapidly purified penicillin in sufficient quantity to perform the experiment that Fleming could not: they successfully treated mice that had been given lethal doses of bacteria. Within a year, their results were published in a seminal paper in the *Lancet*. As the world took notice, they swiftly demonstrated that injections of penicillin caused miraculous recoveries in patients with a variety of infections.

The Oxford team did not stop there. Rushing to meet the needs of World War II, they helped the government set up a network of "minifactories" for penicillin production. Florey also played a crucial role in galvanizing the large-scale production of penicillin by U.S. pharmaceutical companies in the early 1940s. By D-day there was enough penicillin on hand to treat every soldier who needed it. By the end of World War II, it had saved millions of lives.

Pneumonia, syphilis, gonorrhea, diphtheria, scarlet fever

and many wound and childbirth infections that once killed indiscriminately suddenly became treatable. As deaths caused by bacterial infections plummeted, a grateful world needed a hero. Fleming alone became such an object of public adulation, probably for two reasons. First, Florey shunned the press, while Fleming seemed to revel in the publicity. Second, and perhaps more important, it was easier for the admiring public to comprehend the deductive insight of a single individual than the technical feats of a scientific team.

AWARDS AND ACCOLADES CAME TO FLEMING IN rapid succession, including a knighthood (with Florey) in 1944 and the Nobel Prize for Medicine (with Florey and Chain) in 1945. By this time, even Fleming was aware that penicillin had an Achilles' heel. He wrote in 1946 that "the administration of too small doses ... leads to the production of resistant strains of bacteria." The problem bedevils us to this day.

When Fleming died of a heart attack in 1955, he was mourned by the world and buried as a national hero in the crypt of St. Paul's Cathedral in London. Although his scientific work in and of itself may not have reached greatness, his singular contribution changed the practice of medicine.

THEN AND NOW: TOP 10 CAUSES OF DEATH

1900
1. Pneumonia and influenza
2. Tuberculosis
3. Diarrhea and enteritis
4. Heart diseases
5. Brain hemorrhage
6. Kidney diseases
7. Accidents
8. Cancer
9. Senility
10. Diphtheria

Number of deaths each year per 100,000 Americans

1,719

872

Source: National Center for Health Statistics

1996
1. Heart diseases
2. Cancer
3. Stroke
4. Pulmonary diseases
5. Accidents
6. Pneumonia and influenza
7. Diabetes
8. AIDS
9. Suicide
10. Chronic liver disease

He deserves our utmost recognition. At the same time, we must bear in mind that the "Fleming Myth," as he called it, embodies the accomplishments of many giants of antibiotic development. Fleming is but a chosen representative for the likes of Florey, Chain, Domagk, Selman Waksman and René Dubos, many of whom remain, sadly, virtual unknowns. Their achievements have made the world a better, healthier place. In commemorating Fleming, we commemorate them all. ∎

Dr. David Ho, TIME's 1996 Man of the Year, is director of the Aaron Diamond AIDS Research Center in New York City.

Philo Farnsworth

The key to the TV picture tube came to him when he was a farm boy of 14; he had a working device at 21. Yet he died in obscurity

By NEIL POSTMAN

FOR THOSE INCLINED TO THINK OF OUR FADING century as an era of the common man, let it be noted that the inventor of one of the century's greatest machines was a man called Phil. Even more, he was actually born in a log cabin, rode to high school on horseback and, without benefit of a university degree (indeed, at age 14), conceived the idea of electronic television—the moment of inspiration coming, according to legend, while he was tilling a potato field back and forth with a horse-drawn harrow and realized that an electron beam could scan images the same way, line by line, just as you read a book. To cap it off, he spent much of his adult life in a struggle with one of America's largest and most powerful corporations. Our kind of guy.

I refer, of course, to Philo Taylor Farnsworth. The "of course" is meant as a joke, since almost no one outside the industry has ever heard of him. But we ought not to let the century expire without attempting to make amends.

Farnsworth was born in 1906 near Beaver City, Utah, a community settled by his grandfather (in 1856) under instructions from Brigham Young himself. When Farnsworth was 12, his family moved to a ranch in Rigby, Idaho, which was four miles from the nearest high school, thus his daily horseback rides. Because he was intrigued with the electron and electricity, he persuaded his chemistry teacher, Justin Tolman, to give him special instruction and to allow him to audit a senior course. You could read about great scientists from now until the 22nd century and not find

another instance where one of them celebrates a high school teacher. But Farnsworth did, crediting Tolman with providing inspiration and essential knowledge.

Tolman returned the compliment. Many years later, testifying at a patent interference case, Tolman said Farnsworth's explanation of the theory of relativity was the clearest and most concise he had ever heard. Remember, this would have been in 1921, and Farnsworth would have been all of 15. And Tolman was not the only one who recognized the young student's genius. With only two years of high school behind him, and buttressed by an intense autodidacticism, Farnsworth gained admission to Brigham Young University.

The death of his father forced him to leave at the end of his second year, but, as it turned out, at no great intellectual cost. There were, at the time, no more than a handful of men on the planet who could have understood Farnsworth's ideas for building an electronic-television system, and it's unlikely that any of them were at Brigham Young. One such man was Vladimir Zworykin, who had emigrated to the U.S. from Russia with a Ph.D. in electrical engineering. He went to work for Westinghouse with a dream of building an all-electronic television system. But he wasn't able to do so. Farnsworth was. But not at once.

He didn't do it until he was 21. By then, he had found investors, a few assistants and a loving wife ("Pem") who assisted him in his research. He moved to San Francisco and set up a laboratory in an empty loft. On Sept. 7, 1927,

BORN Aug. 19, in Indian Creek, Utah

1927 Transmits first electronic image

1935 U.S. Patent Office awards "priority of invention"

TUBULAR
Holding a "TV transmission tube," circa 1939

1906

1921 Has idea for how to create images using electrons

1934 Stages first demonstration of his TV system

1939 After seven years of litigation, RCA agrees to pay him royalties

1947 Patents begin to expire; he is hospitalized for depression

DIES March 11 in Holladay, Utah

1971

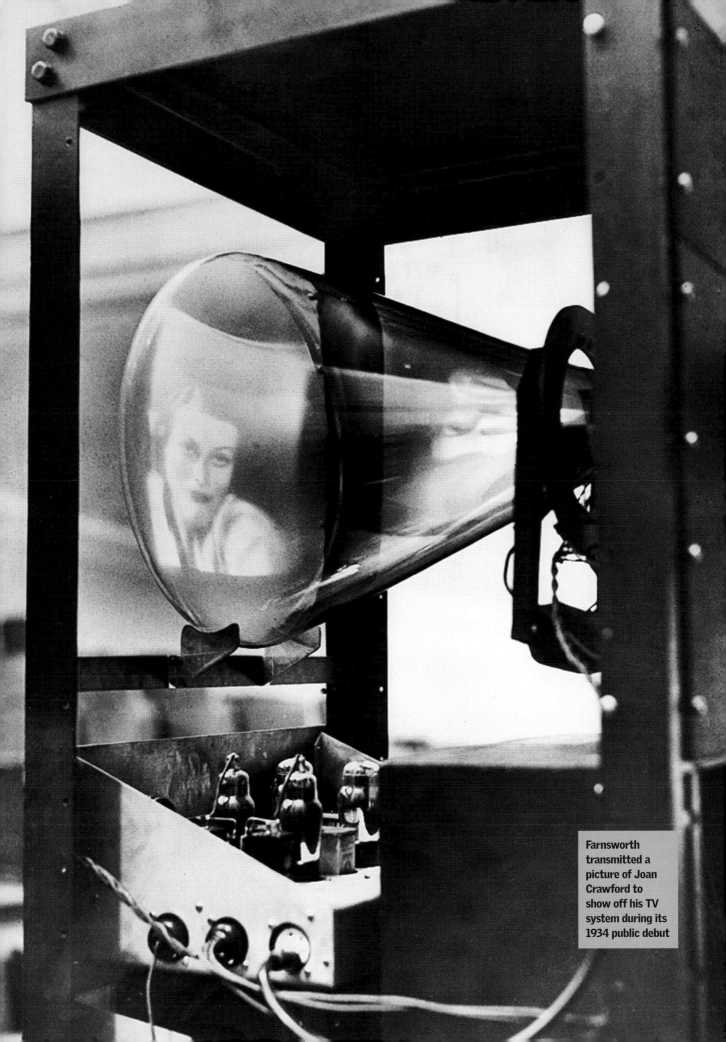

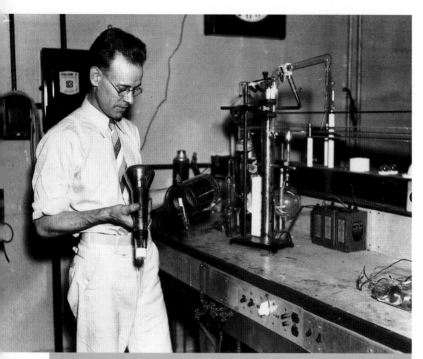

Farnsworth working on the Image Dissector and Conical Receiver in 1935

Farnsworth painted a square of glass black and scratched a straight line on the center. In another room, Pem's brother, Cliff Gardner, dropped the slide between the Image Dissector (a camera tube that Farnsworth had invented earlier that year) and a hot, bright, carbon arc lamp. Farnsworth, Pem and an investor, George Everson, watched the receiver. They saw the straight-line image and then, as Cliff turned the slide 90°, they saw it move—which is to say they saw the first all-electronic television picture ever transmitted.

HISTORY SHOULD TAKE NOTE OF FARNSWORTH'S reaction. After all, we learn in school that Samuel Morse's first telegraph message was "What hath God wrought?" Edison spoke into his phonograph, "Mary had a little lamb." And Don Ameche—I mean, Alexander Graham Bell—shouted for assistance: "Mr. Watson, come here, I need you!" What did Farnsworth exclaim? "There you are," said Phil, "electronic television." Later that evening, he wrote in his laboratory journal: "The received line picture was evident this time." Not very catchy for a climactic scene in a movie. Perhaps we could use the telegram George Everson sent to another investor: "The damned thing works!"

At this point in the story, things turn ugly. Physics, engineering and scientific inspiration begin to recede in importance as lawyers take center stage. Zworykin had made a patent application in 1923, and by 1933 he had developed a camera tube he called an Iconoscope. It also happens that Zworykin was by then connected with the Radio Corporation of America, whose chief, David Sarnoff, had no intention of paying royalties to Farnsworth for the right to manufacture television sets. "RCA doesn't pay royalties," he allegedly said, "we collect them."

And so there ensued a legal battle over who invented television. RCA's lawyers contended that Zworykin's 1923 patent had priority over any of Farnsworth's patents, including the one for his Image Dissector. RCA's case was not strong, since it could produce no evidence that in 1923 Zworykin had produced an operable television transmitter. Moreover, Farnsworth's old teacher, Tolman, not only testified that Farnsworth had conceived the idea when in high school, but also produced the original sketch of an electronic tube that Farnsworth had drawn for him at that time. It was almost an exact replica of an Image Dissector.

In 1934 the U.S. patent office rendered its decision, awarding priority of invention to Farnsworth. RCA appealed and lost, but litigation continued for many years until Sarnoff finally agreed to pay Farnsworth royalties. He didn't have to for very long. During World War II, the government suspended sales of TV sets, and by the war's end, Farnsworth's key patents were close to expiring. When they did, RCA was quick to take charge of the production and sales of TV sets, and in a vigorous public-relations campaign, promoted both Zworykin and Sarnoff as the fathers of television. Farnsworth withdrew to a house in Maine, suffering from depression, which was made worse by excessive drinking. He had a nervous breakdown, spent time in hospitals and had to submit to shock therapy. And in 1947, as if he were being punished for having invented television, his house in Maine burned to the ground.

One wishes that this was the final indignity Farnsworth had to suffer, but it was not. Ten years later, he appeared as a mystery guest on the TV program *What's My Line?* He was referred to as Dr. X and the panel had the task of discovering what he had done to merit his appearance on the show. One of the panelists asked Dr. X if he had invented some kind of a machine that might be painful when used. Farnsworth answered, "Yes. Sometimes it's most painful."

He was just being characteristically polite. His attitude toward the uses that had been made of his invention was more ferocious. His son Kent said, "I suppose you could say that he felt he had created kind of a monster, a way for people to waste a lot of their lives." He added, "Throughout my childhood his reaction to television was 'There's nothing on it worthwhile, and we're not going to watch it in this household, and I don't want it in your intellectual diet.'"

So we may end Farnsworth's story by saying that he was not only the inventor of television but also one of its earliest and most perceptive critics. ∎

Neil Postman is the Paulette Goddard Professor of Media Ecology at New York University.

Jean
Piaget

He found the secrets of human learning and knowledge hidden behind the cute and seemingly illogical notions of children

By SEYMOUR PAPERT

"[He is] one of the two towering figures of 20th century psychology.

JEROME BRUNER, **Founder of the Harvard Center for Cognitive Studies**

J EAN PIAGET, THE PIONEERING SWISS PHILOSOPHER and psychologist, spent much of his professional life listening to children, watching children and poring over reports of researchers around the world who were doing the same. He found, to put it most succinctly, that children don't think like grownups. After thousands of interactions with young people often barely old enough to talk, Piaget began to suspect that behind their cute and seemingly illogical utterances were thought processes that had their own kind of order and their own special logic. Einstein called it a discovery "so simple that only a genius could have thought of it."

Piaget's insight opened a new window into the inner workings of the mind. By the end of a wide-ranging and prolific research career that spanned nearly 75 years—from his first scientific publication at age 10 to work in progress when he died at 84—Piaget had developed several new fields of science: developmental psychology, cognitive theory and what came to be called genetic epistemology. Although not an educational reformer, he championed a way of thinking about children that provided the foundation for today's education-reform movements. It was a shift comparable to the displacement of stories of "noble savages" and "cannibals" by modern anthropology. One might say that Piaget was the first to take children's thinking seriously.

Others who shared this respect for children—John Dewey in the U.S., Maria Montessori in Italy and Paulo Freire in Brazil—fought harder for immediate change in the schools, but Piaget's influence on education is deeper and more pervasive. He has been revered by generations of teachers inspired by the belief that children are not empty vessels to be filled with knowledge (a traditional pedagogical theory) but active builders of knowledge—little scientists who are constantly creating and testing their own theories of the world. As computers and the Internet give children greater autonomy to explore ever larger digital worlds, the ideas he pioneered become ever more relevant.

Piaget grew up near Lake Neuchâtel in a quiet region of French Switzerland known for its wines and watches. His father was a professor of medieval studies and his mother a strict Calvinist. Piaget was a child prodigy who soon became interested in the scientific study of nature. When, at age 10, his observations led to questions that could be answered only by access to the university library, Piaget wrote and

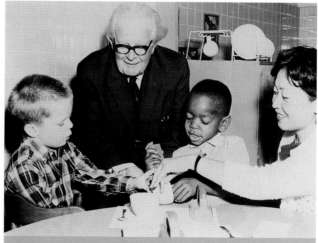

A lifetime of listening helped Piaget to unravel children's minds

published a short note on the sighting of an albino sparrow, hoping the librarian would stop treating him like a child. It worked. Piaget was launched on a path that would lead to his doctorate in zoology and a lifelong conviction that the way to understand anything is to understand how it evolves.

After World War I, Piaget became interested in psychoanalysis. He moved to Zurich, where he attended Carl Jung's lectures, and then to Paris to study logic and abnormal psychology. Working with Théodore Simon in Alfred Binet's child-psychology lab, he noticed that Parisian children of the same age made similar errors on true-false intelligence tests. Fascinated by their reasoning processes, he began to suspect that the key to human knowledge might be discovered by observing how the child's mind develops.

Back in Switzerland, the young scientist began watching children play, scrupulously recording their words and actions as their minds raced to find reasons for why things are the way they are. In one of his most famous experiments, Piaget asked children, "What makes the wind?"

Piaget: What makes the wind?

Julia: The trees.

P: How do you know?

J: I saw them waving their arms.

P: How does that make the wind?

J: (waving her hand in front of his face): Like this.

BORN Aug. 9, in Switzerland

1918 Obtains doctorate in zoology, studies psychoanalysis

1929 Appointed director of the International Bureau of Education

1896

1980

1907 Publishes first paper at age 10

1920 Studies children's intelligence in Paris

1923 First of nearly 60 scholarly books published

1955 Establishes Center for Genetic Epistemology

DIES in Geneva

Only they are bigger. And there are lots of trees.

P: What makes the wind on the ocean?

J: It blows there from the land. No. It's the waves …

Piaget recognized that five-year-old Julia's beliefs, while not correct by any adult criterion, are not "incorrect" either. They are entirely sensible and coherent within the framework of the child's way of knowing. Classifying them as "true" or "false" misses the point and shows a lack of respect for the child. What Piaget was after was a theory that could find in the wind dialogue coherence, ingenuity and the practice of a kind of explanatory principle (in this case by referring to body actions) that stands young children in very good stead when they don't know enough or have enough skill to handle the kind of explanation that grownups prefer.

Piaget was not an educator and never enunciated rules about how to intervene in such situations. But his work strongly suggests that the automatic reaction of putting the child right may well be abusive. Practicing the art of making theories may be more valuable for children than achieving meteorological orthodoxy; and if their theories are always greeted by "Nice try, but this is how it really is … " they might give up after a while on making theories. As Piaget put it, "Children have real understanding only of that which they invent themselves, and each time that we try to teach them something too quickly, we keep them from reinventing it themselves."

Disciples of Piaget are fascinated by children's primitive laws of physics: that things disappear when they are out of sight; that the moon and the sun follow you around; that big things float and small things sink. Einstein was intrigued by Piaget's finding that seven-year-olds insist that going faster can take more time—perhaps because Einstein's own thories of relativity ran so contrary to common sense.

Although every teacher in training memorizes Piaget's four stages of childhood development (sensorimotor, preoperational, concrete operational, formal operational), the better part of Piaget's work is less well known, perhaps because schools of education regard it as "too deep" for teachers. Piaget never thought of himself as a child psychologist. His real interest was epistemology—the theory of knowledge—which, like physics, was considered a branch of philosophy until Piaget came along and made it a science.

Piaget explored a kind of epistemological relativism in which multiple ways of knowing are acknowledged and examined nonjudgmentally, yet with a philosopher's analytic rigor. Since Piaget, the territory has been widely colonized by those who write about women's ways of knowing, Afrocentric ways of knowing, even the computer's ways of

Father knows best: Piaget's subjects included his own three children

knowing. Indeed, artificial intelligence and the information-processing model of the mind owe more to Piaget than its proponents may realize.

The core of Piaget is his belief that looking carefully at how knowledge develops in children will elucidate the nature of knowledge in general. Whether this has in fact led to deeper understanding remains controversial. In the past decade Piaget has been vigorously challenged by the current fashion of viewing knowledge as an intrinsic property of the brain. Ingenious experiments have shown that newborn infants already have some of the knowledge he believed children constructed. But for those, like me, who still see Piaget as the giant in the field of cognitive theory, the difference between what the baby brings and what the adult has is so immense that the new discoveries do not significantly reduce the gap but only increase the mystery. ∎

M.I.T. professor Seymour Papert, creator of the Logo computer language, worked with Piaget in Geneva.

Putting Science to Work

Sometimes the greatest inventions are the ones with the most mundane uses. These ideas quickly found their way into everyday life

Microwave Oven

Percy Spencer didn't know better than to bring candy with him into his microwave lab in 1946. When the American engineer, who was developing radar components for the Raytheon Corp., let his chocolate bar get too close to a piece of equipment, it turned into chocolate goo. Cooking would never be the same. Within a year, Raytheon had introduced the first commercial microwave oven—a clunky, 750-lb. thing that required plumbing to prevent overheating but that managed nonetheless to do the job: heat food by electromagnetically stimulating the water, fat and sugar molecules within it. It was 20 years before Amana introduced a household model; by 1975 microwave ovens outsold gas ones. By 1997, 90% of American households owned one.

High-Yield Crops

Working in Mexico from 1944 to 1960—long before the advent of modern biotechnology—U.S. biologist Norman Borlaug developed a hybrid strain of wheat that was enormously more prolific than its natural cousins. Borlaug's "miracle wheat" allowed Mexico to triple its grain production in a matter of years, and when his hybrid was introduced in south Asia in the mid-1960s, wheat yields there jumped 60%. Miracle strains of rice and other grains followed in short order, triggering a global green revolution that earned Borlaug the Nobel Prize for Peace in 1970.

Birth Control Pill

Biologist Gregory Pincus had his hands full in 1950, when Planned Parenthood gave him $30,000 to develop a contraceptive that was "harmless, entirely reliable, and aesthetically satisfactory to husband and wife." Within 10 years, however, Pincus and his colleagues delivered, inventing the drug that sparked the sexual revolution. Introduced in the U.S. in 1960, the birth control pill, known simply as the Pill, was an ovulation-suppressing mix of estrogen and progestin that was 99% effective. Not surprisingly, the magic contraceptive bullet was an instant best seller. Within five years, 5 million women were "on the Pill."

Laser

What good is a brilliantly intense, tightly focused beam of light? Today lasers are used for, among other things, dentists' drills and delicate eye surgery, playing compact discs, measuring the distance to the moon, creating and viewing holograms, sending voices and data through the air and down optical fibers, surveying roads, "painting" dots on a drum in laser printers and as fancy pointers for lecturers.

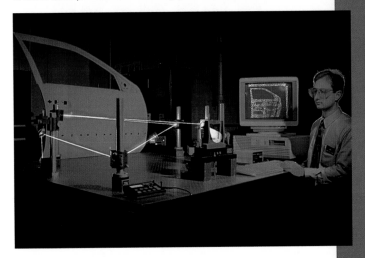

Instant Photography

Edwin Land had long since dropped out of Harvard, founded a successful corporation and come up with scores of inventions when he took on the challenge of instant photography just after World War II. Until then, photographers had to develop their film and then print it on paper—or send it off to a lab—before they actually had a picture in hand. Land aimed to shortcut this laborious process by creating a camera that did all the work itself, and by 1947 he had done it. The Polaroid Land Camera was loaded with photographic paper coated with a paste of light-sensitive chemicals. A mere 60 sec. after the shutter was tripped, out popped a snapshot. The first Polaroids were black-and-white; the company introduced color in 1963.

Radar

An application of electromagnetic radiation, radar changed the nature of travel, warfare and even space exploration. In the early 1900s engineers first appreciated how easily radio waves can be bounced off almost any object. In 1925 physicists took advantage of this, firing signals at the ionosphere and using the reflection to measure its altitude. By World War II, British scientists had refined the technology, and the coast of England was dotted with civil-defense radar stations. As the hardware got simpler, radar found its way into airplanes, boats and air-traffic-control towers, improving navigation and safety. By the end of the century, the same basic technology was being used to steer spacecraft, track storms and help police catch speeders—proof that even the most arcane science can pay very pedestrian dividends.

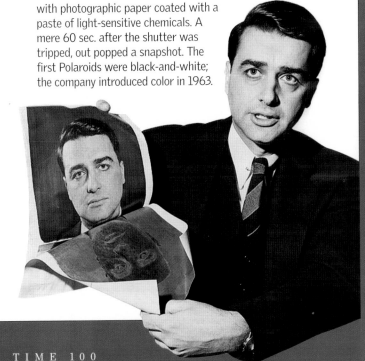

Kurt
Gödel

Turning the lens of mathematics on itself, his "incompleteness theorem" drove a stake through the heart of formalism

By DOUGLAS HOFSTADTER

ÖDEL WAS BORN IN 1906 IN BRUNN, THEN PART of the Austro-Hungarian Empire and now part of the Czech Republic, to a father who owned a textile factory and had a fondness for logic and reason and a mother who believed in starting her son's education early. By age 10, Gödel was studying math, religion and several languages. By 25 he had produced what many consider the most important result of 20th century mathematics: his famous "incompleteness theorem." His astonishing and disorienting discovery, published in 1931, proved that nearly a century of effort by the world's greatest mathematicians was doomed to failure.

To appreciate Gödel's theorem, it is crucial to understand how mathematics was perceived at the time. After many centuries of being a typically sloppy human mishmash in which vague intuitions and precise logic coexisted on equal terms, mathematics at the end of the 19th century was finally being shaped up. So-called formal systems were devised (the prime example being Russell and Whitehead's *Principia Mathematica*) in which theorems, following strict rules of inference, sprouted from axioms like limbs from a tree. This process of theorem sprouting had to start somewhere, and that is where the axioms came in: they were the primordial seeds, the *Ur*-theorems from which all others sprang.

The beauty of this mechanistic vision of mathematics was that it eliminated all need for thought or judgment. As long as the axioms were true statements and as long as the rules of inference were truth preserving, mathematics could not be derailed; falsehoods simply could never creep in. Truth was an automatic hereditary property of theoremhood.

The set of symbols in which statements in formal systems were written generally included, for the sake of clarity, standard numerals, plus signs, parentheses and so forth, but they were not a necessary feature; statements could equally well be built out of icons representing plums, bananas, apples and oranges, or any utterly arbitrary set of chicken scratches, as long as a given chicken scratch always turned up in the proper places and only in such proper places. Mathematical statements in such systems were, it then became apparent, merely precisely structured patterns made up of arbitrary symbols.

Soon it dawned on a few insightful souls, Gödel foremost among them, that this way of looking at things opened up a new branch of mathematics—metamathematics. The familiar methods of mathematical analysis could be brought to bear on the very pattern-sprouting processes that formed the essence of formal systems—of which mathematics itself was supposed to be the primary example. Thus mathematics twists back on itself, like a self-eating snake.

Bizarre consequences, Gödel showed, come from focusing the lens of mathematics on mathematics itself. One way to make this concrete is to imagine that on some far planet (Mars, let's say) all the symbols used to write math books happen—by some amazing coincidence—to look like our numerals 0 through 9. Thus when Martians discuss in their textbooks a certain famous discovery that we on Earth

BORN April 28 in Brunn, Moravia, Austria

1930 Receives doctorate in mathematics

1939 Flees Europe and finds refuge in U.S. at the Institute for Advanced Study, where he works with Einstein

1906

1978

1916 At 10, studies math and languages

1924 Enters University of Vienna to study physics and philosophy

1931 Publishes "incompleteness theorem"

DIES in Princeton, N.J., at 72

attribute to Euclid and that we would express as follows: "There are infinitely many prime numbers," what they write down turns out to look like this: "4453298445087878 63070005766619463864545067111." To us it looks like one big 46-digit number. To Martians, however, it is not a number at all but a statement; indeed, to them it declares the infinitude of primes as transparently as that set of 34 letters forming six words a few lines back does to you and me.

Now imagine that we wanted to talk about the general nature of all theorems of mathematics. If we look in the Martians' textbooks, all such theorems will look to our eyes like mere numbers. And so we might develop an elaborate theory about which numbers could turn up in Martian textbooks and which numbers would never turn up there. Of course we would not really be talking about numbers, but rather about strings of symbols that to us look like numbers.

And yet, might it not be easier for us to forget about what these strings of symbols mean to the Martians and just look at them as plain old numerals?

By such a simple shift of perspective, Gödel wrought deep magic. The Gödelian trick is to imagine studying what might be called "Martian-producible numbers" (those numbers that are in fact theorems in the Martian textbooks), and to ask questions such as, "Is or is not the number 8030974 Martian-producible (M.P., for short)?" This question means, Will the statement "8030974" ever turn up in a Martian textbook?

Gödel, in thinking very carefully about this admittedly surreal scenario, soon realized that the property of being M.P. was not all that different from such familiar notions as "prime number," "odd number" and so forth. Thus earthbound number theorists could, with their standard tools, tackle such questions as, "Which numbers are M.P. numbers, and which are not?" or "Are there infinitely many non-M.P. numbers?" Advanced mathematics textbooks—on Earth, and in principle on Mars as well—might have whole chapters about M.P. numbers.

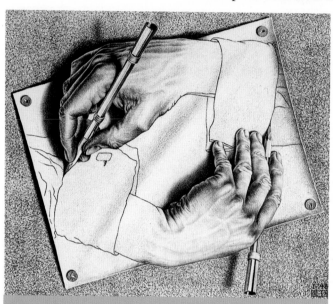

Gödel and artist M.C. Escher shared a fascination with recursion —strange loops and metasystems that chase their own tail

AND THUS, IN ONE OF THE KEENEST INSIGHTS IN the history of mathematics, Gödel devised a remarkable statement that said simply, "X is not an M.P. number" where X is the exact number we read when the statement "X is not an M.P. number" is translated into Martian math notation. Think about this for a little while until you get it. Translated into Martian notation, the statement "X is not an M.P. number" will look to us like just some huge string of digits—a very big numeral. But that string of Martian writing is our numeral for the number X (about which the statement itself talks). Talk about twisty; this is really twisty! But twists were Gödel's specialty—twists in the fabric of space-time, twists in reasoning, twists of all sorts.

By thinking of theorems as patterns of symbols, Gödel discovered that it is possible for a statement in a formal system not only to talk about itself but also to deny its own theoremhood. The consequences of this unexpected tangle lurking inside mathematics were rich, mind-boggling and— rather oddly—very sad for the Martians. Why sad? Because the Martians—like Russell and Whitehead—had hoped with all their hearts that their formal system would capture all true statements of mathematics. If Gödel's statement is true, it is not a theorem in the Martians' mathematics textbooks and will never, ever show up—because it says it won't! If it did show up in their textbooks, then what it says about itself would be wrong, and who—even on Mars—wants math textbooks that preach falsehoods as if they were true?

The upshot of all this is that the cherished goal of formalization is revealed as chimerical. All formal systems—at least ones that are powerful enough to be of interest—turn out to be incomplete because they are able to express statements that say of themselves that they are unprovable. And that, in a nutshell, is what is meant when it is said that Gödel in 1931 demonstrated the "incompleteness of mathematics." It's not really math itself that is incomplete, but any formal system that attempts to capture all the truths of mathematics in its finite set of axioms and rules. To you that may not come as a shock, but to mathematicians in the 1930s, it upended their entire world view, and math has never been the same since.

Gödel's 1931 article did something else: it invented the theory of recursive functions, which today is the basis of a powerful theory of computing. Indeed, at the heart of Gödel's article lies what can be seen as an elaborate computer program for producing M.P. numbers, and this "program" is written in a formalism that strongly resembles the programming language Lisp, which wasn't invented until nearly 30 years later.

Gödel the man was every bit as eccentric as his theories. He and his wife Adele, a dancer, fled the Nazis in 1939 and settled at the Institute for Advanced Study in Princeton, where he worked with Einstein. In his later years Gödel grew paranoid about the spread of germs, and he became notorious for compulsively cleaning his eating utensils and wearing ski masks with eye holes wherever he went. He died at age 72 in a Princeton hospital, essentially because he refused to eat. Much as formal systems, thanks to their very power, are doomed to incompleteness, so living beings, thanks to their complexity, are doomed to perish, each in its own unique manner. ∎

Douglas Hofstadter is the author of Gödel, Escher, Bach, *which was awarded the Pulitzer Prize.*

Goddard with a circular tube he used to study the properties of thrust in a vacuum

Robert
Goddard

He blasted Earthlings into the space age with a 10-ft. rocket named Nell that he launched from a New England cabbage field

By **JEFFREY KLUGER**

A CAPTURED V-2 SCIENTIST, asked how Germany learned to build rockets

ROBERT GODDARD WAS NOT A HAPPY MAN WHEN HE read his copy of the New York *Times* on Jan. 13, 1920. For some time, he had feared he might be in for a pasting in the press, but when he picked up the paper that day, he was stunned. Not long before, Goddard, a physics professor at Clark University in Worcester, Mass., had published an arid little paper on an outrageous topic, rocket travel. Unlike most of his colleagues, Goddard believed rocketry was a viable technology, and his paper, primly titled "A Method of Reaching Extreme Altitudes," was designed to prove it.

For the lay reader, there wasn't much in the writing to excite interest, but at the end, the buttoned-up professor unbuttoned a bit. If you used his technology to build a rocket big enough, Goddard argued, and if you primed it with fuel that was powerful enough, you just might be able to reach the moon with it.

When the *Times* saw Goddard's innocent moon musings, it pounced. As anyone knew, the paper explained with an editorial eye roll, space travel was impossible, for without atmosphere to push against, a rocket could not move so much as an inch. Professor Goddard, it was clear, lacked "the knowledge ladled out daily in high schools."

Goddard seethed. It wasn't just that the editors got the science all wrong. It wasn't just that they didn't care for his work. It was that they had made him out a fool. On that day, Goddard—who would ultimately be hailed as the father of modern rocketry—sank into a quarter-century sulk from which he never fully emerged. And from that sulk came some of the most incandescent achievements of his age.

Born in 1882, Goddard was a rocket man before he was a man at all. From childhood, he had an instinctive feel for all things pyrotechnic; he was intrigued by the infernal powders that fuel firecrackers and sticks of TNT. Figure out how to manage that chemical violence, he knew, and you could do some ripping-good flying.

As a student and professor at Worcester Polytechnic Institute and later at Clark, Goddard tried to figure out just how. Fooling around with the arithmetic of propulsion, he calculated the energy-to-weight ratio of various fuels. Fooling around with airtight chambers, he found that a rocket could indeed fly in a vacuum, thanks to Newton's laws of action and reaction. Fooling around with basic chemistry, he learned, most important, that if he hoped to launch a missile very far, he could never do it with the poor black powder that had long been the stuff of rocketry. Instead, he would need something with real propulsive oomph—a liquid like kerosene or liquid hydrogen, mixed with liquid oxygen to allow combustion to take place in the airless environment of space. Fill a missile with that kind of fuel, and you could retire black powder for good.

For nearly 20 years, Goddard's theories were just theories. The rockets he built never flew anywhere at all. When he'd return to Clark, fizzled missile in hand, he'd be greeted by a colleague asking, as was his habit, "Well, Robert, how goes your moongoing rocket?" When he steeled himself to publish his work, the *Times* made him wish he hadn't.

Finally, all that changed. On March 16, 1926, Goddard finished building a spindly, 10-ft. rocket he dubbed Nell, loaded it into an open car and trundled it out to his aunt Effie's nearby farm. He set up the missile in a field, then summoned an assistant, who lit its fuse with a blowtorch attached to a long stick. For an instant the rocket did

BORN
Oct. 5 in Worcester, Mass.

1915 Proves that rocket engines can produce thrust in a vacuum

1930 Begins working in Roswell, N.M.; develops supersonic and multi-stage rockets and fin-guided steering

1882

1945

1908 Begins studying physics at Clark University

1926 Launches the first liquid-fueled rocket to an altitude of 41 ft.

DIES at age 62, holding 214 patents

TESTING Goddard, left, with a crashed rocket in 1927

nothing at all, then suddenly it leaped from the ground and screamed into the sky at 60 m.p.h. Climbing to an altitude of 41 ft., it arced over, plummeted earthward and slammed into a frozen cabbage patch 184 ft. away. The entire flight lasted just 2½ sec.—but that was 2½ sec. longer than any liquid-fueled rocket had ever managed to fly before.

Goddard was thrilled with his triumph but resolved to say little about it. If people thought him daft when he was merely designing rockets, who knew what they'd say when the things actually started to fly? When word nonetheless leaked out about the launch and inquiries poured into Clark, Goddard answered each with a pinched, "Work is in progress; there is nothing to report." When he finished each new round of research, he'd file it under a deliberately misleading title—"Formulae for Silvering Mirrors," for example—lest it fall into the wrong hands.

But rockets are hard to hide, and as Goddard's Nells grew steadily bigger, the town of Worcester caught on. In 1929, an 11-ft. missile caused such a stir the police were

By 1932, Goddard, second from right, was building rockets fitted with gyroscopes. Three years later he went supersonic

called. Where there are police there is inevitably the press, and next day the local paper ran a horse-laughing headline: MOON ROCKET MISSES TARGET BY 238,799½ MILES. For Goddard, the East Coast was clearly becoming cramped. In 1930 he and his wife Esther headed west to Roswell, N.M., where the land was vast and the launch weather good, and where the locals, they were told, minded their business.

In the open, roasted stretches of the Western scrub, the fiercely private Goddard thrived. Over the next nine years, his Nells grew from 12 ft. to 16 ft. to 18 ft., and their altitude climbed from 2,000 ft. to 7,500 ft. to 9,000 ft. He built a rocket that exceeded the speed of sound and another with fin-stabilized steering, and he filed dozens of patents for everything from gyroscopic guidance systems to multistage rockets.

By the late 1930s, however, Goddard grew troubled. He had noticed long before that of all the countries that showed an interest in rocketry, Germany showed the most. Now and then, German engineers would contact him with a technical question or two, and he would casually respond. But in 1939 the Germans suddenly fell silent. With a growing concern over what might be afoot in the Reich, Goddard paid a call on Army officials in Washington and brought along films of his various Nells. He let the generals watch a few of the launches in silence, then turned to them. "We could slant it a little," he said simply, "and do some damage." The officers thanked the missile man for his time and sent him on his way. The missile man, however, apparently knew what he was talking about. Five years later, the first of Germany's murderous V-2 rockets blasted off for London. By 1945, more than 1,100 of them had rained down on the ruined city.

Rebuffed by the Army, Goddard spent World War II on sabbatical from rocketry, designing experimental airplane engines for the Navy. When the war ended, he quickly returned to his preferred work. As his first order of business, he hoped to get his hands on a captured V-2. From what he had heard, the missiles sounded disturbingly like his more peaceable Nells. Goddard's trusting exchanges with German scientists had given Berlin at least a glimpse into what he was designing. What's more, by 1945 he had filed more than 200 patents, all of which were available for inspection. When some V-2s finally made their way to the U.S. and Goddard had a chance to autopsy one, he instantly recognized his own handiwork. "Isn't this your rocket?" an assistant asked as they poked around its innards. "It seems to be," Goddard replied flatly.

Goddard accepted paternity of his bastard V-2, and that, as it turned out, was the last rocket he fathered while alive. In 1945 he was found to have throat cancer, and before the year was out, he was dead. His technological spawn, however, did not stop. American scientists worked alongside émigré German scientists to incorporate Goddard's innovations into the V-2, turning the killer missile into the Redstone, which put the first Americans into space. The Redstone led directly to the Saturn moon rockets, and indirectly to virtually every other rocket the U.S. has ever flown.

Though Goddard never saw a bit of it, credit would be given him, and—more important to a man who so disdained the press—amends would be made. After Apollo 11 lifted off en route to humanity's first moon landing, the New York Times took a bemused backward glance at its tart little 1920 editorial. "Further investigation," said the paper, "[has] confirmed ... that a rocket can function in a vacuum as well as in an atmosphere. The Times regrets the error." The grim Goddard might not have appreciated the humor, but he would almost certainly have accepted the apology. ∎

TIME *senior writer Jeffrey Kluger is the co-author, along with astronaut Jim Lovell, of* Apollo 13.

Edwin Hubble

He discovered a vast universe beyond the Milky Way, then found the first hints that it began with a Big Bang

By MICHAEL D. LEMONICK

DURING THE PAST 100 YEARS, ASTRONOMERS HAVE discovered quasars, pulsars, black holes and planets orbiting distant suns. But all these pale next to the discoveries Edwin Hubble made in a few remarkable years in the 1920s. At the time, most of his colleagues believed the Milky Way galaxy, a swirling collection of stars a few hundred thousand light-years across, made up the entire cosmos. But peering deep into the reaches of space from the chilly summit of Mount Wilson, in Southern California, Hubble realized that the Milky Way is not unique, but is just one of millions of galaxies that dot an incomparably larger setting.

Hubble went on to trump even that achievement by showing that this galaxy-studded cosmos is expanding—inflating majestically like an unimaginably gigantic balloon—a finding that prompted Albert Einstein to acknowledge and retract what he called "the greatest blunder of my life." Hubble did nothing less, in short, than invent the idea of the universe and then provide the first evidence for the Big Bang theory, which describes the birth and evolution of the universe. He discovered the cosmos, and in doing so he founded the science of cosmology.

Hubble's astronomical triumphs earned him worldwide scientific honors and made him the toast of Hollywood during the 1930s and '40s—the confidant of Aldous Huxley and a friend to Charlie Chaplin, Helen Hayes and William Randolph Hearst. Yet nobody (except perhaps Hubble) could have imagined such a future when the 23-year-old Oxford graduate, who was born in a small town in southern Missouri, began his first job, in New Albany, Ind., in 1913.

Hubble majored in science as an undergraduate at the University of Chicago. A tall, powerfully built young man, he excelled at basketball and boxing (fight promoters reportedly tried to talk him into turning pro), and his combination of academic and athletic prowess earned him a Rhodes scholarship to Oxford. In England, Hubble stayed active: he fought, ran track and played on one of the first baseball teams ever organized in the British Isles.

His official academic focus shifted, thanks to a promise made to his dying father that he would study law rather than science (he also took up literature and Spanish). On his return to America, he took a position as a high school Spanish teacher. Though he was popular with students—especially, according to Hubble biographer Gale Christianson, with the girls, who were evidently charmed by his affected British diction and "Oxford mannerisms"—Hubble longed to return to science.

After a year, he signed on as a graduate student at Yerkes Observatory in Wisconsin and embarked on the work that would one day make him famous: studying faint, hazy blobs of light called nebulae (from the Latin word for cloud) that are visible through even a modest telescope.

Hubble's skills as an astronomer were impressive enough to earn him an offer from the prestigious Mount Wilson Observatory. World War I kept him from accepting right away, but in 1919 the newly discharged Major Hubble—as

BORN
In Marshfield, Mo.

1910 Enters Oxford as a Rhodes scholar

1919 Joins the staff of the prestigious Mount Wilson Observatory after serving in World War I

1923 Proves that the universe extends beyond the edges of the Milky Way galaxy

1925 Creates the first useful scheme for classifying galaxies

1929 Proves that the universe is expanding

1936 Publishes *The Realm of the Nebulae,* a huge popular success

1943 Becomes temporary head of Army ballistics research

1889

1953

DIES Sept. 28

> ## [Hubble's] discovery that the universe is expanding was one of the great intellectual revolutions of the 20th century.

STEPHEN HAWKING, *A Brief History of Time*

he invariably introduced himself—arrived at observatory headquarters, still in uniform but ready to start scanning the skies with the just completed 100-in. Hooker Telescope, the most powerful on earth.

Up on the mountain, Hubble encountered his greatest scientific rival, Harlow Shapley, who had already made his reputation by measuring the size of the Milky Way. Using bright stars called Cepheid variables as standardized light sources, he had gauged the galaxy as being an astounding 300,000 light-years across—10 times as big as anyone had thought. Yet Shapley claimed that the Milky Way was the whole cosmic ball of wax. The luminous nebulae were, he insisted, just what they looked like: clouds of glowing gas that were relatively nearby.

Hubble wasn't so sure. And in 1924, three years after Shapley departed to take over the Harvard Observatory, Hubble found proof to the contrary. Spotting a Cepheid variable star in the Andromeda nebula, Hubble used Shapley's technique to show that the nebula was nearly 1 million light-years away, far beyond the bounds of the Milky Way.

It's now known to be the full-fledged galaxy closest to our own in a universe that contains tens of billions of galaxies. "I do not know," Shapley wrote Hubble in a letter quoted by biographer Christianson, "whether I am sorry or glad to see this break in the nebular problem. Perhaps both." (Hubble was not entirely magnanimous in victory. To the end he insisted on using the term nebulae instead of Shapley's preferred galaxies.)

HUBBLE'S SCIENTIFIC REPUTATION WAS MADE almost overnight by his discovery that the universe is vast and the Milky Way relatively insignificant. But he had already moved on to a new problem. For years, astronomers had noted that light from the nebulae was redder than it should be. The most likely cause of this so-called red shifting was motion away from the observer. (The same sort of thing happens with sound: a police car's siren seems to drop in pitch abruptly as the car races past a listener.)

Hubble and his assistant, Milton Humason, began measuring the distances to these receding nebulae and found what is now known as Hubble's Law: the farther away a galaxy is from Earth, the faster it's racing away. Could it be that the universe as a whole is rapidly expanding? That conclusion was extraordinary, mind-blowing, yet inescapable.

When Einstein heard of Hubble's discovery, he was elated. More than a decade earlier, Einstein's new general theory of relativity had told him that the universe must either be expanding or contracting, yet astronomers had assured him it was doing neither. Against his better judgment, he had uglied up his elegant equations with an extra factor he called the cosmological term—a sort of antigravity force that kept the universe from collapsing in on itself.

But suddenly, the cosmological term was unnecessary. Einstein's instincts had been right, after all. His great blunder had been to doubt himself, and in 1931, during a visit to Caltech, the great and grateful physicist traveled to the top of Mount Wilson to see the telescope and thank Hubble personally for delivering him from folly.

With the greatest scientific superstar of the age paying him homage, Hubble became a popular superstar in his own right. His 1936 book on his discoveries, *The Realm of the Nebulae,* cemented his celebrity. Tourists and

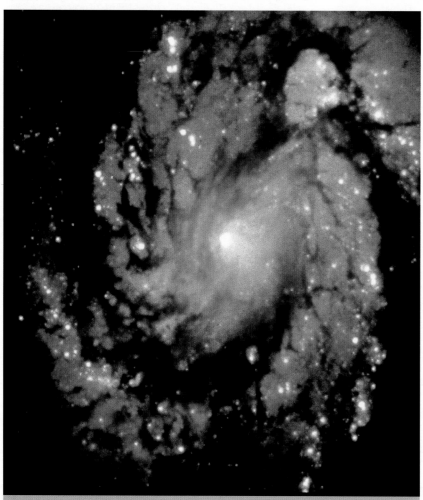

The M100 galaxy, 56 light-years away, in an image from the Hubble Space Telescope

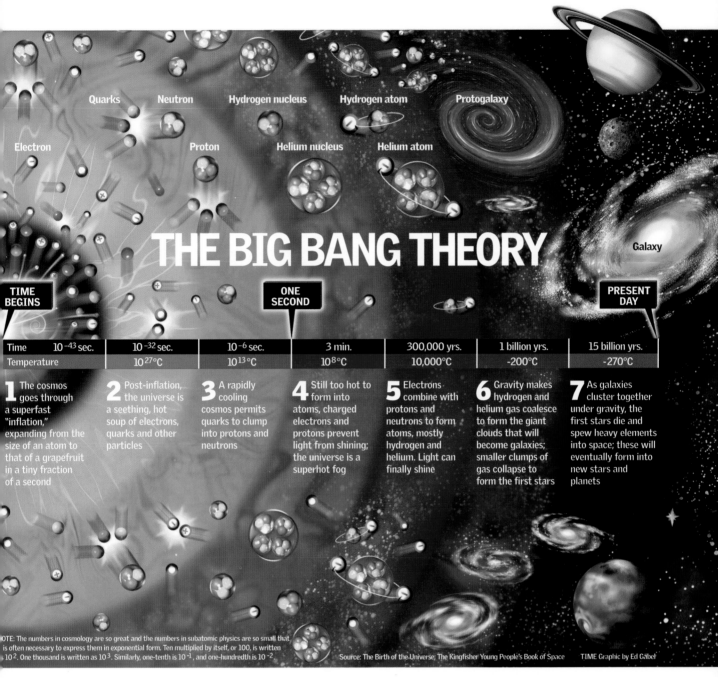

THE BIG BANG THEORY

Quarks Neutron Hydrogen nucleus Hydrogen atom Protogalaxy

Electron Proton Helium nucleus Helium atom

Galaxy

TIME BEGINS

ONE SECOND

PRESENT DAY

Time	10^{-43} sec.	10^{-32} sec.	10^{-6} sec.	3 min.	300,000 yrs.	1 billion yrs.	15 billion yrs.
Temperature		10^{27}°C	10^{13}°C	10^{8}°C	10,000°C	-200°C	-270°C

1 The cosmos goes through a superfast "inflation," expanding from the size of an atom to that of a grapefruit in a tiny fraction of a second

2 Post-inflation, the universe is a seething, hot soup of electrons, quarks and other particles

3 A rapidly cooling cosmos permits quarks to clump into protons and neutrons

4 Still too hot to form into atoms, charged electrons and protons prevent light from shining; the universe is a superhot fog

5 Electrons combine with protons and neutrons to form atoms, mostly hydrogen and helium. Light can finally shine

6 Gravity makes hydrogen and helium gas coalesce to form the giant clouds that will become galaxies; smaller clumps of gas collapse to form the first stars

7 As galaxies cluster together under gravity, the first stars die and spew heavy elements into space; these will eventually form into new stars and planets

NOTE: The numbers in cosmology are so great and the numbers in subatomic physics are so small that is often necessary to express them in exponential form. Ten multiplied by itself, or 100, is written 10^2. One thousand is written as 10^3. Similarly, one-tenth is 10^{-1}, and one-hundredth is 10^{-2}.

Source: The Birth of the Universe; The Kingfisher Young People's Book of Space   TIME Graphic by Ed Gabel

Hollywood luminaries alike would drive up the mountain to marvel at the observatory where Hubble had discovered the universe, and he and his wife Grace were embraced by the élite of California society.

Hubble's last great contribution to astronomy was his central role in the design and construction of the Hale Telescope on Palomar Mountain. Four times as powerful as the Hooker, the Hale would be the largest telescope on Earth for four decades. The mammoth scope would have been even longer, but its completion was interrupted by World War II. So was Hubble's career. The ex-major from the Great War signed on as head of ballistics at Aberdeen Proving Ground in Maryland. (At one point the eminent astronomer spent an afternoon test-firing bazookas, at great personal risk, to pinpoint a design flaw.)

Hubble finally got his hands on the Hale when it went into service in 1949. But his prime was past; he had suffered a major heart attack, and he never fully regained the stamina it took to spend all night in a freezing-cold observatory.

However, his reputation required no further polishing.

The only recognition that eluded the aging skywatcher was a Nobel Prize—and not for lack of effort on his part. He tried everything. In the late 1940s he even hired a publicity agent to promote his cause. Alas, there was no prize for astronomy, and by the time the Nobel committee decided astronomy could be viewed as a branch of physics, it was too late. Insiders say Hubble was on the verge of winning when he died, in 1953.

Hubble would have been consoled by the fact that his name adorns the Hubble Space Telescope, which probes the cosmos to depths he could not have imagined but would have fully appreciated. Whatever marvels the Hubble telescope reveals, they're all played out on the vast stage Edwin Hubble first glimpsed in a wild surmise on a silent mountain peak in California.   ■

TIME *senior writer Michael D. Lemonick is the author of* Other Worlds: The Search for Life in the Universe.

The Century of the Countdown

Robert Goddard was not the first to conceive of liquid-fueled rockets, but he was the first to make one fly. The descendants of his invention put machines into space and humans on the moon

1957 The First Satellite in Earth Orbit

The U.S.S.R. launches Sputnik 1, the first satellite, thus taking a commanding—and surprising—lead in the exploration of space. In the tense climate of the cold war, the "race to space" becomes a duel between superpowers, as America's space program accelerates.

1903 A Roadmap for Rockets

Russia's Konstantin Tsiolkovsky publishes "Exploring Space with Reactive Devices," the first great rocketry study. Soviet propagandists would later become notorious for their bogus claims of Russian scientific genius, but Tsiolkovsky was a true pioneer.

1944 Rain of Death

Germany, inspired in part by homegrown rocketeer Hermann Oberth and in part by Goddard, launches the first V-2 rockets against London and Paris.

1961 The First Man in Space

The U.S.S.R.'s Yuri Gagarin becomes the first human being in space; America's Alan Shepard follows the next month. But Gagarin completed a complete orbit of the planet, while Shepard's brief sub-orbital journey only broadcast to the world that the U.S. was lagging far behind the Soviet Union in the rush to conquer space.

1969 **The First Men on the Moon**

Apollo 11, launched by a Saturn V rocket, puts the first men on the moon in the *Eagle* landing module. The triumph for the U.S. NASA program comes only eight years after President John F. Kennedy committed the U.S. to landing a man on the moon within a decade.

1986 **A Tragedy in Space**

The shuttle *Challenger* explodes, killing seven U.S. astronauts, including schoolteacher Christa McAuliffe, whom NASA had heavily promoted as the first in a new program of sending civilians into space. Shuttle launches are halted for months as NASA struggles to discover the reason for the system failure.

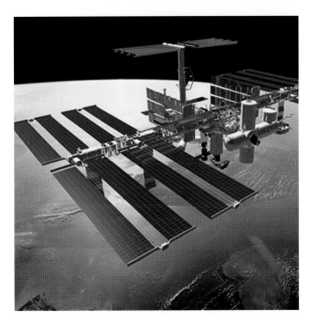

1998 **An International Station**

Assembly begins on a long-planned, 16-nation International Space Station. The first two pieces, Russia's Zarya and America's United modules, reach orbit late in the year, where they are linked together and powered up by U.S. astronatuts.

1981 **Dawn of the Shuttle Age**

The U.S. launches the first shuttle, a revolutionary vehicle that is the first re-usable space transportation: it blasts into orbit atop a rocket, but then returns to Earth and employs its stubby wings to land like an airplane.

BORN Sept. 29
in Rome

1932 Writes key
paper on beta decay

1938 Awarded
Nobel Prize
for Physics

1942 Achieves
man-made
nuclear chain
reaction

1949 Argues
against
development
of the H-bomb

1901

1954

1926 Develops
Fermi-Dirac statistics

1934
Discovers slow
neutrons

1939 Moves to
the U.S. with
Jewish wife

DIES in
Chicago

Enrico
Fermi

He was the last of the double-threat physicists: a genius at creating both the most esoteric theories and the most elegant experiments

By RICHARD RHODES

IF THE 19TH CENTURY WAS THE CENTURY OF CHEMISTRY, the 20th was the century of physics. The burgeoning science supported a cornucopia of transforming applications: medical imaging, nuclear reactors, atom and hydrogen bombs, radio and television, transistors, computers and lasers. Physical knowledge increased so rapidly after 1900 that theory and experiment soon divided into separate specialties. Enrico Fermi, a supremely self-assured Italian American born in Rome in 1901, was the last great physicist to bridge the gap.

Fermi's theory of beta decay introduced the last of the four basic forces known in nature (gravity, electromagnetism and, operating within the nucleus of the atom, the strong force and his new "weak force"). Fermi also co-invented and designed the first man-made nuclear reactor, starting it up in a historic secret experiment at the University of Chicago on Dec. 2, 1942. In the famous code that an administrator used to report the success of the experiment by open phone to Washington, Fermi was "the Italian navigator" who had "landed in the new world."

This Columbus of the nucleus had personally landed in the new world four years earlier, with a newly minted Nobel Prize gold medal in his pocket, pre-eminent among a distillation of outstanding scientists who immigrated to the U.S. in the 1930s to escape anti-Semitic persecution in both Hitler's Germany and Mussolini's Italy—in Fermi's case, of his Jewish wife Laura.

A dark, compact man with mischievous gray-blue eyes, Fermi was the son of a civil servant, an administrator with the Italian national railroad. He discovered physics at 14, when he was left bereft by the death of his cherished older brother Giulio during minor throat surgery. Browsing through the bookstalls in Rome's Campo dei Fiori, the grieving boy found two antique volumes of elementary physics, carried them home and read them through, sometimes correcting the mathematics. Later, he told his older sister Maria that he had not even noticed they were written in Latin. Einstein characterized his own commitment to science as a flight from the I and the we to the it. Physics may have offered Enrico more consolatory certitudes than religion.

He progressed so quickly, guided by an engineer who was a family friend, that his competition essay for university admission was judged worthy of a doctoral examination. By 1920 he was teaching his teachers at the University of Pisa; he worked out his first theory of permanent value to physics while still an undergraduate. His only setback was a period of postdoctoral study in Germany in 1923 among such talents as Wolfgang Pauli and Werner Heisenberg, when his gifts went unrecognized. He disliked pretension, preferring simplicity and concreteness, and the philosophic German style may have repelled him. "Not a philosopher," the American theorist J. Robert

Thirty months after Fermi and his Chicago team achieved fission, the U.S. tested the first A-bomb in Alamagordo, N.M.

" Passion for clarity. He was simply unable to let things be foggy. Since they always are, this kept him pretty active. "

J. ROBERT OPPENHEIMER, on the nature of Fermi's genius

Fermi, front left, reunites with Manhattan Project scientists at the University of Chicago 16 months after Hiroshima

Oppenheimer later sketched him. "Passion for clarity. He was simply unable to let things be foggy. Since they always are, this kept him pretty active." He won appointment as professor of theoretical physics at the University of Rome at 25 and quickly assembled a small group of first-class young talents for his self-appointed task of reviving Italian physics. Judging him infallible, they nicknamed him "the Pope."

The Pope and his team almost found nuclear fission in 1934 in the course of experiments in which, looking for radioactive transformations, they systematically bombarded one element after another with the newly discovered neutron. They missed by the thickness of the sheet of foil in which they wrapped their uranium sample; the foil blocked the fission fragments that their instruments would otherwise have recorded. It was a blessing in disguise. If fission had come to light in the mid-1930s, while the democracies slept, Nazi Germany would have won a long lead toward building an atom bomb. In compensation, Fermi made the most important discovery of his life, that slowing neutrons by passing them through a light-element "moderator" such as paraffin increased their effectiveness, a finding that would allow for the release of nuclear energy in a reactor.

If Hitler had not hounded Jewish scientists out of Europe, the Anglo-American atom bomb program sparked by the discovery of fission late in 1938 would have found itself shorthanded. Most Allied physicists had already been put to work developing radar and the proximity fuse, inventions of more immediate value. Fermi and his fellow émigrés—Hungarians Leo Szilard, Eugene Wigner, John von Neumann and Edward Teller, German Hans Bethe— formed the heart of the bomb squad. In 1939, still officially enemy aliens, Fermi and Szilard co-invented the nuclear reactor at Columbia University, sketching out a three-dimensional lattice of uranium slugs dropped into holes in black, greasy blocks of graphite moderator, with sliding neutron-absorbing cadmium control rods to regulate the chain reaction. Fermi, still mastering English, dubbed this elegantly simple machine a "pile."

The work moved to the University of Chicago when the Manhattan Project consolidated its operations there, culminating in the assembly of the first full-scale pile, CP-1, on a doubles squash court under the stands of the university football field in late 1942. Built up in layers inside wooden framing, it took the shape of a doorknob the size of a two-car garage—a flattened graphite ellipsoid 25 ft. wide and 20 ft. high, weighing nearly 100 tons.

Dec. 2 dawned to below-zero cold. That morning the State Department announced that 2 million Jews had perished in Europe and 5 million more were in danger; American boys and Japanese were dying at Guadalcanal. It was cold inside the squash court, and the crowd of scientists who assembled on the balcony kept on their overcoats.

Fermi proceeded imperturbably through the experiment, confident of the estimates he had charted with his pocket slide rule. At 11:30 a.m., as was his custom, he stopped for lunch. The pile went critical in midafternoon with the full withdrawal of the control rods, and Fermi allowed himself a grin. He had proved the science of a chain reaction in uranium; from then on, building a bomb was mere engineering. He shut the pile down after 28 minutes of operation. Wigner had thought to buy a celebratory fiasco of Chianti, which supplied a toast. "For some time we had known that we were about to unlock a giant," Wigner would write. "Still, we could not escape an eerie feeling when we knew we had actually done it."

From that first small pile grew production reactors that bred plutonium for the first atom bombs. Moving to Los Alamos in 1944, Fermi was on hand in the New Mexico desert for the first test of the brutal new weapon in July 1945. He estimated its explosive yield with a characteristically simple experiment, dropping scraps of paper in the predawn stillness and again when the blast wind arrived and comparing their displacement.

Fermi died prematurely of stomach cancer in Chicago in 1954. He had argued against U.S. development of the hydrogen bomb when that project was debated in 1949, calling it "a weapon which in practical effect is almost one of genocide." His counsel went unheeded, and the U.S.-Soviet arms race that ensued put the world at mortal risk. But the discovery of how to release nuclear energy, in which he played so crucial a part, had long-term beneficial results: the development of an essentially unlimited new source of energy and the forestalling, perhaps permanently, of world-scale war. ∎

Richard Rhodes is the Pulitzer-prizewinning author of The Making of the Atomic Bomb.

Behind the Bomb

Along with Fermi, a cluster of brilliant scientists ushered in a new age of power—and peril

J. Robert Oppenheimer

Brilliant and charismatic, Oppenheimer directed the team at Los Alamos that created the first atom-bombs, but in 1954 he lost his security clearance for opposing the H-bomb.

Hans Bethe

After fleeing Nazi Germany for the U.S. in 1935, he discovered the fusion reactions that power the stars. The reliable Bethe guided work on the first A-bombs and worked on the H-bomb—before concluding that scientists shouldn't build such weapons.

Andrei Sakharov

Ordered by the KGB to work on the H-bomb, the young physicist exploded a kiloton-yield weapon only 13 months after the first U.S. test. He later led a dissident movement that helped topple Soviet communism.

Edward Teller

The volatile, Russia-fearing Hungarian began espousing a hydrogen bomb in 1942 and never wavered. He lobbied for a crash program after the first Soviet A-bomb test and encouraged Reagan's ambitious "Star Wars" initiative in the '80s.

John Maynard
Keynes

His radical idea that governments should spend money they don't possess mystified politicians—and may have saved capitalism

By **ROBERT B. REICH**

HE HARDLY SEEMED CUT OUT TO BE A WORKING-man's revolutionary. A Cambridge University don with a flair for making money, a graduate of Eton, a collector of modern art, the darling of Virginia Woolf and her intellectually avant-garde Bloomsbury group, the chairman of a life-insurance company, later a director of the Bank of England, married to a ballerina, John Maynard Keynes—tall, charming and self-confident—nonetheless transformed the dismal science into a revolutionary engine of social progress.

Before Keynes, economists were gloomy naysayers. "Nothing can be done," "Don't interfere," "It will never work," they intoned with Eeyore-like pessimism. But Keynes was an unswerving optimist. Of course we can lick unemployment! There's no reason to put up with recessions and depressions! The "economic problem is not—if we look into the future—*the permanent problem of the human race,*" he wrote (liberally using italics for emphasis).

Born in Cambridge, England, in 1883, the year Karl Marx died, Keynes probably saved capitalism from itself and surely kept latter-day Marxists at bay. His father John Neville Keynes was a noted Cambridge economist. His mother Florence Ada Keynes became mayor of

Cambridge. Young John was a brilliant student but didn't immediately aspire to either academic or public life. He wanted to run a railroad. "It is so easy ... and fascinating to master the principles of these things," he told a friend, with his usual modesty. But no railway came along, and Keynes ended up taking the civil service exam. His lowest mark was in economics. "I evidently knew more about Economics than my examiners," he later explained.

Keynes was posted to the India Office, but the civil service proved deadly dull, and he soon left. He lectured at Cambridge, edited an influential journal, socialized with his Bloomsbury friends, surrounded himself with artists and writers and led an altogether dilettantish life until Europe was plunged into World War I. Keynes was called to Britain's Treasury to work on overseas finances, where he quickly shone. Even his artistic tastes came in handy. He figured a way to balance the French accounts by having Britain's National Gallery buy paintings by Manet, Corot and Delacroix at bargain prices.

His first brush with fame came soon after the war, when he was selected to be a delegate to the Paris Peace Conference of 1918-19. The young Keynes held his tongue as Woodrow Wilson, David Lloyd George and Georges Clemenceau imposed vindictive war reparations on Germany. But he let out a roar when he returned to England, writing a short book, *The Economic Consequences of the Peace.* The Germans, he wrote acerbically, could not possibly pay what the victors were demanding. Calling Wilson a "blind, deaf Don Quixote" and Clemenceau a xenophobe with "one illusion—France, and one disillusion—mankind" (and only at the last moment scratching the purple prose he had reserved for Lloyd George: "this goat-footed bard, this half-human visitor to our age from the hag-ridden magic and enchanted woods of Celtic antiquity"), an outraged Keynes prophesied that the reparations would keep Germany impoverished and ultimately threaten all Europe.

His little book sold 84,000 copies, caused a huge stir and made Keynes an instant celebrity. But its real import was to be felt decades later, after the end of World War II. Instead

Keynes, far left, hits the airwaves in 1946 to tout the postwar economy

BORN June 5
in Cambridge,
England

1919 Representative at
Paris Peace Conference

1936 *The General Theory of
Employment, Interest and
Money* appears

1944
Delegate at
Bretton Woods

1883

CHIPPER
Keynes
in 1945

1946

1915 Accepts
position in
the British
Treasury

1919 Returns to
Cambridge to teach; *The
Economic Consequences
of the Peace* is published

1942 Named
Baron Keynes
of Tilton

DIES
April 21,
in Firle,
England

of repeating the mistake made almost three decades before, the U.S. and Britain bore in mind Keynes' earlier admonition. The surest pathway to a lasting peace, they then understood, was to help the vanquished rebuild. Public investing on a grand scale would create trading partners that could turn around and buy the victors' exports, and also build solid middle-class democracies in Germany, Italy and Japan.

Yet Keynes' largest influence came from a convoluted, badly organized and in places nearly incomprehensible tome published in 1936, during the depths of the Great Depression. It was called *The General Theory of Employment, Interest and Money.* Keynes' basic idea was simple. In order to keep people fully employed, governments have to run deficits when the economy is slowing. That's because the private sector won't invest enough. As their markets become saturated, businesses reduce their investments, setting in motion a dangerous cycle: less investment, fewer jobs, less consumption and even less reason for business to invest. The economy may reach balance, but at a cost of high

Keynes, center, at the Bretton Woods conference in 1944

unemployment and social misery. Better for governments to avoid the pain in the first place by taking up the slack.

The notion that government deficits are good has an odd ring these days. For most of the past two decades, America's biggest worry has been inflation due to excessive demand. Inflation soared into double digits in the 1970s, budget deficits ballooned in the '80s, and in 1998 Bill Clinton was cheering a budget surplus that he wanted to use to pay down the debt. But some 60 years ago, when 1 out of 4 adults couldn't find work, the problem was lack of demand.

Even then, Keynes had a hard sell. Most economists of the era rejected his idea and favored balanced budgets. Most politicians didn't understand his idea to begin with. In the 1932 presidential election, Franklin D. Roosevelt had blasted Herbert Hoover for running a deficit, and promised he'd balance the budget if elected. Keynes' visit to the White House two years later to urge F.D.R. to do more deficit spending wasn't exactly a blazing success. "He left a whole rigmarole of figures," a bewildered F.D.R. complained to Labor Secretary

Frances Perkins. "He must be a mathematician rather than a political economist." Keynes was equally underwhelmed, telling Perkins that he had "supposed the President was more literate, economically speaking."

As the Depression wore on, Roosevelt tried public works, farm subsidies and other devices to restart the economy, but he never completely gave up trying to balance the budget. In 1938 the Depression deepened. Reluctantly, F.D.R. embraced the only new idea he hadn't yet tried, that of the bewildering British "mathematician." As the President explained in a fireside chat, "We suffer primarily from a failure of consumer demand because of a lack of buying power." It was therefore up to the government to "create an economic upturn" by making "additions to the purchasing power of the nation."

Yet not until the U.S. entered World War II did F.D.R. try Keynes' idea on a scale necessary to pull the nation out of the doldrums—and Roosevelt, of course, had little choice. The big surprise was just how productive America could be when given the chance. Between 1939 and 1944 (the peak of wartime production), the nation's output almost doubled, and unemployment plummeted—from more than 17% to just over 1%.

Never before had an economic theory been so dramatically tested. Even granted the special circumstances of war mobilization, it seemed to work exactly as Keynes predicted. The grand experiment even won over many Republicans. America's Employment Act of 1946—the year Keynes died—codified the new wisdom, making it "the continuing policy and responsibility of the Federal Government ... to promote maximum employment, production, and purchasing power."

And the Federal Government did just that, for the next quarter-century. As the U.S. economy boomed, the government became the nation's economic manager and the President its Manager in Chief. It became accepted wisdom that government could "fine-tune" the economy, pushing the twin accelerators of fiscal and monetary policy in order to avoid slowdowns, and applying the brakes when necessary to avoid overheating. In 1964 Lyndon Johnson cut taxes to expand purchasing power and boost employment. "We are all Keynesians now," Richard Nixon proclaimed.

Were Keynes alive today he would surely admire the vigor of the U.S. economy, but he would be mystified that the International Monetary Fund is requiring troubled Third World nations to raise taxes and slash spending, that "euro" membership demands budget austerity, and that a U.S. President wants to hold on to budget surpluses. You can bet he wouldn't be silent. Dapper and distinguished as he was, he'd enter the fray with both fists and a mighty roar. Keynes had no patience with economists who assumed that everything would work out in the long run. "This long run is a misleading guide to current affairs," he wrote early in his career. "*In the long run* we are all dead." ∎

Robert B. Reich, professor of economic and social policy at Brandeis, was U.S. Secretary of Labor from 1993 to 1997.

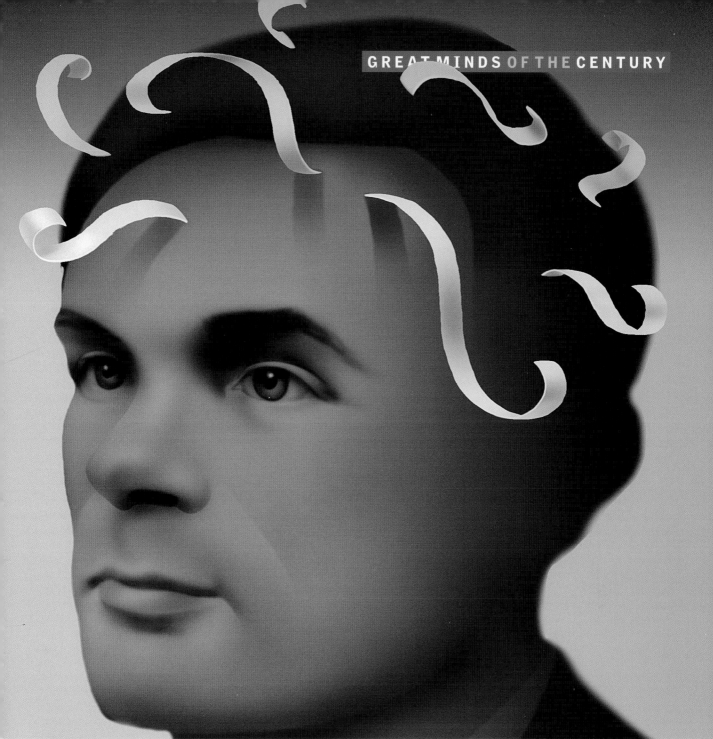

Alan
Turing

While addressing a problem in the arcane field of mathematical logic, he imagined a machine that could mimic human reasoning

By PAUL GRAY

I F ALL ALAN TURING HAD DONE WAS ANSWER, IN THE negative, a vexing question in the arcane realm of mathematical logic, few nonspecialists today would have any reason to remember him. But the method Turing used to show that certain propositions in a closed logical system cannot be proved within that system—a corollary to the proof that made Kurt Gödel famous—had enormous consequences in the world at large. For what this eccentric young Cambridge don did was to dream up an imaginary machine—a fairly simple typewriter-like contraption capable somehow of scanning, or reading, instructions encoded on a tape of theoretically infinite length. Turing demonstrated that as the scanner moved from one square of the tape to the next—responding to the sequential commands and modifying its mechanical response if so ordered—its output could replicate logical human thought.

The device in this inspired mind-experiment quickly acquired a name: the Turing machine. And so did another of Turing's insights. Since the instructions on the tape governed the behavior of the machine, by changing those instructions, one could induce the machine to perform the functions of all such machines. In other words, depending on the tape it scanned, the same machine could calculate numbers or play chess or do anything else of a comparable nature. Hence his device acquired a new and even grander name: the Universal Turing Machine.

Does this concept—a fairly rudimentary assemblage of hardware performing prodigious and multifaceted tasks according to the dictates of the instructions fed to it—sound familiar? It certainly didn't in 1937, when Turing's seminal paper, "On Computable Numbers, with an Application to the *Entscheidungs* Problem," appeared in *Proceedings of the London Mathematical Society.* Turing's thoughts were recognized by the few readers capable of understanding them as theoretically interesting, even provocative. But no one recognized that Turing's machine provided a blueprint for what would eventually become the electronic digital computer. So many ideas and technological advances converged to create the modern computer that it is foolhardy to give one person the credit for inventing it. But the fact remains that everyone who taps at a keyboard or clicks on a mouse is working on an incarnation of a Turing machine.

Turing's 1937 paper changed the direction of his life and embroiled a shy and vulnerable man ever more directly in the affairs of the external world, ultimately with tragic consequences. Alan Mathison Turing was born in London in 1912, the second of his parents' two sons. His father was a member of the British civil service in India, an environment that his mother considered unsuitable for her boys. So John and Alan Turing spent their childhood in foster households in England, separated from their parents except for occasional visits hom. Alan's loneliness during this period may have inspired his lifelong interest in the operations of the human mind, how it can create a world when the world it is given proves barren or unsatisfactory.

At 13 he enrolled at the Sherbourne School in Dorset and there showed a flair for mathematics, even if his papers were criticized for being "dirty," i.e., messy. Turing recognized his homosexuality while at Sherbourne and fell in love, albeit undeclared, with another boy at the school, who suddenly died of bovine tuberculosis. This loss shattered Turing's religious faith and led him into atheism and the conviction that all phenomena must have materialistic explanations. There was no soul in the machine nor any mind behind a brain. But how, then, did thought and consciousness arise?

After twice failing to win a fellowship at the University of Cambridge's Trinity College, a lodestar at the time for mathematicians from around the world, Turing received a fellowship from King's College, Cambridge. King's, under the guidance of such luminaries as John Maynard Keynes and E.M. Forster, provided a remarkably free and tolerant environment for Turing, who thrived there even though he was not considered quite elegant enough to be initiated into King's inner circles. When he completed his degree requirements, Turing was invited to remain at King's as a tutor. And there he might happily have stayed, pottering about with problems in mathematical logic, had not his invention of the Turing machine and World War II intervened.

Turing, on the basis of his published work, was recruited to serve in the Government Code and Cypher School, located in a Victorian mansion called Bletchley Park in Buckinghamshire. The task of all those so assembled—mathematicians, chess champions, Egyptologists, whoever might have something to contribute about the possible permutations of formal systems—was to break the Enigma codes used by the Nazis in communications between headquarters and troops. Because of secrecy restrictions, Turing's role in this

BORN June 23 in London

1937 Landmark paper introduces the imaginary Turing machine

SPEEDY The avid runner finishes a three-mile race, 1946

1952 Convicted of "gross indecency" for homosexual acts

1912

1931-5 Studies mathematical logic at Cambridge

1939-45 Secretly works with team breaking the Nazis' Enigma codes

1950 Paper in journal *Mind* predicts artificial intelligence

1954

SUICIDE at age 41

A German Enigma machine: Turing helped crack its codes

pick up the quiet academic life he had intended. But the newly created mathematics division of the British National Physical Laboratory asked him to create an actual Turing machine, the ACE (Automatic Computing Engine), and Turing accepted.

But the emergency spirit that had short-circuited so many wartime problems had dissipated. Red tape and bureaucracy again were the order of the day. Finding that most of his suggestions were ignored, dismissed or overruled, Turing eventually left the NPL for another stay at Cambridge and then accepted an offer from the University of Manchester, where a new computer was being constructed along the lines he had suggested in 1937.

Since his original paper, Turing had considerably broadened his thoughts on thinking machines. He now proposed the idea that a machine could learn from and thus modify its own instructions. In a famous 1950 article in the British philosophical journal *Mind*, Turing proposed what he called an "imitation test," which later was called the "Turing test." Imagine an interrogator in a closed room hooked up in some manner with two subjects, one human and the other a computer. If the questioner cannot determine by the responses to queries posed to them which is the human and which the computer, then the computer can be said to be "thinking" as well as the human.

Turing remains a hero to proponents of artificial intelligence in part because of his blithe assumption of a rosy future: "One day ladies will take their computers for walks in the park and tell each other, 'My little computer said such a funny thing this morning!'"

Unfortunately, reality caught up with Turing well before his vision would, if ever, be realized. In Manchester, he told police investigating a robbery at his house that he was having "an affair" with a man who was probably known to the burglar. Always frank about his sexual orientation, Turing this time got himself into real trouble. Homosexual relations were still a felony in Britain, and Turing was tried and convicted of "gross indecency" in 1952. Although he was spared prison, he was subjected to injections of female hormones intended to dampen his lust. "I'm growing breasts!" Turing told a friend. On June 7, 1954, he committed suicide by eating an apple laced with cyanide. He was 41. ∎

enterprise was not acknowledged until long after his death. And like the invention of the computer, the work done by the Bletchley Park crew was very much a team effort. But it is now known that Turing played a crucial role in designing a primitive, computer-like machine that could decipher at high speed Nazi codes to U-boats in the North Atlantic.

After the war, Turing returned to Cambridge, hoping to

TIME *senior writer Paul Gray works on a Turing machine.*

Homeric Hackers

Alan Turing helped conceive the computer; here are some other forefathers of the digital domain

Robert Noyce

The gifted son of an Iowa minister had worked with William Shockley, but with Gordon Moore and six others left to form Fairchild Semiconductor. There he made the first integrated circuit, or michrochip, printing transistors on silicon wafers. He and Moore later founded Intel.

John von Neumann

The Hungarian-born math prodigy and *Ur*-hacker laid out the basic architecture of the computer in the 1940s. He threw his boundless genius into problems ranging from quantum mechanics to building the A-bomb to weather prediction—and invented game theory.

Alan Kay

Who designed the first personal computer? Steve Jobs and Steve Wozniak of Apple get a lot of the credit —aided by a 1979 "daylight raid" on the Xerox Palo Alto Research Center, where Alan Kay and his team had created a new computer, the Alto. Its language, Smalltalk, made files accessible through pop-up menus and sported other user-friendly features. Five years later, the first Mac brought those ideas to the world.

John Mauchly & Presper Eckert

Their ENIAC was the first true all-purpose electronic computer. Unveiled in 1946, the 30-ton machine had 19,000 vacuum tubes. Rival John Atanasoff's ABC machine was another early model, but while it used binary numbers rather than ENIAC's decimals, it was never fully operational and could not be reprogrammed.

William Shockley

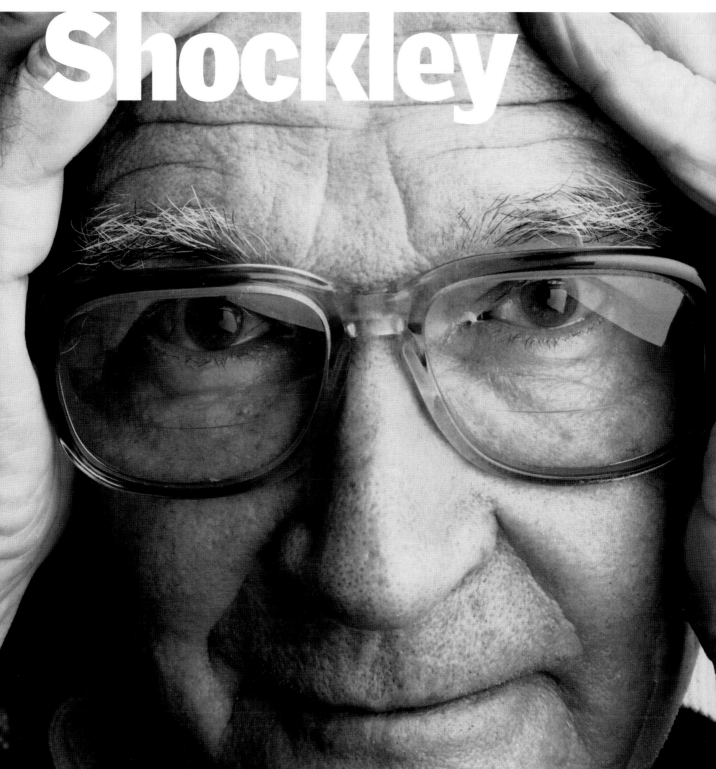

He fathered the transistor and brought the silicon to Silicon Valley but is remembered by many only for his noxious racial views

By GORDON MOORE

THE TRANSISTOR WAS BORN JUST BEFORE CHRISTMAS 1947 when John Bardeen and Walter Brattain, two scientists working for William Shockley at Bell Telephone Laboratories in Murray Hill, N.J., observed that when electrical signals were applied to contacts on a crystal of germanium, the output power was larger than the input. Shockley was not present at that first observation. And though he fathered the discovery in the same way Einstein fathered the atom bomb, by advancing the idea and pointing the way, he felt left out of the momentous occasion.

Shockley, a very competitive and sometimes infuriating man, was determined to make his imprint on the discovery. He searched for an explanation of the effect from what was then known of the quantum physics of semiconductors. In a remarkable series of insights made over a few short weeks, he greatly extended the understanding of semiconductor materials and developed the underlying theory of another, much more robust amplifying device—a kind of sandwich made of a crystal with varying impurities added, which came to be known as the junction transistor. By 1951 Shockley's co-workers made his semiconductor sandwich and demonstrated that it behaved much as his theory had predicted.

For the next couple of decades advances in transistor technology drove the industry, as several companies jumped on the idea and set out to develop commercially viable versions of the device. New ways to create Shockley's sandwich were invented, and transistors in a vast variety of sizes and shapes flooded the market. Shockley's invention had created a new industry, one that underlies all modern electronics, from supercomputers to talking greeting cards. Today the world produces about as many transistors as it does printed characters in all the newspapers, books, magazines and computer and electronic-copier pages combined.

William Bradford Shockley was born in London, where his father, a mining engineer, and mother, a mineral surveyor, were on a business assignment. Home-schooled in Palo Alto, Calif., before attending Palo Alto Military Acade-

The inventors of the transistor: from left, Shockley, Brattain and Bardeen

my and Hollywood High School, he found his interest in physics sparked by a neighbor who taught the subject at Stanford University. Shockley earned a bachelor's degree from Caltech, and a Ph.D. at M.I.T.

At Bell Labs, Shockley recognized early on that the solution to one of the technological nightmares of the day—the cost and unreliability of the vacuum tubes used as valves to control the flow of electrons in radios and telephone-relay systems—lay in solid-state physics. Vacuum tubes were hot, bulky, fragile and short-lived. Crystals, particularly crystals that can conduct a bit of electricity, could do the job faster, more reliably and with 1 million times less power—if only someone could get them to function as electronic valves. Shockley and his team accomplished this trick.

Understanding of the significance of the invention of what came to be called the transistor (for transfer resistance) spread quite rapidly. In 1956 Shockley, Bardeen and Brattain shared a Nobel Prize for Physics—an unusual awarding of the Nobel for the invention of a useful article.

Not content with his lot at Bell Labs, Shockley set out to capitalize on his invention. In doing so, he played a key role in the industrial development of the region at the base of the San Francisco Peninsula. It was Shockley who brought the silicon to Silicon Valley.

In February 1956, financed by Beckman Instruments Inc., led by Arnold Beckman, he founded Shockley Semiconductor Laboratory with the goal of developing and producing a silicon transistor. He chose to establish this start-up near Palo Alto, where he had grown up and where his mother still lived. He set up operations in a storefront—little more than a Quonset hut—and hired a group of young scientists (I was one of them) to develop the necessary technology. By the spring of 1956 he had a small staff in place and was beginning to undertake research and development.

Until this time, nearly all transistors had utilized germanium because it was easier to prepare in pure form. Silicon offered advantages, at least in theory: devices made from it could operate at higher temperatures. Also, silicon is a very

BORN Feb. 13 in London

1942 Directs U.S. Navy submarine research

1947 Invents first transistor, below, with Bardeen and Brattain

1955 Quits Bell Labs

1963 Appointed professor at Stanford; begins research on intelligence

1910

1989

1936 Earns doctorate from M.I.T. and is hired by Bell Laboratories

1945 Returns to Bell Labs

1956 Founds company; is awarded Nobel Prize

DIES Aug. 12 in San Francisco

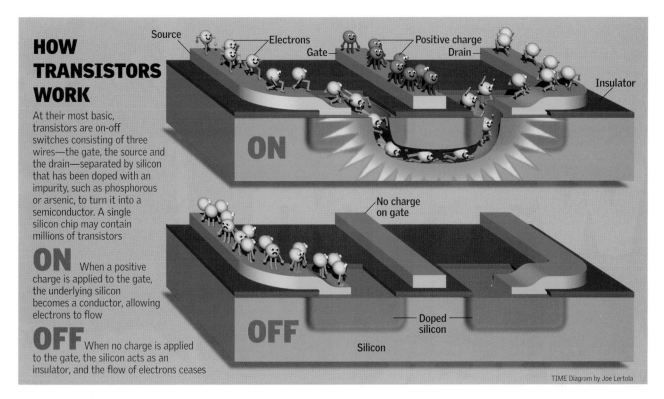

HOW TRANSISTORS WORK

At their most basic, transistors are on-off switches consisting of three wires—the gate, the source and the drain—separated by silicon that has been doped with an impurity, such as phosphorous or arsenic, to turn it into a semiconductor. A single silicon chip may contain millions of transistors

ON When a positive charge is applied to the gate, the underlying silicon becomes a conductor, allowing electrons to flow

OFF When no charge is applied to the gate, the silicon acts as an insulator, and the flow of electrons ceases

Source — Electrons — Gate — Positive charge — Drain — Insulator — ON

No charge on gate — Doped silicon — Silicon — OFF

TIME Diagram by Joe Lertola

common chemical element, whereas germanium is relatively rare. Silicon, however, melts at a much higher temperature, making its purification and processing more difficult. Shockley's group set to work to learn about the materials and processes that would be required. Only a few of the scientists had any previous experience with semiconductors, so it was an intense learning time for most of us.

Working for Shockley was a particular challenge. He extended his competitive nature even to his working relationships with the young physicists he supervised. Beyond that, he developed traits that we came to view as paranoid. He suspected that members of his staff were purposely trying to undermine the project and prohibited them from access to some of the work. He viewed several trivial events as malicious and assigned blame. He felt it necessary to check new results with his previous colleagues at Bell Labs, and he generally made it difficult for us to work together.

In what was probably the final straw, he decided the entire laboratory staff should undergo polygraph tests to determine who was responsible for a minor injury experienced by one of the office workers. While the group was making real progress in developing the technology needed to produce silicon transistors, Shockley's management style proved an increasing burden. The group was in danger of breaking up. In fact, a few of the first recruits had already abandoned the lab for other jobs. To try to stabilize the organization, several of us went over Shockley's head, directly to Arnold Beckman, who had financed the start-up, suggesting that Shockley be removed from direct management of the lab and function only as a technical consultant.

We grossly overestimated our power. Shockley survived our insurrection, and we felt we had to look elsewhere for jobs. In the process of searching, we became convinced that our best course was to set up a company to complete Shockley's original goal—which he had abandoned by this time in favor of another semiconductor device he had also invented—to make a commercial silicon transistor.

This new company, financed by Fairchild Camera & Instrument Corp., became the mother organization for several dozen new companies in Silicon Valley. Nearly all the scores of companies that are or have been active in semiconductor technology can trace the technical lineage of their founders back through Fairchild to the Shockley Semiconductor Laboratory. Unintentionally, Shockley contributed to one of the most spectacular and successful industry expansions in history.

IN 1963 SHOCKLEY LEFT THE ELECTRONICS INDUSTRY and accepted an appointment at Stanford. There he became interested in the origins of human intelligence. Although he had no formal training in genetics or psychology, he began to formulate a theory of what he called dysgenics. Using data from the U.S. Army's crude pre-induction IQ tests, he concluded that African Americans were inherently less intelligent than Caucasians—an analysis that stirred wide controversy among laymen and experts in the field alike.

Nonetheless, Shockley pursued his inflammatory ideas. In speeches regularly interrupted by boos and catcalls, he argued that remedial educational programs were a waste of time. He suggested that individuals with IQs below 100 be paid to undergo voluntary sterilization. He donated openly and repeatedly to a so-called Nobel sperm bank designed to pass on the genes of geniuses. He filed a $1.25 million libel suit against the Atlanta *Constitution*, which had compared his ideas to Nazi genetic experiments; the jury awarded him $1 in damages. He ran for the U.S. Senate on the dysgenics platform and came in eighth. Sadly, when he died at 79 of cancer, he regarded his work in genetics as more important than any role he played in creating the $130 billion semiconductor industry. ∎

Intel co-founder Gordon Moore posited Moore's Law: chip power doubles every 18 months as prices decline.

James
Watson
& Francis
Crick

An ex-physicist and a former ornithology student—with some unwitting help from a competitor—cracked the secret of life

By **ROBERT WRIGHT**

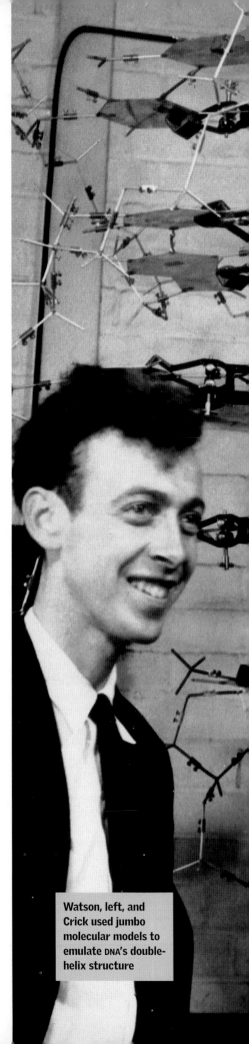

N FEB. 28, 1953, FRANCIS CRICK WALKED INTO THE EAGLE PUB IN Cambridge, England, and, as James Watson later recalled, announced that "we had found the secret of life." Actually, they had. That morning, Watson and Crick had figured out the structure of deoxyribonucleic acid, DNA. And that structure—a "double helix" that can "unzip" to make copies of itself—confirmed suspicions that DNA carries life's hereditary information.

Not until decades later, in the age of genetic engineering, would the Promethean power unleashed that day become vivid. But from the beginning, the Watson and Crick story had traces of hubris. As told in Watson's classic memoir, *The Double Helix*, it was a tale of boundless ambition, impatience with authority and disdain, if not contempt, for received opinion. ("A goodly number of scientists," Watson explained, "are not only narrow-minded and dull but also just stupid.") Yet the Watson and Crick story is also one of sublime harmony, an example, as a colleague put it, of "that marvelous resonance between two minds—that high state in which 1 plus 1 does not equal 2 but more like 10."

The men were in some ways an odd pair. The British Crick, at 35, still had no Ph.D. The American Watson, 12 years Crick's junior, had graduated from the University of Chicago at 19 and nabbed his doctorate at 22. But they shared a certain wanderlust, an indifference to boundaries. Crick had migrated from physics into chemistry and biology, fascinated by the line "between the living and the nonliving." Watson had studied ornithology, then forsook birds for viruses, and then, doing postdoctoral work in Europe, took another sharp career turn.

At a conference in Naples, Watson saw a vague, ghostly image of a DNA molecule rendered by X-ray crystallography. DNA, he had heard, might be the stuff genes are made of. "A potential key to the secret of life was impossible to

Watson, left, and Crick used jumbo molecular models to emulate DNA's double-helix structure

> # The structure was too pretty not to be true.

JAMES WATSON, *The Double Helix*

The young researchers at Cambridge; in 1953 TIME described their office as "a magpie's nest."

estrangement led Wilkins to show Watson one of Franklin's best pictures yet, which hadn't been published. "The instant I saw the picture my mouth fell open," Watson recalled. The sneak preview "gave several of the vital helical parameters."

Franklin died of cancer in 1958, at 37. In 1962 the Nobel Prize, which is not given posthumously, went to Watson, Crick and Wilkins. In Crick's view, if Franklin had lived, "it would have been impossible to give the prize to Maurice and not to her" because "she did the key experimental work." And her role didn't end there. Her critique of an early Watson and Crick theory had sent them back to the drawing board, and her notebooks show her working toward the solution until they found it; she had narrowed the structure down to some sort of double helix. But she never employed a key tool—the big 3-D molecular models that Watson and Crick were fiddling with at Cambridge.

push out of my mind," he later wrote. "It was certainly better to imagine myself becoming famous than maturing into a stifled academic who had never risked a thought."

This theme of Watson's book—the hot pursuit of glory, the race against the chemist Linus Pauling for the Nobel Prize that DNA would surely bring—got bad reviews from the (relatively) genteel Crick. He didn't recall anyone mentioning a Nobel Prize. "My impression was that we were just, you know, mad keen to solve the problem," he later said. But whatever their aims, Watson and Crick shared an attraction to DNA, and when they wound up in the same University of Cambridge lab, they bonded.

Fatefully, such amity did not prevail at a laboratory over at King's College, London, where a woman named Rosalind Franklin was creating the world's best X-ray diffraction pictures of DNA. Maurice Wilkins, a colleague who was also working on DNA, disliked the precociously feminist Franklin, and the feeling was mutual. By Watson's account, this

It was Watson who fit the final piece into place. He was in the lab, pondering cardboard replicas of the four bases that, we now know, constitute DNA's alphabet: adenine, thymine, guanine and cytosine, or A, T, G and C. He realized that "an adenine-thymine pair held together by two hydrogen bonds was identical in shape to a guanine-cytosine pair." These pairs of bases could thus serve as the rungs on the twisting ladder of DNA.

Here—in the "complementarity" between A and T, between C and G—lay the key to replication. In the double helix, a single strand of genetic alphabet—say, CAT—is paired, rung by rung, with its complementary strand, GTA. When the helix unzips, the complementary strand becomes a template; its G, T and A bases naturally attract bases that

Crick BORN on June 8 in Northampton, England;		**1951 Collaboration begins**	**1961 Crick's team finds genetic code for proteins**	**1968 Watson's *The Double Helix* is published**	**1988 Watson named head of U.S. Human Genome Project; later resigns**
1916	**1928**				**1999**
	Watson BORN, on April 6, 1928, in Chicago	**1953 The double helix is described**	**1962 Nobel Prize, shared with Maurice Wilkins**	**1968 Watson is director of Cold Spring Harbor**	**1977 Crick begins brain research at Salk Institute**

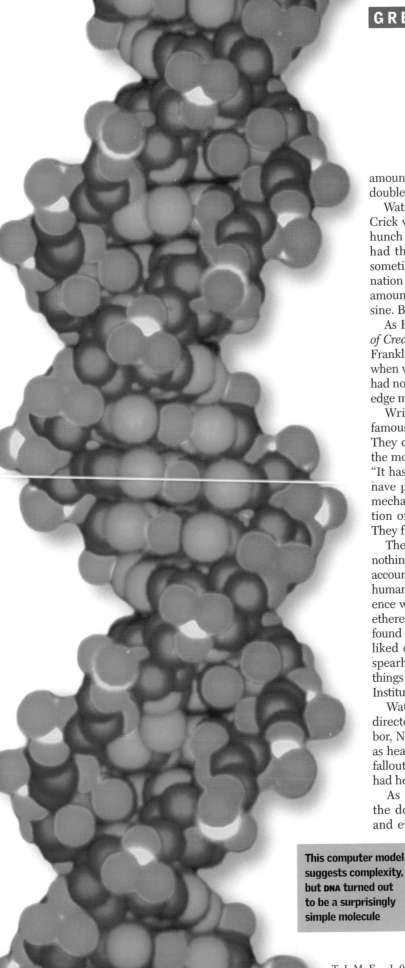

This computer model suggests complexity, but DNA turned out to be a surprisingly simple molecule

amount to a carbon copy of the original strand, CAT. A new double helix has been built.

Watson's "Aha!" was but the last in a long chain. It was Crick who had fastened onto a chemist friend's theoretical hunch of a natural attraction between A and T, C and G. He had then championed the complementarity scenario—sometimes against Watson's resistance—as a possible explanation of "Chargaff's rules," the fact that DNA contains like amounts of adenine and thymine and of guanine and cytosine. But it was Watson who had first learned of these rules.

As Horace Freeland Judson observed in *The Eighth Day of Creation*, this sort of synergy is, above all, what Rosalind Franklin lacked. Working in a largely male field in an age when women weren't allowed in the faculty coffee room, she had no one to bond with—no supportive critic whose knowledge matched her gaps, whose gaps her knowledge matched.

Writing up their findings for the journal *Nature*, the famously brash Watson and Crick donned a British reserve. They capped a dry account of DNA's structure with one of the most famous understatements in the history of science: "It has not escaped our notice that the specific pairing we have postulated immediately suggests a possible copying mechanism for the genetic material." They faced the question of byline: Watson and Crick, or Crick and Watson? They flipped a coin.

The double helix—both the book and the molecule—did nothing to slow this century's erosion of innocence. Watson's account, depicting researchers as competitive and spiteful—as human—helped de-deify scientists and bring cynicism to science writing. And DNA, once unveiled, left little room for the ethereal, vitalistic accounts of life that so many people had found comforting. Indeed, Crick, a confirmed agnostic, rather liked deflating vitalism—a mission he pursued with zeal, spearheading decades of work on how exactly DNA builds things before he moved on to do brain research at the Salk Institute for Biological Studies in La Jolla, Calif.

Watson drifted from pure science into administration. As director of the molecular-biology lab at Cold Spring Harbor, N.Y., he turned it into a scientific powerhouse. Serving as head of the Human Genome Project, he absorbed some fallout from the high-energy ethical debates whose fuse he had helped light nearly four decades earlier.

As the practical and philosophical issues opened by the double helix continue to unfold, policy, philosophy and even religion will evolve in response. But one truth seems likely to endure. It emerges with equal clarity whether you examine the DNA molecule or the way it was revealed. The secret of life is complementarity. ∎

Robert Wright is the author of The Moral Animal: Evolutionary Psychology and Everyday Life.

Jonas Salk

Many scientists were racing to make a polio vaccine in the '50s—but he got there first

By WILFRID SHEED

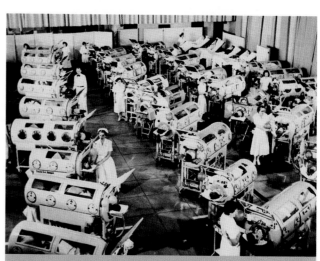

Iron lungs were widely used in the 1950s to ventilate victims of polio whose paralysis left them incapable of breathing

HOW MANY CASES MAKE AN EPIDEMIC? SURVIVORS of the great polio plagues of the 1940s and '50s will never believe that in the U.S. the average toll in those years was "only" 1 victim out of every 5,000 people. Was that really all it took to scare the nation out of its wits, sending families scurrying in all directions—to the mountains, to the desert, to Europe—in vain hope of sanctuary?

Perhaps polio's other name, infantile paralysis, played a role. Images of babies in wheelchairs and tots on crutches tend to skew one's perception. And in case anyone wasn't scared enough, the National Foundation for Infantile Paralysis hammered the nightmare home with photos that seemed to show up everywhere of sad-looking children in leg braces. "Please give to the March of Dimes." Oh, yes, indeed, five times at the same movie—or so it sometimes felt.

It was inevitable that whoever was first to allay such fears would become a national hero. "The Man Who Saved the Children" should be good for a statue in every town in the world. And since the odds of a microbiologist's becoming even a little bit famous are a lot worse than 5,000 to 1, it was perhaps inevitable that this hero's achievements would immediately be disputed. In a scientific field so heavily manned, findings routinely crisscross, and even minor discoveries can leave a trail of claims and counterclaims, not to mention envy and acrimony, that are truly incurable.

Thus a monument to the conquest of polio that is faithful to the facts would consist of not one man in a white lab coat but two of them glaring at each other. Both Drs. Jonas Salk and Albert Sabin could and did make convincing cases for themselves and pretty good ones against each other too. But since the public usually prefers one hero to two, and since Salk did get there first, he got the monument.

Between occasional shouts of "Eureka!" even the heroes of science tend to have quiet careers. But Salk's career stands out in at least two respects: the sheer speed with which he outraced all the other tortoises in the field and the honors he did not receive for doing so. How could the Man Who Saved the Children be denied a Nobel Prize? Or summarily be turned down for membership in the National Academy of Sciences? What was it about Salk that so annoyed his fellow scientists?

That he was fast, there was no doubt. And hungry too. After taking brilliant advantage of the amazing public education available to New Yorkers in the first half of this century, this son of Orthodox Polish-Jewish immigrants whizzed through his medical training and received an enviable University of Michigan fellowship to study virology under the distinguished Dr. Thomas Francis—who, incidentally, would remain in Salk's corner for life.

BORN Oct. 28 in East Harlem, N.Y.	**1939 Graduates** from New York University College of Medicine	**1955 Announces** success of his polio vaccine. Mass immunization begins		**PIONEERS Children** who helped test the vaccine got a button with their booster

1914 —————————————————————————————— **1995**

1942 Begins work on first commercial flu vaccine	**1949 Starts polio** research with funding from the March of Dimes	**1960 Founds Salk** Institute for Biological Studies in La Jolla, Calif.	**DIES at 80**

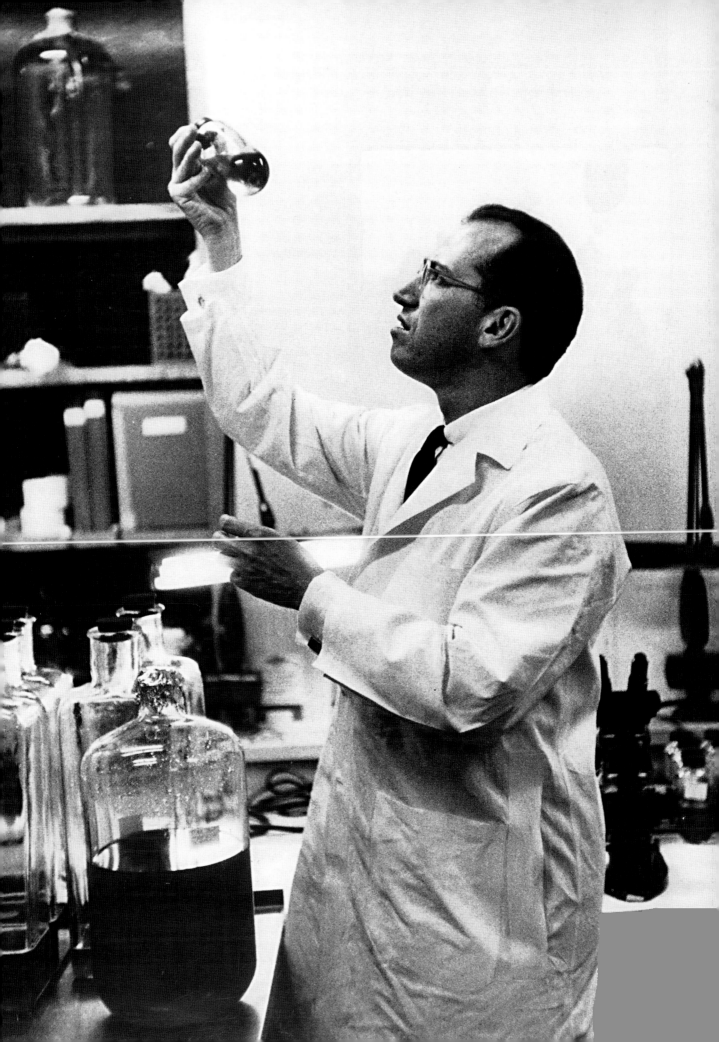

" He shows the world how to eliminate paralytic polio, and you'd think he had halitosis or had committed a felony. "

BASIL O'CONNOR, National Foundation for Infantile Paralysis

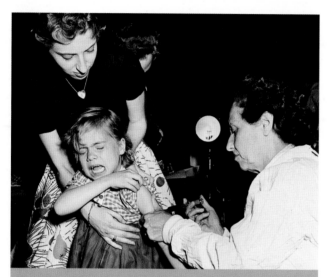

Ouch! Mothers—if not their kids—were thrilled with the shots

Salk's major patron at Michigan, however, proved to be no one man but the whole U.S. Army, which needed a flu vaccine at once to help win World War II and was happy to complete Salk's education in speed under pressure. After that, it was a snap for him to set up his own peacetime lab at the University of Pittsburgh and equip it to the gills for the Great Crusade—the one that every immunologist in the world then had his eye on—against the Great White Whale itself, poliomyelitis.

Fortunately, Salk had somehow found time to do basic research on the virus and write a few theoretical papers, and it was these that caught the eye of Basil O'Connor, the zealous head of the National Foundation for Infantile Paralysis, who decided to play a hunch and shove some dimes in Salk's direction with instructions to get going.

With that, the seeds of resentment, deep and abiding, were sown. By then, dozens of worthy researchers had been toiling far longer than Salk in the fields of polio and would have given their microscopes for such funding and freedom. Who was this hired gun who appeared from nowhere with a bankroll the size of a special prosecutor's, plus free use of all the backbreaking work that had gone before?

In fact, the key piece of research, available to all, was completed a few years earlier by the one undisputed hero of this story, Harvard's John Enders. It was his team that figured out how to grow polio in test tubes—suddenly giving vaccine hunters everywhere enough virus to work with.

Now the goal was truly in sight, and who got there first was largely a matter of speed—Salk's forte—and luck. "Salk was strictly a kitchen chemist," Sabin used to gripe. "He never had an original idea in his life." But imaginative people perennially underrate efficient ones, and at the time, the kitchen chemist—who prepared his vaccine by marinating the virus in formalin—was just what the doctor ordered.

Salk and Sabin came from the two competing schools of vaccine research. Sabin, like Louis Pasteur, believed the

way to produce immunity was to create a mild infection with a "live" but crippled virus, and he concocted his competing vaccine accordingly. Salk, from his flu-fighting days, knew the immune system could be triggered without infection, using deactivated, or "killed," viruses. And, as it turned out, his quick-and-dirty killed viruses were better suited to a crash program than Sabin's carefully attenuated live ones. By 1954, Salk and Francis were ready to launch the largest medical experiment yet carried out in the U.S., vaccinating more than 1 million kids ages six to nine, some with the vaccine, some with a placebo. The children weren't told which they were getting.

The Salk vaccine worked. But the world of science has a protocol for releasing such findings: first publish them in a medical journal, and then spread the credit as widely as possible. Salk took part in a press conference and went on radio but gave credit to nobody, including himself—of course, he was going to get the credit anyway.

That was the mistake that would haunt him. Radio was right; vanity was wrong. This was not some breakthrough in carbuncle research but hot news that couldn't wait one more minute. Within the brotherhood of researchers, however, Salk had sinned unforgivably by not saluting either Enders or, more seriously, his colleagues at the Pittsburgh lab. Everything he did after that was taken as showboating—when he opened the Salk Institute, a superlab in La Jolla, Calif., for the world's scientists to retreat to and bask in, and even when not long before his death in 1995, he started a search for an AIDS vaccine, to a flourish of trumpets and welcome new funding.

Just as some politicians are at their best when running for office, so Salk came into his own as a spokesman for vaccination. Although it is generally accepted in the field that the real man on the monument should be Enders (who in 1954 shared the only Nobel Prize given for polio research), it seems unlikely that either he or the pugnacious Sabin would have performed half so patiently as Salk the ceremonial chores expected of monuments or would have sat so politely through so many interviews, indefatigably spreading the gospel of disease prevention far and wide.

And one last thing. Like the millions of American veterans who have never ceased thanking Harry Truman for dropping the Bomb and ending World War II, the folks who got their polio shot between the first Salk vaccine and the Sabin model have never had any quarrel with Salk's high place in history. (The two vaccines are now given in alternating booster shots.) There are times when even genius has to give way to the old Yankee virtues of know-how and can do. And if in this instance these happened to be embodied in the son of a couple of Polish-Jewish immigrants ... well, that kind of thing happens in America. ■

Novelist and essayist Wilfrid Sheed wrote about his battle with polio in In Love with Daylight *(1995).*

Rachel
Carson

Before the dawn of the environmental movement,
there was one brave woman and her very brave book

By PETER MATTHIESSEN

"To stand at the edge of the sea ... is to have knowledge of things that are as eternal as any earthly life can be."

RACHEL CARSON, *Under the Sea-Wind*

SHE WAS ALWAYS A WRITER, AND SHE ALWAYS KNEW that. Like Faulkner, Fitzgerald, e.e. cummings, Edna Millay and E.B. White, 10-year-old Rachel Louise Carson, born in 1907 in the Allegheny Valley town of Springdale, Pa., was first published in the *St. Nicholas* literary magazine for children. A reader and loner and devotee of birds and indeed of all nature, the slim, shy girl of plain face and dark curly hair continued writing throughout adolescence, chose an English major at Pennsylvania College for Women and continued to submit poetry to periodicals. Not until junior year, when a biology course reawakened the "sense of wonder" with which she had always encountered the natural world, did she switch her major to zoology, not yet aware that her literary and scientific passions might be complementary.

Graduating magna cum laude in 1929, Carson won her master's degree in zoology at Johns Hopkins, but family responsibilities caused her to abandon her quest for a doctorate. For a few years she would teach zoology at the University of Maryland, continuing her studies in the summer at the Marine Biological Laboratories at Woods Hole, Mass. It was there, in her early 20s, that she first saw—and was enchanted by—the enormous mysteries of the sea.

In 1935 "Ray" Carson, as some friends knew her, took part-time work writing science radio scripts for the old Bureau of Fisheries, a job that led, in 1936, to a full-time appointment as a junior aquatic biologist. To eke out her small income, she wrote feature articles for the Baltimore *Sun*, most of them related to marine zoology. Though her poetry was never to be published, a strong lyrical prose was already evolving, and one of her pieces for a government publication seemed to the editor so elegant and unusual that he urged her to submit it to the *Atlantic Monthly*.

"Undersea," the young writer's first publication in a national magazine (September 1937), was seminal in theme and tone. Together with an evocative *Sun* feature, "Chesapeake Eels Seek the Sargasso Sea" ("From every river and stream along the whole Atlantic Coast, eels are hurrying to the ..."), it was the starting point for her first book. *Under the Sea-Wind* (1941), Carson's favorite among her books, passed almost unnoticed. Meanwhile, her editorial duties at what would become the Fish and Wildlife Service (FWS) had increased. In 1946 she was promoted to information specialist; in 1949 she became chief editor of publications.

In their first meeting, the naturalist Louis Halle found Carson "quiet, diffident, neat, proper and without affectation." Nothing written about her since seems to dispute this. But for all her modesty and restraint, she was not prim. She had a mischievous streak, a tart tongue and confidence in her own literary worth.

A decade after her first book, her agent circulated a second work in progress that proposed to explore the origins and geological aspects of the sea. The material was rejected by 15 magazines, including the *Saturday Evening Post* and *National Geographic*. Eventually the work came into the hands of Edith Oliver at the *New Yorker;* she recommended it to William Shawn, who recognized its exceptional quality at once. Much of it was serialized as "A Profile of the Sea," and in July 1951 it was published in book form as *The Sea Around Us*. It won the National Book Award, and within the year sold more than 200,000 copies in hard cover.

Success permitted Carson to retire from the FWS in 1952 to write full time. That summer she bought land and built a cottage on the Sheepscot River on the coast of Maine, where she and her mother had visited since 1946. Her new celebrity also gave her the opportunity to speak out on concerns she felt strongly about. As early as 1945, Carson and her close colleague Dr. Clarence Cottam had become alarmed by government abuse of new chemical pesticides such as DDT, in particular the "predator" and "pest" control programs, which were broadcasting poisons with little regard for the welfare of other creatures. That same year, she offered an article to *Reader's Digest* on insecticide experiments going on at Patuxent, Md., not far from her home in Silver Spring, to determine the effects of DDT on all life in affected areas. Apparently the *Digest* was not interested. Carson went back to her government job and her sea trilogy, and not until after the third volume had been completed did she return to this earlier preoccupation.

Meanwhile, the insecticide barrage had been augmented by a host of fearful compounds many times stronger than DDT, all of which the government planned to distribute for public use and commercial manufacture. "The more I learned about the use of pesticides, the more appalled I became," Carson recalled. "I realized that here was the material for a book. What I discovered was that everything which meant most to me as a naturalist was being threatened, and that nothing I could do would be more important."

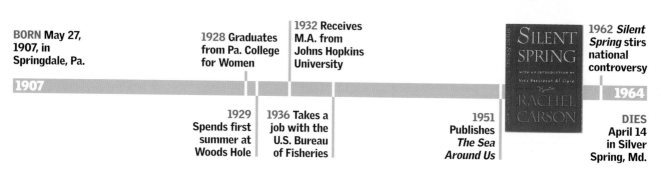

BORN **May 27, 1907, in Springdale, Pa.**

1928 Graduates from Pa. College for Women

1932 Receives M.A. from Johns Hopkins University

1907

1962 *Silent Spring* stirs national controversy

1964

1929 Spends first summer at Woods Hole

1936 Takes a job with the U.S. Bureau of Fisheries

1951 Publishes *The Sea Around Us*

DIES April 14 in Silver Spring, Md.

Carson's work as a marine biologist prompted her first magazine article, which eventually led to her landmark book, *Silent Spring*

With her fame, eloquence and reputation for precision, Carson could count on the support of leading scientists and conservation groups, and was well positioned to command a hearing. Even so, the *Digest* and other magazines had little interest in this gloomy subject. Then, in 1957, there was a startling wildlife mortality in the wake of a mosquito-control campaign near Duxbury, Mass., followed by a needless spraying of a DDT/fuel-oil mix over eastern Long Island for eradication of the gypsy moth. Next, an all-out war in the Southern states against the fire ant did such widespread harm to other creatures that its beneficiaries cried for mercy; and after that a great furor arose across the country over the spraying of cranberry plants with aminotriazole, which led to an Agriculture Department ban against all cranberry marketing just in time for Thanksgiving 1959.

SILENT SPRING, SERIALIZED IN THE *NEW YORKER* IN June 1962, gored corporate oxen all over the country. Even before publication, Carson was violently assailed by threats of lawsuits and derision, including suggestions that this meticulous scientist was a "hysterical woman" unqualified to write such a book. A huge counterattack was organized, led by the chemical industry and duly supported by the Agriculture Department as well as the more cautious in the media. (TIME's reviewer deplored Carson's "oversimplifications and downright errors … Many of the scary generalizations—and there are lots of them—are patently unsound.")

By year's end, *Audubon* and *National Parks Magazine* had published more excerpts from the book, and all but the most self-serving of Carson's attackers were backing rapidly toward safer ground. In their ugly campaign to reduce a brave scientist's protest to a matter of public relations, the

chemical interests had only increased public awareness. *Silent Spring* became a runaway best seller, with international reverberations. Nearly 40 years later, it is still regarded as the cornerstone of the new environmentalism.

Carson was not a born crusader but an intelligent and dedicated woman who rose heroically to the occasion. She was rightly confident about her facts as well as her ability to present them. Secure in the approval of her peers, she remained remarkably serene in the face of her accusers. Perhaps the imminence of her own mortality had helped her find this precious balance and perspective. In most photographs, the pensive face appears a little sad, but this was true long before she knew that she had cancer. She was 56 when she died in April 1964.

"The beauty of the living world I was trying to save," she wrote in a letter to a friend in 1962, "has always been uppermost in my mind—that, and anger at the senseless, brutish things that were being done. I have felt bound by a solemn obligation to do what I could—if I didn't at least try I could never be happy again in nature. But now I can believe that I have at least helped a little."

True, the damage being done by poison chemicals today is far worse than it was when she wrote the book. Yet one shudders to imagine how much more impoverished our habitat would be had *Silent Spring* not sounded the alarm. Well crafted, fearless and succinct, it remains her most celebrated book, although her wonderful essays on the sea may be remembered longer. Even if she had not inspired a generation of activists, Carson would prevail as one of the greatest nature writers in American letters.　■

Peter Matthiessen is an environmentalist and writer. His latest novel, Bone by Bone, *was published in April 1999.*

Cranks ... Villains ... And Unsung Heroes

Along with scientific superstars like Einstein, the century brought us charlatans, saints and sinners

CRANKS **Stanley Pons & Martin Fleischmann**

In 1989 the two chemists announced to great fanfare that they had built a simple bench-top percolator made up of two electrodes and a slug of heavy water that, like our sun, produced limitless amounts of fusion energy. But when other scientists tried to duplicate the pair's results, they ended up with beakers filled with ... chilly water.

CRANK **Wilhelm Reich**

The Austrian-born psychoanalyst, an early disciple of Freud's, pioneered the study of body language, dabbled with Marxism, then began theorizing about a universal life-giving "orgone energy"— which was expressed through neurosis-free orgasms. Reich ended up blaming UFOs for a deadly counter-energy and claiming red fascists were out to get him.

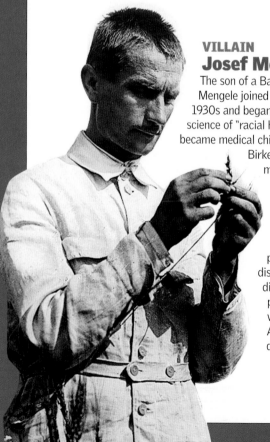

VILLAIN **Josef Mengele**

The son of a Bavarian industrialist, Mengele joined the Nazi Party in the 1930s and began studying the sham science of "racial hygiene." In 1943 he became medical chief at Auschwitz-Birkenau; there he sent more than 400,000 prisoners to the gas chambers. He also engaged in all manner of butchery, even exposing prisoners to infectious diseases to watch how different races react to pathogens. After the war, he fled to South America, where he died in 1979.

VILLAIN **Trofim Lysenko**

The agronomist and Marxist ideologue earned Stalin's acclaim by rejecting Gregor Mendel's ideas on heredity, believing organisms passed on to succeeding generations characteristics acquired in their lifetime. Through what he called vernalization, he hoped to "train" spring wheat to be winter wheat and thus increase the number of annual harvests. Result: both Soviet agriculture and biology were set back.

HERO **Eugene Shoemaker**

Probing Arizona's Meteor Crater in 1956, the crusading geologist found a form of quartz that is created only by strong impacts and concluded it had been formed not by volcanoes, as most scientists thought, but by large objects hitting the earth. The public paid heed when, in 1994, Comet Shoemaker-Levy 9 (which he co-discovered) crashed into Jupiter in an awesome display of what could happen here.

HERO **Alfred Wegener**

Geologists dismissed as preposterous his theory that the earth's major land masses had once been huddled together in a single supercontinent, then began drifting apart. For years continental drift was held up to derision—until studies of the movement of the ocean floor in the 1960s offered proof for his ideas. Renamed plate tectonics, they gave geology a single unifying theory.

UNSUNG HERO
Srinivasa Ramanujan

A minor bureaucrat in Madras, India, he failed to interest serious mathematicians in his spare-time dabbling with numbers—until Cambridge don G.H. Hardy deciphered the young man's scrawls and realized he was a genius. He brought Ramanujan to England in 1914, where they worked to prove the Indian's brilliant conjectures before his death at age 32.

HERO **Elisabeth Kübler-Ross**

The Swiss-born psychiatrist was determined to overthrow medicine's taboo against discussing death with patients—including the terminally ill. After interviewing hundreds of dying patients, sometimes in the presence of startled medical students, she compiled her findings in her best-selling 1969 book, *On Death and Dying.* In it she identified the five psychological stages of dying: denial, anger, bargaining, depression and, finally, acceptance.

The Leakeys

Without the groundbreaking—and backbreaking—efforts of one family, the story of how we evolved would still be largely untold

By DONALD C. JOHANSON

LOUIS LEAKEY'S ENTHUSIASM FOR AFRICA AND THE search for earliest man were infectious. Speaking before a packed lecture hall in his staccato-like voice, punctuated by rapid inhales, he cast a spell, making each listener believe he was speaking only to him. His following in America was cultlike. Consumed with devotion and swept up in his charisma, many developed a desire to follow somehow in his footsteps, to please him.

No wonder Leakey became the patriarch of a family that dominated anthropology as no family has dominated a scientific field before or since. Not only did Louis, his wife Mary and their second son Richard make the key discoveries that shaped our understanding of human origins, but they also inspired a generation of researchers (myself included) to pick up where they left off.

I recall with great fondness my first visit to Nairobi in 1970; Louis ceremoniously led me to the room housing the crown jewels of human evolution. Each fossil took on a mythical cast as he waxed eloquent about how it revealed a magic moment of our origins. Here he was, the grand master, sharing his passion, knowledge and intuition with a new disciple. He was often like that: generous, open, supportive, always trying to win new converts to his way of working, his way of interpreting the past.

Born in Kenya of English missionaries, Louis was initiated by tribal elders into the native Kikuyu society. As a young man he was adventurous, impulsive, driven, ruggedly handsome and romantically African. Fresh out of Cambridge, Louis set out to prove Darwin's theory that Africa was humankind's homeland—and to discover evidence for his own belief that true man, *Homo*, had a very ancient origin.

In 1933, when Louis met and fell in love with 20-year-old Mary Nicol, he already had a family, but in flagrant disregard of the social norms of the time, he divorced. The synergy of Louis and Mary's union was obvious from the outset. In contrast to Louis' charming, gregarious, outgoing nature, Mary was shy, reserved, socially uncomfortable. Mary was a careful evaluator of scientific evidence; Louis was often impulsive and cavalier in his proclamations. Rigorous, intensely focused and remarkably diligent, Mary quickly set new standards in the study of African prehistory, culminating in her stunning monographs on the archaeology of Olduvai Gorge.

Digging into time: Richard and Mary at Olduvai Gorge in 1961

Mary's 1959 discovery of the *Zinjanthropus* cranium at Olduvai captured worldwide attention, made the Leakeys a household name, attracted a multidisciplinary team of specialists to work at Olduvai and launched the modern science of paleoanthropology, the study of human origins.

Following the success of *Zinjanthropus*, Louis began spending less time at Olduvai, which became Mary's domain. For most of the next 25 years she worked there with her staff, her dogs and selected visitors. Until his death in 1972, Louis visited occasionally but spent most of his time traveling, lecturing and raising funds to support an ever expanding list of research projects, including notable field studies of the living great apes: Jane Goodall's chimps, Dian Fossey's gorillas and Biruté Galdikas' orangutans.

In 1978 Mary made what may have been her greatest find. Her team was re-exploring a site in Tanzania called Laetoli—40 years after Louis had incorrectly assumed that

Richard poses with the reconstruction of a skull his team found in Kenya in 1972

When the first men were fashioned in the Good Lord's forge,/ He sent them, it seems, to Olduvai Gorge.

Attributed to the British magazine *Punch*

the absence of tools there implied that hominid fossils would not be found—when they discovered a trail of remarkably clear ancient hominid footprints impressed and preserved in volcanic ash. It was a stunning glimpse of the world 3.6 million years ago. If only Louis had lived to see it.

A detailed study of the Laetoli hominid fossils confirmed that they belonged to a new hominid species, best represented by the 3.2 million-year-old "Lucy" skeleton I had found four years earlier at Hadar, Ethiopia. When I presented these findings in 1978 at a Nobel symposium in Sweden, Mary had already agreed to be one of the co-authors on the paper defining the new species, *Australopithecus afarensis*. A few months later, however, she cabled me demanding removal of her name. I respected her wishes and had the title page redone. Like Louis, she did not believe *Australopithecus* was our ancestor; if her finds at Laetoli were our ancestors, they had to be *Homo*.

IT WAS A BLUSTERY, WINTRY AFTERNOON IN 1970 AT the University of Chicago when I first met Louis and Mary's son Richard. He had just completed a presentation on his new finds from Lake Turkana (then Lake Rudolf). I told him I would be in Nairobi the next summer, and wanted to see his exciting hominid fossils. A year younger than I, he had chosen, following disenchantment with the safari business, to follow in his parents' footsteps. He too seemed to possess the "Leakey luck" and was well on the way to stardom in paleoanthropology.

Our first meeting in Nairobi was cordial, and Richard dazzled me with remarkable specimens; a friendship was simmering. Beginning preparations for my research in Ethiopia's Afar region, I was a frequent visitor to Nairobi, and Richard offered suggestions and appeared supportive of my efforts. But our conversation always had a dimension of competition, and even though we offered each other advice, in retrospect it was as if we were looking for chinks in each other's armor. Both of us were strong in character and ultimately, almost inevitably, this led to our estrangement in 1981. We were the Young Turks of anthropology in those days, staunchly defending our interpretations of human evolution. Perhaps now, with the mellowing of age, it is time to break the silence.

Much like his father, Richard has strong opinions and is often hasty to make pronouncements about his discoveries.

This was especially true when he presented, in 1972, a *Homo* skull that he believed was 2.9 million years old. Adhering to his father's belief in very early *Homo*, this find, older than all *Australopithecus* fossils then known, was a welcome and stunning endorsement of Louis' views. Louis and Richard had been feuding over museum matters, and this discovery brought them together again in a final meeting shortly before Louis died. He spent his last days comforted by the knowledge that he had been proved correct. Since then, however, the skull has been correctly dated to 1.8 million years, and most anthropologists today believe *Australopithecus* is indeed one of our ancestors.

Richard, meanwhile, continued his rise to prominence. Fossil finds such as the astonishingly complete 1.6 million-year-old skeleton of an African *Homo erectus* (*Homo ergaster* to some) and the 2.5 million-year old "Black Skull" have added immeasurably to our knowledge of human origins. Paleoanthropology has not been his only passion, however. He will probably be best remembered in Africa for founding an opposition political party in Kenya in 1995, after which he suffered public humiliation, including being beaten with leather whips. But Richard is resilient. Even after a life-saving kidney transplant in 1979 (a gift from his estranged brother Philip) and the partial loss of both legs in a 1993 plane crash, he continues to exude confidence.

In 1989 President Daniel arap Moi appointed Richard head of what is now the Kenya Wildlife Service. Richard raised hundreds of millions of dollars and revamped wildlife conservation in Kenya, heavily arming antipoaching units and instituting a controversial edict permitting the shooting of poachers on sight. He resigned in 1994 amid politically motivated charges of corruption, racism and mismanagement—only to be reinstated by Moi 4½ years later.

Nevertheless, the Leakeys will forever be synonymous with paleoanthropology and even today show all signs of being alive, well and contributing productively to the field. In 1999 Richard's wife Meave, a trained zoologist, and their eldest daughter Louise were leading teams to northern Kenya, where hominids in excess of 4 million years old are being found. The stage is set for the first family of anthropology to continue well into the next century. ∎

Donald C. Johanson, discoverer of "Lucy," is director of the Institute of Human Origins at Arizona State University.

UNION Louis and Mary meet in England. They marry in 1936	1959 Mary finds *Zinjanthropus*	1972 Richard finds 1.8 million-year-old skull at Koobi Fora; Louis dies in London on Oct. 3, at 69		1984 Mary retires	1989 Richard takes up career in wildlife conservation
1933					**1996**
1944 Richard is born in Kenya	1964 Louis unveils *Homo habilis,* "handy man," who made stone tools	1978 Mary's Laetoli footprint trail	1985 Richard finds "Black Skull" at Lake Turkana		DIES Mary passes away in Nairobi, Dec. 9, at 83

The Delvers

Digging into mankind's fossil record and social mores, these scientists gave us new insights into what it means to be human

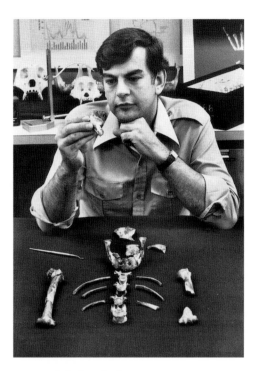

Donald C. Johanson

In 1974 the American anthropologist and French colleague Maurice Taieb unearthed 3 million-year-old "Lucy," the earliest hominid ever found. The *Australopithecus* woman had a large face, a small brain, stood 3½ ft. tall—and walked erect.

Margaret Mead

The century's foremost woman anthropologist, she became an icon. Studying primitive societies in the field, she found evidence (later challenged) to support her belief that cultural conditioning, not genetics, molded human behavior.

Claude Lévi-Strauss

The Belgian-born French anthropologist became a leading exponent of structural anthropology, which argues that certain innate mental structures, like language, are common to human behavior in all societies and account for behavior. A gifted writer, Lévi-Strauss brought a literary sensibility to such seminal works as *Tristes Tropiques* (1955) and *The Savage Mind* (1962) .

Howard Carter

After a 15-year search, in 1922 the British archaeologist uncovered the untouched burial tomb of the 14-year-old Egyptian Pharaoh Tutankhamen, who reigned in the 14th century B.C. In the hoard: the solid-gold mask of "King Tut."

Tim Berners-Lee

From the thousands of interconnected threads of the Internet, he wove the World Wide Web, a mass medium for the 21st century

By JOSHUA QUITTNER

WANT TO SEE HOW MUCH THE WORLD HAS changed in the past decade? Log on to the Internet, launch a search engine and type in the word enquire (British spelling, please). You'll get about 30,000 hits. It turns out you can "enquire" about nearly anything online these days, from used Harley Davidsons for sale in Australia ("Enquire about touring bikes. Click here!"), to computer-training-by-e-mail courses in India ("Where excellence is not an act but a habit"). Click once to go to a site in Nairobi and enquire about booking shuttle reservations there. Click again, and zip off to Singapore, to a company that specializes in "pet moving." Enquire about buying industrial-age nuts and bolts from "the Bolt Boys" in South Africa, or teddy bears in upstate New York. Exotic cigar labels! Tantric sex guides! Four-poster beds for dogs!

So what, you say? Everybody knows that with a mouse, a modem and access to the Internet, these days you can point-and-click anywhere on the planet, unencumbered by time or space or long-distance phone tariffs.

Ah, but scroll down the list far enough, hundreds of entries deep, and you'll find this hidden *Rosebud* of cyberspace: "Enquire Within Upon Everything"—a nifty little computer program written nearly 20 years ago by a lowly software consultant named Tim Berners-Lee. Who knew then that from this modest hack would flow the civilization-altering, millionaire-spawning, information suckhole known as the World Wide Web?

Unlike so many of the inventions that have moved the world, this one truly was the work of one man. Thomas Edison got credit for the light bulb, but he had dozens of people in his lab working on it. William Shockley may have fathered the transistor, but two of his research scientists actually built it. And if there ever was a thing that was made by committee, the Internet—with its protocols and packet switching—is it. But the World Wide Web is Berners-Lee's alone. He designed it. He loosed it on the world. And he more than anyone else has fought to keep it open, non-proprietary and free.

It started, of all places, in the Swiss Alps. The year was 1980. Berners-Lee, doing a six-month stint as a software engineer at CERN, the European Laboratory for Particle Physics, in Geneva, was noodling around with a way to organize his far-flung notes. He had always been interested in programs that dealt with information in a "brain-like way" but that could improve upon that occasionally memory-constrained organ. So he devised a piece of software that could, as he put it, keep "track of all the random associations one comes across in real life and brains are supposed to be so good at remembering but sometimes mine wouldn't." He christened it Enquire, short for *Enquire Within Upon Everything*, a Victorian-era encyclopedia he remembered from childhood.

Building on ideas that were current in software design at the time, Berners-Lee fashioned a kind of "hypertext" notebook. Words in a document could be "linked" to other files

BORN June 8 in London

1955

1976 Graduates from Queen's College, Oxford

WEBMASTER In 1976, soldering one of his first computers

1980 At CERN, he writes Enquire

1989 Proposes global hypertext project called "WorldWideWeb"

1991 The Web debuts on the Internet

1994 Joins M.I.T. to direct the W3 Consortium

1993 University of Illinois releases Mosaic browser

1999 nearly 150 million people log on to the Internet each week

Pictures of
2,304 different
websites were
combined to
make this
photo-mosaic
of Berners-Lee

The wizard of the World Wide Web poses in Switzerland with the first Web browser

The World Wide Web debuted in 1991, instantly bringing order and clarity to the chaos that was cyberspace. From that moment on, the Web and the Internet grew as one, often at exponential rates. Within five years, the number of Internet users jumped from 600,000 to 40 million. At one point, it was doubling every 53 days.

Growing up in the '60s, Berners-Lee was the quintessential child of the computer age. His parents met while working on the Ferranti Mark I, the first computer sold commercially. They taught him to think unconventionally; he'd play games over the breakfast table with imaginary numbers (what's the square root of minus 4?). He made pretend computers out of cardboard boxes and five-hole paper tape and fell in love with electronics. Later,

on Berners-Lee's computer; he could follow a link by number (there was no mouse to click back then) and automatically pull up its related document. It worked splendidly in its solipsistic, Only-On-My-Computer way.

But what if he wanted to add stuff that resided on someone else's computer? First he would need that person's permission, and then he would have to do the dreary work of adding the new material to a central database. An even better solution would be to open up his document—and his computer—to everyone and allow them to link their stuff to his. He could limit access to his colleagues at CERN, but why stop there? Open it up to scientists everywhere! Let it span the networks! In Berners-Lee's scheme there would be no central manager, no central database and no scaling problems. The thing could grow like the Internet itself, open-ended and infinite. "One had to be able to jump," he later wrote, "from software documentation to a list of people to a phone book to an organizational chart to whatever."

S
O HE COBBLED TOGETHER A RELATIVELY EASY-TO-learn coding system—HTML (HyperText Markup Language)—that has come to be the lingua franca of the Web; it's the way Web-content creators put those little colored, underlined links in their text, add images and so on. He designed an addressing scheme that gave each Web page a unique location, or URL (universal resource locator). And he hacked a set of rules that permitted these documents to be linked together on computers across the Internet. He called that set of rules HTTP (HyperText Transfer Protocol).

And on the seventh day, Berners-Lee cobbled together the World Wide Web's first (but not last) browser, which let users anywhere view his creation on their computer screen.

at Oxford, he built his own working electronic computer out of spare parts and a TV set. He also studied physics, which he thought would be a lovely compromise between math and electronics. "Physics was fun," he recalls. "And in fact a good preparation for creating a global system."

It's hard to overstate the impact of the global system he created. It's almost Gutenbergian. He took a powerful communications system that only the élite could use and turned it into a mass medium. "If this were a traditional science, Berners-Lee would win a Nobel Prize," Eric Schmidt, CEO of Novell, once told the New York *Times*. "What he's done is that significant."

You'd think he would have at least got rich; he had plenty of opportunities. But at every juncture, Berners-Lee chose the nonprofit road, both for himself and his creation. Marc Andreessen, who helped write the first popular Web browser, Mosaic—which, unlike the master's browser, put images and text in the same place, like pages in a magazine—went on to co-found Netscape and become one of the Web's first millionaires. Berners-Lee, by contrast, headed off in 1994 to an administrative and academic life at the Massachusetts Institute of Technology. From a sparse office at M.I.T., he directs the W3 Consortium, the standard-setting body that helps Netscape, Microsoft and anyone else agree on openly published protocols rather than hold one another back with proprietary technology. The rest of the world may be trying to cash in on the Web's phenomenal growth, but Berners-Lee is content to labor quietly in the background, ensuring that all of us can continue, well into the 21st century, to Enquire Within Upon Anything. ∎

Joshua Quittner, TIME's *Personal Technology columnist, is the new editor of* TIME DIGITAL.

Weavers of the Web

Thanks to their efforts, cyberspace is now everywhere (and nowhere)

Linus Torvalds

Like Tim Berners-Lee (and unlike the billionaires of the browser wars), Torvalds embraces the idealistic "shareware" philosophy that animated the early days of computing. In 1991 the young Finn began offering his potent (and ever more popular) Linux operating system for free on the Internet.

Marc Andreessen

As a student in Illinois, he built a browser, Mosaic, that brought new graphic capabilities to the Web. The "golden geek" went on to co-found Netscape, helping turn browsers from hackers' toys into commercial dynamos.

Vannevar Bush

Franklin D. Roosevelt's science czar in World War II, he organized the Manhattan Project. But the onetime professor at M.I.T.—where he built a massive, gear-driven analog computer—was also a prophet who foresaw a desktop machine that would display text and pictures electronically.

William Gibson

Someone had to give the virtual realm that unites computers via telephone lines a name—and the honors went to sci-fi writer Gibson, who coined the term "cyberspace" in his 1984 novel *Neuromancer*.

Index

A

ABC machine, 142
ABC Sports, 71
A-bomb, 133, 134, 135
ACE (Automatic Computing Engine), 141
Adams, Ansel, 77
Adams, Henry, 87
Adler, Alfred, 104
advertising, 55-56
AFL-CIO, 51
Africa, 158-60
African Americans
    barred from Levittown, 48
    in big business, 4
    Shockley's theory of intelligence, 145
Agnelli, Giovanni, 3
AIDS, 4
AIF-COLA formula, 51
air conditioning, 26-27
airplanes
    airlines, 40-42
    impact of, 92
    Wright brothers, 92-93
Alaska pipeline, 33
Ali, Muhammad, 73
Allen, Paul, 83, 84
Altair 8800, 83
Alto computer, 142
Amazon.com, 81
America Eats Out (Mariani), 64
American Express, 81
American Federation of Labor (AFL), 51
American Football League (AFL), 71
American Meat Institute, 56
America Online, 4
aminotriazole, 155
Andreessen, Marc, 4, 164, 165
anthropology, 158-60, 161
antibiotics, 110-11
antitrust laws
    National Football League and, 72
Apollo 11, 131
Apple Computer, 4, 61, 83, 142
archaeology, 158-60, 161
architecture, 34
Arden, Elizabeth, 4
Arledge, Roone, 71, 72
Ash, Mary Kay, 4
astronauts, 130-31
astronomy, 127-29
Atanasoff, John, 142
atomic structure, 98
Auden, W.H., 104
Auschwitz-Birkenau, 156
automobiles, 4, 88
    Henry Ford, 6-9
    significant models, 10-11
Australopithecus afarensis, 160, 161

B

Baekeland, Leo, 106-108
Baeyer, Adolf von, 108
Bakelite, 106, 108
Bancitaly Corp., 21
Band-Aid, 29
bank accounts, 20-21
BankAmericard, 81
bank credit cards, 81
banking, 20-21, 25
Bank of America, 20, 21, 81
Bank of Italy, 20, 21
Barbie doll, 69
Bardeen, John, 144
BASIC, 83
basketball, 73
Bechtel, Riley, 33
Bechtel, Stephen, 30-33

Bechtel, Warren, 32
Bechtel company, 32-33
Beckman, Arnold, 144, 145
Beckman Instruments, 144
Bell Telephone Laboratories, 144, 145
Bernays, Edward, 56
Bernbach, William, 55
Berners-Lee, Tim, 162-64, 165
Bernstein, Carl, 68
beta decay, 133
Bethe, Hans, 134, 135
Big Bang theory, 88, 127, 129
Binet, Alfred, 116
birth control pills, 88, 118
Birth of a Nation, The, 12
"Black Skull," 160
Bluestone, Irving
    on Walter Reuther, 49-51
Boeing, 42
Bohr, Niels, 97, 98
boxing, 73
Bradley, Major General Follett, 58
Brattain, Walter, 144
broadcast news, 19
Broglie, Louis de, 95
Browne, Joe, 72
Brownie box camera, 77
browsers, 83, 84, 162, 164, 165
Buffalo Forge Co., 27
Burnett, Leo, 55-56
Bush, Vannevar, 165

C

cable television, 19
Cadillac, 11
cameras, 77, 119
capitalism, 2-5
Carrier, Willis, 26-27
Carson, Rachel, 153-55
Carter, Howard, 161
Carter, Jimmy, 60
Case, Steve, 4
CBS, 19
cellular phones, 77
celluloid, 108
Cepheid variable stars, 128
CERN (European Laboratory for Particle
    Physics), 162, 164
Chain, Ernst Boris, 111
Challenger shuttle, 131
Chicago Bulls, 73
children
    child psychology, 116
    child rearing, 105
    thought processes of, 116-17
chlorofluorocarbons (CFCS), 27
Christianson, Gale, 127
Chrysler, Walter, 5
Chrysler Airflow, 11
Channel Tunnel (Chunnel), 35
Citroën 7CV, 11
Civilization and Its Discontents (Freud), 104
civil rights
    United Auto Workers and, 51
Claude, Georges, 29
Clemenceau, Georges, 136
Cleveland NFL franchise, 72
Clinton, Bill, 138
CNN, 19
Coca-Cola, 4
cold fusion, 156
"collective unconscious," 105
Columbus Savings & Loan Society, 21
comets, 157
compact discs (CDs), 77
computers, 88
    Alan Turing, 141

Bill Gates, 82-84
    development of, 142
    discount retailing and, 80
    IBM, 58-60
    mathematical logic and, 101
Condensite, 108
Congress of Industrial Organizations (CIO),
    51
Cooper, Martin, 77
Corvair, 11
cosmetics, 65-67
Cottam, Clarence, 154
Country Club Plaza (Kansas City, Mo.), 81
Crabgrass Frontier (Jackson), 46
cranberries, insecticide poisoning, 155
Crawford, Joan, 14
credit cards, 81
Crick, Francis, 146-49
crops, high-yield, 118
cyberspace, 165

D

Dallas Cowboys, 72, 73
Darwin, Charles, 87, 158
Dayton Hudson, 80
DDT, 154-55
deficit spending, 138
deoxyribonucleic acid (DNA), 146-49
Depression, 138
detergents, 28
Dewey, John, 116
Dewey, Thomas E., 45
Dickson, Earle, 29
Diners Club, 81
discount retailing, 78-80
Disney, Elias, 36, 38
Disney, Roy, 38
Disney, Walt, 4, 5, 21, 36-39
Disneyland, 39
Dodge brothers, 5
Dodge Touring Car, 11
Domagk, Gerhard, 111
DOS, 83
Double Helix, The (Watson), 146
dreams, interpretation of, 104, 105
Dreft, 28
Drexel Burnham, 4
Dubos, Réné, 111
Dupont, 28
Durant, Will, 5
dysgenics, 145

E

Eastman, George, 106
Eastman Kodak, 77
Eckert, J. Presper, 142
Economic Consequences of the Peace, The
    (Keynes), 136
economics, 136-38
Eddington, Arthur, 96
Edison, Thomas Alva, 5, 8, 108, 162
Edison Illuminating Co., 8
Edison Institute, 8
Education of Henry Adams, The (Adams), 87
Eighth Day of Creation, The (Judson), 149
Einstein, Albert, 87, 88, 94-97, 116, 117, 122,
    128
Eisenhower, Dwight D., 15, 18, 35
Eisner, Michael, 5, 18
Ellison, Larry, 61
Empire State Building, 34
Employment Act of 1946, 138
Enders, John, 152
engineering
    air conditioning, 26-27
    monuments, 34-35
    Stephen Bechtel, 30-33

ENIAC computer, 142
Enigma codes, 140-41
Enquire, 162
Escher, M.C., 122
"euro" community, 138
Exxon, 78

F
Fairchild Camera & Instrument Corp., 145
Fairchild Semiconductor, 142
Faisal, King, 33
Fantasia, 39
Farnsworth, Kent, 114
Farnsworth, "Pem," 112
Farnsworth, Philo, 112-14
fast-food industry, 63-64
Father of Air Conditioning (Ingels), 27
Federal Housing Administration, 47
Federal Reserve Board, 4
Fermi, Enrico, 132-34
Feynman, Richard, 98
Fidelity, Magellan Fund, 4
Filo, David, 61
Fisher, Alva J., 29
Fleischmann, Martin, 156
Fleming, Alexander, 109-111
Florey, Howard, 111
flu vaccine, 152
football, 70-72, 73
Forbes, Steve, 5
Ford, Henry, 3, 4, 5, 6-9
Ford, Henry II, 5, 9
Ford Model A, 9
Ford Model T, 6-7, 8, 10
Ford Motor Co., 5, 7-9, 78
    United Auto Workers and, 50
formaldehyde, 108
FORTUNE, 4
Fossey, Dian, 158
Forster, E.M., 140
Francis, Thomas, 150, 152
Frankin, Rosalind, 148, 149
Frazier, Joe, 73
Freire, Paulo, 116
Freud, Anna, 104
Freud, Sigmund, 87, 101-104, 105, 156
Friedman, Milton, 4-5

G
Gable, Clark, 14
Gagarin, Yuri, 130
Galdikas, Biruté, 158
Gardner, Cliff, 114
Gates, Bill, 3, 82-84
Gekko, Gordon, 2
General Bakelite Corp., 108
General Electric, 5, 28, 29, 52
General Motors, 2, 5, 9, 50, 52, 78
General Theory of Employment, Interest and Money, The (Keynes), 137, 138
George, David Lloyd, 136
germanium, 144
Germany
    atom bomb and, 134
    concentration camps, 156
    Enigma codes, 140-41
    rocket science, 125
Getty, J. Paul, 53
Giannini, A.P., 4, 20-21
Gibson, Herb, 78
Gibson, William, 165
Gilbert, Jack, 14
Glaser, Rob, 84
Goddard, Esther, 125
Goddard, Robert, 123-25, 130
Gödel, Adele, 122
Gödel, Kurt, 87, 120-22, 140

Goldman Sachs, 4
Goodall, Jane, 158
Goodrich, B.F., 28
Graduate, The, 106
Graham, Katharine, 68
Graham, Philip, 68
Gratia, D.A., 110
Great Crash of 1929, 22, 24
Green Bay Packers, 73
Green Revolution, 88
Greenspan, Alan, 4
grocery stores, self-serve, 81
gypsy moth, 155

H
Hale telescope, 129
Halle, Louis, 154
Hammer, Armand, 53
Handler, Ruth, 69
Harvey, Thomas, 97
Hawking, Stephen, 128
HBO, 19
H-bomb, 135
Heinz, H.J., 4, 68
Heisenberg, Werner, 98, 133
Helmsley, Harry, 53
Helmsley, Leona, 53
high-yield crops, 118
Hiraiwa, Gaishi, 76
Hitchcock, Alfred, 38
Hock, Dee, 4
hockey
    U.S. 1980 Olympic team, 73
Hoddeson, Lillian, 144
Hoffman, Dustin, 106
Holden, Fay, 15
Homer McGee ad agency, 55
Homo erectus (*Homo ergaster*), 160
homosexuality, 141
Honda, Soichiro, 3
Hooker telescope, 128
Hoover, Herbert, 14-15, 138
Hoover Dam, 31, 33
housing, 46-48
Howard Johnson Co., 63
HTML (HyperText Markup Language), 164
HTTP (HyperText Transfer Protocol), 164
Hubble, Edwin, 126-29
Hubble's Law, 128
Hubble Space Telescope, 127-29
Hughes, Howard, 53
Human Genome Project, 88, 149
Hunt, H.L., 53
Hunt, Lamar, 71
Huxley, Aldous, 88
hypertext, 162-63

I
Iacocca (Iacocca), 5
IBM, 58-60, 83, 84
Ibuka, Masaru, 74-75
Iconoscope, 114
Image Dissector, 114
"imitation test," 141
Indianapolis NFL franchise, 72
Industrial Revolution, 8
infantile paralysis, 150
inferiority complex, 104
Ingels, Margaret, 27
insecticides, 154-55
installment credit, 20
instant photography, 119
Institute for Advanced Study, 122
Intel, 142
intelligence theory, 145
International Air Transport Association, 42

International Business Machines (IBM), 58-60
International Monetary Fund, 138
International Space Station, 131
Internet, 81, 83, 88, 162-64
Interpretation of Dreams, The (Freud), 104
interstate highway system, 35
investment banking, 22-24
iron lungs, 150
ITT Corp., 48

J
Jackson, Kenneth T., 46
Japan, 75
Java, 61, 83
jet aircraft, 42
Jobs, Steve, 4, 61, 142
Johnson, Howard Deering, 63
Johnson, Lyndon, 138
Johnson, Ned, 24
Johnson & Johnson, 29
Jolly Green Giant, 56
Jones, Jerry, 72
Jordan, Michael, 73
Judson, Horace Freeland, 149
Jung, Carl, 104, 105, 116

K
Kaiser, Henry J., 5
Kay, Alan, 142
Kennedy, John F., 131
Kettering, Charles, 5
Keynes, Florence Ada, 136
Keynes, John Maynard, 4, 136-38, 140
Keynes, John Neville, 136
King, Martin Luther, Jr., 51
King Kullen, 81
Kinsey, Alfred, 105
Kitty Hawk, N.C., 92
K Mart, 80
Kresge, S.S., 80
Kroc, Ray, 8, 63-64
Kübler-Ross, Elisabeth, 157

Laetoli hominid fossils, 158, 160
Laker, Sir Freddie, 42
Land, Edwin, 119
Lansky, Meyer, 44-45
laser, 119
Lauder, Estée, 4, 65-67
Lauder, Leonard, 66
Laybourne, Geraldine, 69
Leakey family, 158-60
Lenin, V.I., 53
Leonardo da Vinci, 93
Letterman, David, 69
Levin, Gerald, 19
Lévi-Strauss, Claude, 161
Levitt, Abe, 48
Levitt, Alfred, 46, 48
Levitt, William, 46-48
Levittown, N.Y., 46-48
Levitt & Sons, 48
Lindbergh, Charles, 7, 42
Linux operating system, 165
Loew, Marcus, 12, 13
Lombardi, Vince, 73
Luce, Henry R., vi, 2
Luciano, Charles ("Lucky"), 3, 43-45
"Lucy" remains, 160, 161
Lynch, Edmund C. ("Eddie"), 22
Lynch, Peter, 4, 24
Lysenko, Trofim, 156

M
Macintosh (computer), 83
Made in Japan (Morita), 76

Index

Mafia, 44-45
Magellan Fund (Fidelity), 4
Manhattan Project, 134, 165
Mao Zedong, 35
Maranzano, Salvatore, 44-45
March of Dimes, 150
Marconi Wireless Telegraph, 16
Marcus, Stanley, 67
Mariani, John, 64
Marlboro Man, 56
Masseria, Giuseppe ("Joe the Boss"), 44
mass production, 8, 63
mathematics
    Kurt Gödel, 120-22
    Srinivasa Ramanujan, 157
    Alan Turing, 139-41
    Ludwig Wittgenstein, 99-101
Matsushita, Konosuke, 52
Mattel, 69
Mauchly, John, 142
Mayer, Jacob, 12
Mayer, Louis B., 4, 12-15
Mayer & Co., 15
McAuliffe, Christa, 131
McCarthy, Joe, 15
McCullough, David, 114
McCone, John, 33
McDonald, Dick, 63
McDonald, Mac, 63-64
McDonald's, 63-64
McNamara, Frank, 81
McNamara, Robert, 5
McNealy, Scott, 61
Mead, Margaret, 161
Mellon, Andrew, 25
Mendel, Gregor, 156
Mengele, Josef, 156
mental structures, 161
Mentzer, Josephine Esther, 66
Merrill, Charles, 4, 22-24
Merrill, James, 22, 24
Merrill Lynch & Co., 22-24
metamathematics, 120
metaphysics, 99-101
Meteor Crater, 157
Metro Goldwyn Mayer (MGM), 12-15
Mickey Mouse, 36, 38
Microsoft, 83-84
Microsoft Internet Explorer, 84
Microsoft Windows, 83, 84
microwave oven, 118
Milken, Michael, 4, 25
Milky Way galaxy, 127, 128
Miller, Arjay, 5
minimum wage, 9
Minkowski, Hermann, 95
Minnesota Vikings, 72
minority groups, 4
Moi, Daniel arap, 160
Monday Night Football, 71
Montessori, Maria, 116
moon, travel to, 124, 131
Moore's Law, 145
Morgan, J.P., 4
Morita, Akio, 3, 74-76
Morita, Yoshiko, 76
Morse, Samuel, 114
Mosaic, 162, 164, 165
Motorola, 77
Mount Palomar Observatory, 129
Mount Wilson Observatory, 127
Mumford, Lewis, 48
Murdoch, Rupert, 3, 19
Murray, Mae, 14
Murrow, Edward R., 19
My Years with General Motors (Sloan), 52

N
NASA, 131
National Basketball Association (NBA), 73
National Broadcasting Co. (NBC), 18, 19, 77
National Football League (NFL), 71-72, 73
National Foundation for Infantile Paralysis, 150, 152
NationsBank, 21
NBC, 18, 19, 77
nebulae, 127, 128
neon, 29
Netscape, 4, 83, 84, 164, 165
Neumann, John von, 60, 134, 142
neurasthenics, 104
Neuromancer (Gibson), 165
Newton, Sir Isaac, 87
New Yorker, The 154, 155
Nickelodeon, 69
Nidetch, Jean, 68
Nixon, Richard, 68, 138
Nobel sperm bank, 145
Noyce, Robert, 142
nuclear fission, 134
nuclear fusion, 156
nuclear reactors, 133, 134
nylon stockings, 28

O
Obeth, Hermann, 130
Occidental Petroleum, 53
O'Connor, Basil, 152
Oedipus complex, 102
Ogilvy, David, 55
O'Kieffe, Dewitt ("Jack"), 56
Olds, Ransom, 5
Oliver, Edith, 154
Olympics
    U.S. 1980 hockey team, 73
On Death and Dying (Kübler-Ross), 157
online shopping, 81
operating systems, 83
Oppenheimer, J. Robert, 133-34, 135
Oracle Computer, 61
organized crime, 43-45
orgone energy, 156
Orwell, George, 88
Oswald the Rabbit, 38
Oxygen Media, 18, 69

P
paleoanthropology, 158-60, 161
Paley, William S., 18, 19
Panama Canal, 34
Pan American Airways Inc., 40-42
Panasonic, 52
paper clips, 29
Paris Peace Conference (1918-19), 136
Pauli, Wolfgang, 133
penicillin, 110-11
Perkins, Frances, 138
Perot, Ross, 5
personal computers, 88, 165
phenol, 108
Philips, 77
Phillips, Carol, 67
Philosophical Investigations (Wittgenstein), 100, 101
philosophy, mathematical, 100-101
photography
    instant, 119
Piaget, Jean, 115-17
Piggly Wiggly, 81
Pillsbury Doughboy, 56
Pincus, Gregory, 118
Pinocchio, 39
Planck, Max, 98
Planned Parenthood, 118

plastics, 106-108
plate tectonics, 157
plutonium, 134
Polaroid Land Camera, 119
polio vaccine, 150-52
Pons, Stanley, 156
Porsche, Ferdinand, 5
Price, Sol, 80
Prince, Earl, 63
Principia Mathematica (Russell and Whitehead), 100
Procter & Gamble, 28
professional football, 70-72, 73
Prontosil, 111
propellers, aircraft, 92
psychoanalysis, 101-104, 156
punch-card tabulators, 60

Q
Q-DOS, 83
quanta, 98
quantum mechanics, 97, 98

R
racial hygiene, 156
radar, 119
radio, 16, 18
Radio Corp. of America (RCA), 114
Radiola, 18
Raft, George, 45
Ramanujan, Srinivasa, 157
Raskob, John, 34
Raytheon Corp., 118
RCA, 18, 77
Reader's Digest, 154, 155
Realm of the Nebulae, The (Hubble), 128
recursive functions, 122
Redmanol, 108
red shifting, 128
refrigerators, 28
Reich, Wilhelm, 156
relativity, theory of, 87, 95, 96-97, 112, 128
retail stores, discount, 78-80
Reuther, Roy, 50
Reuther, Victor, 50
Reuther, Walter, 3, 49-51
Rock, Arthur, 25
rocketry, 123-25, 130
Rolls-Royce, 55
Ronald McDonald, 63-64
Rooney, Mickey, 14-15
Roosevelt, Eleanor, 50
Roosevelt, Franklin D., 50, 60, 138, 165
Root, A.R., 93
Rozelle, Pete, 3, 70-72
Rubinstein, Helena, 4
Russell, Bertrand, 87, 100, 101, 138
Rutherford, Ann, 14

S
Sabin, Albert, 150, 152
Sakharov, Andrei, 135
Salk, Jonas, 150-52
Salk Institute, 152
San Francisco–Oakland Bay Bridge, 33
Sarnoff, David, 16-18, 114
satellites, 130
Saudi Arabian oil pipeline, 33
Scatena, Lorenzo, 21
Schary, Dore, 15
Schenck, Nick, 15
Schmidt, Eric, 164
Schulberg, B.P., 12
Schwab, Charles, 25
Sea Around Us, The (Carson), 154
Sears, 4, 28
Seattle Computer Products, 83

self-serve grocery stores, 81
semiconductors, 144-45
sexual behavior
    psychoanalysis and, 102
    study of, 105
Shapley, Harlow, 128
shareware, 165
Shawn, William, 154
shellac, synthetic, 106, 107
Shepard, Alan, 130
Sherman Anti-Trust Act
    National Football League and, 71
Shockley, William, 142, 143-45, 162
Shockley Semiconductor Laboratory, 144
Shoemaker, Eugene, 157
Shoemaker-Levy 9, comet, 157
shopping centers, 81
Siegel, Benjamin ("Bugsy"), 45
Silent Spring (Carson), 155
silicon, 144-45
Silicon Valley, 144-45
Silverman, Fred, 18
Simon, Théodore, 116
Sinatra, Frank, 45
Skinner, B.F., 105
skyscrapers, 34
Sloan, Alfred P., 5, 52
Smalltalk (computer language), 142
Snow White and the Seven Dwarfs, 21, 36, 39
Sony America, 76
Sony Corp., 74-76, 77
Sony Walkman, 76
Soviet Union
    space program, 130, 131
space shuttles, 131
space station, 131
space-time, 95, 97
Spencer, Percy, 118
Sperry Rand, 60
Spock, Benjamin, 105
Sputnik 1, 130
Staphylococcus bacteria, 110
steam engine, 87
Stewart, Anita, 12
Stewart, Martha, 69
stock market, 22-24
Stone, Lewis, 15
structural anthropology, 161
Studebaker, Clement, 5
suburbia, 46-48
Sundback, Gideon, 28
Sun Microsystems, 61, 83
Super Bowl, 70-72
supermarkets, 81
surfactants, 28
System/360 (IBM), 60
Szilard, Leo, 134

T
Taylor, Robert, 12, 14
TBS, 19
telephones
    cell phones, 77
telescopes, 127-29
television, 4, 19
    advertising, 56

David Sarnoff, 16-18
    development of, 77
    invention of, 112-14
    sports, 73
    Walt Disney, 39
Thalberg, Irving, 12, 13, 15
Thomson, J.J., 87
Thomson, David, 39
Thornton, Charles, 5
thought processes of children, 116-17
Three Essays on the Theory of Sexuality
    (Freud), 104
Three Gorges Dam, 35
Tide, 28
Time Warner, 19
Titanic, 16
Tokyo Telecommunications Engineering,
    Inc., 74
Tolman, Justin, 112, 114
Torvalds, Linus, 165
Toyoda, Eiji, 3
Toyota Corona, 10
Tractatus Logico-philosophicus
    (Wittgenstein), 100, 101
Tracy, Spencer, 12
TransAmerica Corp., 21
transistors, 60
    development of, 143-45
    radios, 75, 77
Travelers Insurance Co., 4
Trippe, Juan, 40-42
Tsiolkovsky, Konstantin, 130
Turing, Alan, 87, 101, 139-41
Turing, John, 140
Turing machine, 140, 141
"Turing test," 141
Turner, Ted, 19
"turnkey" construction contracts, 33
Tutankhamen, tomb of, 161
Tyndall, John, 110

U
Under the Sea-Wind (Carson), 154
unionism, 49-51
United Auto Workers (U.A.W.), 49
United Technologies, 27
Univac, 60
Universal Turing Machine, 101, 140
universe, study of, 88, 127-29
U.S. Bureau of Narcotics, 45
U.S. Justice Department, 84
U.S. Maritime Commission, 32

V
Vaaler, Johan, 29
vacuum tubes, 144
Veblen, Oswald, 122
Velox, 106
Veterans Administration, 47
Virgin Atlantic, 42
Virtuous Wives (film), 13
Visa credit card, 4, 81
Volkswagen, 55
    Beetle, 10
V-2 rockets, 125, 130

W
Wachner, Linda, 69
Wagner, Jeanette, 67
Waksman, Selman, 111
Walker, C.J., 68
Walkman (Sony), 76
Wall Street, 22-24
Wal-Mart, 4, 78-80
Walton, Sam, 78-80
Wampler, Cloud, 27
Warnaco Group, 69
washing machines, 29
Washington Post, 68
Watson, Dick, 60
Watson, James, 146-49
Watson, Thomas, 60
Watson, Thomas, Jr., 58-60
W3 Consortium, 162, 164
"weak force," 133
Wegener, Alfred, 157
Weight Watchers International, 68
Welch, Jack, 5, 52
Wells, H.G., 95
What's My Line?, 114
Whitehead, Alfred North, 87
Wigner, Eugene, 134
wildlife conservation, 160
Wilkins, Maurice, 148
Willys Jeep, 10
Wilson, Charles E., 2
Wilson, Woodrow, 136
Wittgenstein, Ludwig, 87, 88, 99-101
Wizard of Oz, 13
Woodward, Bob, 68
Woolf, Virginia, 136
Woolworth, F.W., 80
World War II, 138
World Wide Web, 83, 88
    development of, 162-64
    growth of, 165
    online shopping, 81
Wozniak, Steve, 142
Wright, Orville, 90-93
Wright, Wilbur, 90-93
Wright Cycle Co., 92

X-Y-Z
Xerox Palo Alto Research Center, 142
Yahoo!, 61
Yang, Jerry, 61
Yangtze River
    Three Gorges Dam, 35
Zinjanthropus, 158
zippers, 28
Zworykin, Vladimir K., 18, 77, 112

THE STARS OF MGM from the L.B. Mayer story, pages 14-15. First row: James Stewart, Margaret Sullavan, Lucille Ball, Hedy Lamarr, Katharine Hepburn, Louis B. Mayer, Greer Garson, Irene Dunne, Susan Peters, Ginny Simms, Lionel Barrymore. Second row: Harry James, Brian Donlevy, Red Skelton, Mickey Rooney, William Powell, Wallace Beery, Spencer Tracy, Walter Pidgeon, Robert Taylor, Jean Pierre Aumont, Lewis Stone, Gene Kelly, Jackie Jenkins. Third row: Tommy Dorsey, George Murphy, Jean Rogers, James Craig, Donna Reed, Van Johnson, Fay Bainter, Marsha Hunt, Ruth Hussey, Marjorie Main, Robert Benchley. Fourth row: Dame May Whitty, Reginald Owen, Keenan Wynn, Diana Lewis, Marilyn Maxwell, Esther Williams, Ann Richards, Martha Linden, Lee Bowman, Richard Carlson, Mary Astor. Fifth row: Blanche Ring, Sara Haden, Fay Holden, Bert Lahr, Frances Gifford, June Allyson, Richard Whorf, Frances Rafferty, Spring Byington, Connie Gilchrist, Gladys Cooper. Sixth row: Ben Blue, Chill Wills, Key Luke, Barry Nelson, Desi Arnaz, Henry O'Neill, Bob Crosby, Rags Ragland

Photo Credits

Photo credits read left to right and from top to bottom of page, except as noted.

Cover

Photo-illustration by Sanjay Kothari. Photographs: Churchill by Yousuf Karsh—Woodfin Camp; Map by The Stock Market; Atom by Gilbert—Photo Researchers; Princess Diana by John Stilwell—PA; Armstrong by Eliot Elisofon—LIFE©Time Inc.; Model T by Ford Motor Co.; Picasso by Edward Quinn—Camera Press/Retna; Vietnam by Eddie Adams—AP/Wide World Photos; F.D.R. by George Skadding—LIFE; Fiber Optics by Hamblin—Gamma Liaison; Dolly by Chris Buck—Outline; Hitler by Archive Photos; 3-D Theater by J.R. Eyerman—LIFE©Time Inc.

Contents

iv Henry Ford Museum; Diana Walker; Culver Pictures; Bill Pierce
v AP—Wide World Photos; Alfred Eisenstaedt—LIFE; Christopher Cormack—Corbis; Alfred Eisenstaedt—LIFE

Builders & Titans

1 Peter Sibbald—Sygma; Allan Grant—LIFE; William Coupon—Gamma Liaison **6** Henry Ford Museum & Greenfield Village **8** Brown Brothers; Henry Ford Museum & Greenfield Village **9** William Vandivert—LIFE **10** Ron Kimball (2); Toyota USA Archives; no credit **11** Cadillac; Chevrolet; Chrysler; Dodge; Cadillac; Citroën **12** Brown Brothers **13** Turner Entertainment—Time Warner **14** Walter Sanders—LIFE **16** RCA **17** Alfred Eisenstaedt—LIFE **18** Corbis **19** Chris Brown—Saba; Britain Hill—Outline; James Leynse—Saba; Chris Sanders—Outline **20** Bank of America **21** Arnold Genthe—Fine Arts Museum of San Francisco—Achenbach Foundation for Graphic Arts; Corbis-Bettmann **22** UPI—Corbis-Bettmann **23** Illustration by Anita Kunz **24** Merrill Lynch **25** Hulton Getty—Liaison Agency; John Chiasson—Gamma Liaison; Doug Menuez—Saba; Andy Freeberg **26** Corbis **27** United Technologies—Carrier Corp. **28** no credit; Friday Historical Business Archives; Du Pont Nylon; no credit **29** Courtesy Stuart R. Blond; no credit; James Keyser for TIME; Maytag Co. **30** Corbis **31** John Bryson **32** Bechtel Corp. (3) **33** Bechtel Corp. **34** Brown Brothers; Berenholtz—The Stock Market **35** Tom Zimberoff; Sygma; Bob Sacha **36** ©Walt Disney Corp. (2) **37** The Granger Collection **38** Hulton-Deutsch Collection—Corbis **39** Alan Grant—LIFE **40** Illustration by Bruce McCall; Courtesy Pan Am Historical Archives **41** Courtesy Pan Am Historical Archives **42** Joseph Scherschel—LIFE **43** NYC Municipal Archives **44** AP/Wide World Photos; Archivio Publifoto—Olympia **45** AP/Wide World Photos **46** Anthony Linck—LIFE **47** Corbis-Bettmann; Emil Reynolds **48** Anthony Linck—LIFE **49** Anthony Linck—LIFE **50** Brown Brothers; UPI-Corbis-Bettmann; AP/Wide World Photos **51** Wide World Photos **52** Louis Psihoyos—Matrix; Dennis Stock—Magnum; Hulton Getty-Gamma Liaison **53** John Bryson—Sygma; Douglas Kirkland—Sygma; J.R. Eyerman—LIFE; no credit **54** Yousuf Karsh—Woodfin Camp **55** The Pillsbury Company **56** no credit **57** Nikolas Muray; no credit; Alain Keler—Matrix; Newspictures **58** Courtesy IBM **59** John Loengard—LIFE **60** IBM Archives **61** William Mercer McLeod—Outline; Louis Psihoyos—Matrix (2); Michael Schumann—Saba **62** Art Shay **63** Michael Justice—The Image Works; AP/Wide World Photos **64** McDonald's Corp. **65** Oberto Gili—©1990 Vogue—Condé Nast Publications Inc. **66** Dallas *Morning News*; Courtesy the Lauder Family **67** Murray Korman—Courtesy the Lauder Family **68** Mark Godfrey—The Image Works; Addison Scurlock; Martha Holmes©Time Inc.; Vicky Kasala—Gamma Liaison **69** John Abbott; Randee St. Nicholas—*Martha Stewart Living*; John Abbott **70** Don Uhrbrock **71** no credit **72** Bob Gomel—LIFE **73** Heinz Kluetmeier—SPORTS ILLUSTRATED; Neil Leifer; John W. McDonough—SPORTS ILLUSTRATED; Walter Iooss Jr.—SPORTS ILLUSTRATED **74** Sony Corp. **75** William Coupon—Gamma Liaison **76** Ethan Hoffman **77** Barbara Puorro Galasso—Courtesy George Eastman House; Friday Historical Business Archives; no credit;

Jay Colton for TIME; no credit **78** no credit **79** Stephen Pumphrey **80** Steven Pumphrey **81** no credit; Bill Luster—Matrix; Courtesy Epoch 5 Marketing; Courtesy Citicorp; no credit **82** Gregory Heisler—Outline **84** Courtesy Lakeside School—Microsoft; Liaison

Great Minds of the Century

85 no credit (2); Library of Congress; **90** Brown Brothers **92** Corbis-Bettmann; George Rinhart—Corbis-Bettmann **93** Hulton Deutsch Collection—Corbis **94** AP/Wide World Photos **95** Albert Einstein Archives—Hebrew University Jerusalem **96** Albert Einstein Archives—Hebrew University Jerusalem; Lotte Jacobi Archive—University of New Hampshire **98** Cynthia Johnson—Gamma Liaison; Wide World Photos; no credit; AP/Wide World Photos **99** Ben Richards—Courtesy Wittgenstein Archive; Cambridge **100** Brenner Archives (2) **101** BPK Berlin **102** Reuters—Corbis-Bettmann; BPK Berlin **103** Illustration by Brad Holland **104** Mary Evans Library—Sigmund Freud copyrights **105** Henri Carter Bresson—Magnum; Ken Hayman; Wallace Kirkland—LIFE; Dmitri Kessel—LIFE **106** Quintet Publishing Ltd. (2) **107** Brown Brothers **108** Dorling Kindersley Ltd., London; Quintet Publishing Ltd. **109** Hans Wild—LIFE **110** Fritz Goro—LIFE; Mary Evans Library **112** UPI-Corbis-Bettmann **113** no credit **114** UPI-Corbis-Bettmann **115** Yves Debraine **116** Wayne Behling—Archives Jean Piaget; Archives Jean Piaget **117** Piaget Family—Archives Jean Piaget **118** Roy Stevens; Art Rickerby—LIFE; no credit **119** U.S. Navy; Ted Thai—TIME; UPI-Corbis **121** ©Arnold Newman **122** *Drawing Hands* by M.C. Escher. All Escher's work ©1999 Cordon Art B.V.-Baarn-Holland. All rights reserved. **123** Clark University Archives **124** Clark University Archives **125** Culver Pictures **126** Margaret Bourke White—LIFE **127** Roger Ressmeyer—Corbis **128** NASA—JPL **130** Culver Pictures; David A. Hardy—Science Photo Library/Photo Researchers; no credit; *Tass* **131** NASA; Bruce Weaver—AP/Wide World Photos; Hank Morgan & Wayne Source; NASA **132** Brown Brothers; DFP Fotocronache **133** U.S. Army **134** DFP Fotocronache **135** Jacob Lofman—Pix Inc.; Alfred Eisenstaedt—LIFE; UPI-Corbis-Bettmann; Yuri Abramochkin **136** Brown Brothers **137** Illustration by Joseph Salina; Brown Brothers **138** Brown Brothers **139** Illustration by Matt Mahurin **140** The Granger Collection **141** National Security Agency—Courtesy Smithsonian Institution; National Archives **142** Alfred Eisenstaedt—LIFE; Ted Streshinsky—TIME; Carol A. Foote; Alfred Eisenstaedt—LIFE **143** Bruce Davidson—Magnum **144** AT&T; Lucent Technologies **147** A. Barrington Brown—Science Photo Library/Photo Researchers **148** Camera Press—Retna; Topham Picturepoint—AP/Wide World Photos **149** Peter Menzel **150** The Granger Collection; no credit **151** Al Fenn—LIFE **152** Brown Brothers **153** Erich Hartmann—Magnum **154** no credit **155** Erich Hartmann—Magnum **156** Tom Smart—Gamma Liaison; no credit; ©1985 Burda GMBH—Bunte; no credit **157** UPI-Corbis; Roger Ressmeyer—Corbis; The Granger Collection; Roy Porello—*San Diego Magazine* **158** UPI—Corbis-Bettmann **159** Carl Fischer **160** William Campbell—Sygma **161** UPI—Corbis-Bettmann; Dale Wittner; Michael Merchant; Harry Burton—Metropolitan Museum of Art **162** Courtesy Tim Berners-Lee **163** Photo-mosaic by Robert Silvers **164** ©CERN **165** Olivier Laude; Andy Freeberg; Boston *Globe*; P.F. Bentley